John Bright

The Public Letters of The Right Hon. John Bright, M.P.

Collected and Edited by H.J. Leech

John Bright

The Public Letters of The Right Hon. John Bright, M.P.
Collected and Edited by H.J. Leech

ISBN/EAN: 9783337818524

Printed in Europe, USA, Canada, Australia, Japan

Cover: Foto ©ninafisch / pixelio.de

More available books at **www.hansebooks.com**

THE
PUBLIC LETTERS
OF
THE RIGHT HON.
JOHN BRIGHT, M.P.

LONDON:
PRINTED BY GILBERT AND RIVINGTON, LIMITED,
ST. JOHN'S SQUARE.

THE
PUBLIC LETTERS

OF

THE RIGHT HON.

JOHN BRIGHT, M.P.

COLLECTED AND EDITED BY

H. J. LEECH.

London:
SAMPSON LOW, MARSTON, SEARLE, & RIVINGTON,
CROWN BUILDINGS, 188, FLEET STREET.
1885.

[*All rights reserved.*]

PREFACE.

THIS collection of letters, which Mr. Bright has written during his political career, has been obtained by a search through the files of several newspapers. Covering a space, as it does, of five-and-thirty years, many of the letters it contains will be new to the bulk of the public; and although this can hardly be claimed for a large portion of the letters, it may be submitted that they are all valuable communications, worthy of being collected and arranged so as to be available for reference and for general perusal.

Most of the letters deal with political questions. The collection would have been simplified if it had included such communications only; but in that case some very interesting letters of a public, though not of a political, nature would have had to be omitted, and it has seemed to me a better course to insert every letter I could find.

An exception to this rule has been made in

the case of the letters included in the Brougham correspondence of 1843. On the 15th of February in that year Lord Brougham wrote to Mr. Bright, asking for a disclaimer of the "atrocious falsehood" published in the Anti-Bread-Tax Circular, to the effect that he had importuned a League deputation to entrust him with a motion in the House of Lords. Mr. Bright, in reply, defended the League generally, and disavowed the authorship of the report. A correspondence, consisting of three letters on either side, followed; but as the whole of the correspondence relates principally to the charges which had been brought against Lord Brougham in the Anti-Bread-Tax Circular, I have not considered it necessary to include it in this volume.

A special interest attaches to these letters from the fact that, with the exception of his speeches, they are the only medium Mr. Bright has used for bringing his opinions before the world. He has neither written books nor contributed to reviews, and it is to his letters that we have to look for whatever of literary effort he has put forth.

I have to express my indebtedness to Mr. Thomas Moss, of Levenshulme, Manchester, who had made a collection of Mr. Bright's letters from the newspapers for several years, and who, hearing of what I was doing, readily placed his list at my disposal, and thus enabled me to include in this collection a number of letters I had failed to find. I also desire to acknowledge the assistance of my friend, Mr. J. Irlam, of Walkden, Lancashire, by whom the idea of making the collection was first suggested to me, and who has rendered me considerable help in the work.

I think it necessary to state, in justice to Mr. Bright, that he is in no degree responsible for the publication of this volume. He has, it is true, given his consent to it, but so far from his having originated the work in any way, the collection was made and completed before any communication on the subject was made to him. Appreciation of the style and contents of the letters, and regard for the character and services of Mr. Bright, have led to the production of the book, and it is given to the world in the belief that it will prove an acceptable addition to the literature of the country; comprising, as it does, the written declarations of one who is confessedly a master of the English language, and containing ideas which have helped to mould the political thought of a nation.

H. J. LEECH.

Manchester, January 17, 1885.

CONTENTS.

	PAGE
Foreign Policy. July 3, 1850	1
The Irish Church Question. October 25, 1852	5
The War with Russia. April 18, 1854	22
To Mr. Absalom Watkin. October 29, 1854	26
On the Representation of Manchester. November 5, 1856	36
On losing his Seat for Manchester. March 31, 1857	39
Reform. May 17, 1857	42
On his being elected a Member for Birmingham. August 10, 1857	44
On being asked to subscribe to a Bazaar. August, 1857	46
The Government of India. December 2, 1857	47
Reform—The Necessity of a Redistribution of Seats and the Ballot. February 1, 1858	49
Mr. Milner Gibson. January 20, 1858	56
The Conspiracy Bill. February 12, 1858	57
The Conspiracy Bill. March 1, 1858	59
The Condition of the Country. March 25, 1858	61
The Representation of Birmingham. May 26, 1858	62
The Necessity for Emigration and its Causes. September 1, 1858	63
The Currency. January 12, 1859	68
Reform—Mr. Bright's Reform Bill. April 9, 1859	69

CONTENTS.

	PAGE
The Government of India. January 14, 1860	75
Strikes, and the Exclusion of the Working Classes from the Suffrage. November 3, 1860	76
The Income-Tax, and Taxation and Representation. March 11, 1862	82
The Income-Tax. March 21, 1862	87
The United States. April 4, 1862	88
Mr. Rubery's Case. January 6, 1864	90
The Malt-Tax. April 11, 1864	92
The Licensing System. June 13, 1864	93
Irish Questions. December 22, 1864	94
Reform. May 15, 1865	96
The United States and Canada. June 10, 1865	97
Reform—Lord Palmerston and Reform. September 10, 1865	99
The Game Laws. September 30, 1865	100
Irish Affairs. March 3, 1866	105
Reform—The Reform Bill of 1866. March 25, 1866	106
The Reform Bill of 1866. May 19, 1866	110
The Hyde Park Demonstration in 1866. July 19, 1866	112
On receiving an Invitation to a Banquet in Dublin. September 1, 1866	114
On an Anticipated Visit to Ireland. September 27, 1866	116
Mr. Garth's Libels. December 24, 1866	117
Reform—The Reform Resolutions of 1867. February 16, 1867	128
The Reform Resolutions of 1867. February 18, 1867	132
The Reform Bill of 1867. March 19, 1867	133
Three-Cornered Constituencies. July 31, 1867	134
The Ballot. August 18, 1867	135
Reform—Redistribution and the Ballot. September 29, 1867	137
The Irish Land Question. November 11, 1867	138

CONTENTS. xi

	PAGE
Irish Questions. January 27, 1868	140
Three-Cornered Constituencies. August 1, 1868	145
The House of Lords. June 9, 1869	145
On becoming President of the Board of Trade. December 9, 1868	147
Free Trade and Tory Pamphleteers. September 8, 1869	148
Home Rule. January 20, 1872	149
The Representation of Birmingham. January 27, 1872	150
The Income-Tax. March 4, 1872	151
Republicanism. April 7, 1872	152
Free Trade—The French Commercial Treaty of 1872. November 22, 1872	153
The Birmingham Conservative Working Men's Mutual Improvement Association. February 28, 1873	156
On the Use of Indian Corn in England. October 10, 1873	159
Free Land. November 2, 1873	160
The Licensing System. November 27, 1873	161
The "Residuum." December 9, 1873	163
The American Jubilee Singers. December 23, 1873	165
Extempore Speaking and Preaching. January, 1874	166
The Liberal Party. March 2, 1874	168
Mr. Charles Sumner. April 4, 1874	169
The Civil Service. April 29, 1874	170
Temperance. June 5, 1874	171
Temperance. June 6, 1874	173
Vaccination. October 6, 1874	174
Free Trade in Relation to the Price of Food. October 12, 1874	175
Canvassing at Elections. October 26, 1874	176
Sunday Closing in Ireland. October 27, 1874	177
Secret Voting in Representative Bodies. January 12, 1875	178

Working-Men Candidates. February 13, 1875	179
Home Rule. February 25, 1875	181
The Tichborne Case. July 15, 1875	183
The Foreign Cattle Trade. September 3, 1875	186
Funeral Reform. October 26, 1875	188
Sunday Closing in Ireland. November 27, 1875	188
The Eastern Question—Turkish Rule in Europe. September 1, 1876	189
The Eastern Question—The Policy of England towards Turkey. September 30, 1876	191
Peace and War. September 22, 1876	193
War. November 25, 1876	195
Mr. Joseph Kay. April 11, 1877	196
Parliamentary Reporting. April 21, 1877	198
Free Trade—A Protective Policy in the English Colonies. July 31, 1877	199
Kindness to Animals. November 22, 1877	203
Consecrated Ground. November 23, 1877	203
India—The Indian Import and Excise Duties. February 7, 1878	205
Free Trade and Armaments. March 18, 1878	207
Irish Members of Parliament in Relation to the Liberal Party. April 4, 1878	209
The Foreign Policy of Lord Beaconsfield's Government. May 2, 1878	210
The Liberal Party in Accrington. May 4, 1878	212
The Foreign Policy of Lord Beaconsfield's Government. May, 1878	213
The Liquor Traffic and the Tory Party. September 4, 1878	214
The Prevention of War. September 23, 1878	216
The Liquor Traffic. October 7, 1878	218
The "Virtuous Poor." November, 1878	219
Protection in the United States. January 21, 1879	222
Juvenile Smoking. February, 1879	223

CONTENTS.

	PAGE
Perpetual Pensions, Septennial Parliaments, and the Beaconsfield Government. March 11, 1879	224
Tory Misrepresentation. March 28, 1879	226
The Condition of England under Free Trade. April 1, 1879	227
Free Trade and the Depression in Trade in 1879. May, 1879	228
The Depression in Trade in 1879 and its Causes. June 26, 1879	231
Free Trade—Its Progress and Results. August 1, 1879	233
Canadian Policy. August 16, 1879	236
War. August 18, 1879	238
The Game Laws. November 16, 1879	239
The Study of Political Questions. November 17, 1879	241
The Crimean War. December 13, 1879	242
Fagot Voting. December 20, 1879	243
Reading the Bible in Board Schools. February 20, 1880	244
The Trade between England and the United States. January 3, 1880	245
The Beaconsfield Government. March, 1880	246
Three-Cornered Constituencies. July, 1880	247
On being elected Lord Rector of Glasgow University. November 22, 1880	248
Monarchs, Aristocracy, and Landowners. December 25, 1880	249
Tory Clergy. January 11, 1881	251
The Policy of the Gladstone Government in the Transvaal, and on the Hon. James Lowther. February, 1881	252
The Transvaal Peace. March 14, 1881	253
The Transvaal Peace. March 23, 1881	254
Free Trade—Mr. Hermon's Protective Proposals. March 18, 1881	255
Free Trade—The French and American Tariffs. March 29, 1881	257

CONTENTS.

	PAGE
Reciprocity. April 15, 1881	260
Liberal Rule. April, 1881	262
The French Treaty. August 10, 1881	263
The Irish Land Bill of 1881. August 19, 1881	264
Reciprocity. September 2, 1881	265
Free Trade. November 20, 1881	266
On completing his Seventieth Year. December 13, 1881	267
National Expenditure. February, 1882	268
Slavery in the United States. March 8, 1882	269
The Salvation Army. May 3, 1882	270
The War in Egypt. September 25, 1882	271
The Rules of Procedure. October 19, 1882	273
On completing his Seventy-First Year. November 21, 1882	274
On an Invitation being sent to Mr. Bright to visit America. January 16, 1883	275
The Oaths Question. February 14, 1883	278
The Income Tax. April 6, 1883	279
The Marriage Laws. May 7, 1883	280
The Government of India. August 25, 1883	281
The Work of Luther. September 3, 1883	282
The Future of Ireland. October 4, 1883	283
Election Fads. October 8, 1883	284
Election Fads—Mr. Hare's Scheme. October 16, 1883	286
Protection in Young Countries. November 20, 1883	287
Vaccination. December, 1883	290
The Factory Acts. January 1, 1884	292
War. February 13, 1884	292
The Land Laws. February 27, 1884	293
America, Peace, and War. March 10, 1884	295
Fair Trade. April 1, 1884	297
A Llandudno Pensioner. April, 1884	300
Free Trade and Depressed Industries. June 19, 1884	300
The House of Lords. July 18, 1884	303

CONTENTS.

	PAGE
Lord Salisbury's Misrepresentation of Mr. Bright's Views. October 9, 1884	304
The Sunday Postal Delivery. October 23, 1884	306
Integrity in Business. November, 1884	308
Indian Government. November, 1884	309
The Results of Free Trade in England. November 17, 1884	311
Land and its Rent. December 19, 1884	315
A Conservative Candidate's Speech. December 27, 1884	320
The Liberal Party in Relation to Agricultural Labourers. December 29, 1884	323

ADDENDUM.

Address to the Working Men of Rochdale. August, 1842	331

THE PUBLIC LETTERS

OF THE

RIGHT HON. JOHN BRIGHT, M.P.

ON FOREIGN POLICY.

ADDRESSED to one of Mr. Bright's constituents, who had written to him expressing his disapproval of his vote against Mr. Roebuck's resolution on the foreign policy of the Russell Government.

Mr. Roebuck's resolution was moved on the 24th of June, 1850. It had reference to the foreign policy of the Government, of which Lord John Russell was Premier and Lord Palmerston Foreign Secretary, and was as follows:—"That the principles which have hitherto regulated the foreign policy of her Majesty's Government are such as were required to preserve untarnished the honour and dignity of this country, and at all times best calculated to maintain peace between this country and the various nations of the world." Mr. Roebuck moved this resolution as a vote of confidence in the Government in reply to an adverse vote in the House of Lords, on the 17th of June, on Lord Stanley's motion, censuring the Government for undue interference in the affairs of Greece. The debate in the Commons lasted four nights. It was remarkable for the brilliant defence which Lord Palmerston made for his policy, and ended in a majority of forty-six for the Government. Among those who spoke in support of the Government was Mr. Alexander Cockburn, afterwards Lord Chief Justice, and the most notable speeches against the resolution were those of Mr. Gladstone and Sir Robert Peel. The latter spoke on this occasion for the last time in the House of Commons. On the following day the lamentable accident occurred which terminated his life.

London, July 3, 1850.

Sir,—I have your letter of yesterday, and regret to find that my vote on a recent occasion has not been such as to meet your views. I cannot, of course, expect on all occasions to find myself in harmony with all the electors of Manchester; but I am most anxious that my votes should be found in accordance with my honest convictions and with the sentiments I expressed in Manchester before and at my election.

The question at issue in the late debate was mainly this: Shall the foreign minister of this country be permitted to interfere in the affairs of other countries in cases where the direct interests of the country do not require it? Shall he advise, and warn, and meddle in matters which concern only the domestic and internal affairs of other countries? I say that such a policy necessarily leads to irritation, and to quarrels with other nations, and may lead even to war; and that it involves the necessity of maintaining greater armaments, and a heavier expenditure and taxation than would otherwise be required. It is a policy, therefore, which I cannot support under any pretence whatever. It is contrary to all I have ever declared in the Free Trade Hall, and in the many speeches in which I have touched upon this subject; and it is contrary to the principles on which I was elected.

With regard to the particular vote, I have only to say that, in giving it, I followed my own convictions, and acted upon opinions long since and constantly avowed. I venture to think that no good could arise to Manchester from its representatives acting on any other principle; and I would not, for a moment, sit in parliament for Manchester, or for any other constituency, if it was to be understood that I am to forget my own character and long-held principles, and what I believe to be the true interests of the country, to abandon all these, and vote as the necessities of *party* may require, at the crack of the treasury whip.

You speak of an alliance with Lord Stanley, and seem to forget that the resolution on which I voted was moved by Mr. Roebuck, a friend of the present Government. It was not a resolution condemning the Government, moved by an opponent, but a resolution approving the Government policy, moved by one of their friends. I was asked to approve it; honestly, I could not do it. You may say that I might have been absent; but the question appeared to me of so grave a character, that I felt I could not shrink from deciding upon it. I took the only honest and manly course, and I am prepared to abide the consequences. To represent Manchester, on such terms as an independent mind can accept, is a position of honour which I hope I can fully appreciate; but to sit in Parliament as the mere instrument of *party* is no object of hope or ambition with me.

It is possible my conduct may be blamed, and my motives called in question by some, but I will rely with confidence on all I have done in public life during the last ten years as my answer to those who suppose me careless of the interests of freedom, whether at home or abroad. I have the satisfaction, too, of having voted with my colleague in the representation of Manchester,[1] and of his judgment, and principles, and political honesty, I have the highest opinion. I voted, too, with Mr. Cobden, whom few men will suspect of a want of political sagacity, or a disregard of the true interests of liberty and of his country. I voted, too, with Mr. Hume, of whose character and labours for the public welfare I need say nothing. I voted, too, with that statesman,[2] since then so suddenly taken from amongst us, whose good disposition towards the existing Government none could doubt, and whose sacrifices in recent years

---

[1] Mr. T. Milner Gibson.
[2] Sir Robert Peel. Died July 2, 1850.

have been such as to make his name sacred among his countrymen, and if on this point there be any distinction among them, most of all to be revered by the inhabitants of your city.

I am fortified, then, by the association of men for whose judgment, and principles, and character, I have the most profound regard,— by the knowledge that I have acted in accordance with every pledge, and with every opinion expressed in times past to my constituents,— and more than all by the consciousness that my vote has been recorded against a policy calculated to engender ill-will between nations, and therefore, in reality, hostile to the true interests of liberty, both at home and abroad.

I have not the pleasure of being personally acquainted with you, but as you are the only person, among all the constituency of Manchester, who has written to me in condemnation of my vote, I take the liberty of writing to you at some length, in justification of the course I have taken.

I am, very respectfully,
JOHN BRIGHT.

To Mr. John Heywood, Manchester.

ON THE IRISH CHURCH QUESTION.

Addressed to Dr. Gray, Editor of the *Freeman's Journal*, afterwards Sir John Gray, M.P.

Rochdale, October 25, 1852.

MY DEAR DR. GRAY,—I observe from the

newspapers that the friends of "religious equality" in Ireland are about to hold a conference in the city of Dublin with a view to consider the existing ecclesiastical arrangements of your country. My engagements will not permit me to be present at your deliberations, and, indeed, I am not sure that your invitations extend further than to Irishmen and Irish representatives; but I feel strongly disposed to address you on the great question you are about to discuss—a question affecting the policy and interests of the United Kingdom, but of vital importance to Ireland.

Let me say, in the first place, that I am heartily glad that any number of the Irish representatives should have resolved to grapple with a question which, in my opinion, must be settled on some just basis, if Ireland is ever to become tranquil and content. The case of the Catholic population of Ireland—and, in truth, it is scarcely more their case than that of every intelligent and just Protestant in the three kingdoms—is so strong, so unanswerable, and so generally admitted, that nothing is wanting to ensure its complete success but the combination of a few able and honest men to concentrate and direct the opinion which exists. If such men are to be found among you—resolute, persevering, and disinterested—a great work is before them, and as certainly a great result. They will meet with insult and calumny in abundance; every engine of the "supremacy" party will be in motion against them; they will be denounced as "conspirators" against the institutions of the country, when, in fact, they combine only against a grievance which it is hard to say whether it is more humiliating in Ireland to endure, or disgraceful in England to inflict; but against all this, having a right cause, and working it by right means, they will certainly succeed.

It would be to insult your understanding were I to imagine that you demand anything more or less than a perfect "equality" before the law for the religious sects which exist in Ireland—that is, for the members or adherents of the Protestant Episcopalian, the Presbyterian, and the Roman Catholic Churches. So entirely is it felt that you are in the right in making this demand, that with regard to it your opponents dare not attempt an argument with you; they prefer to say that you claim something else—namely, a supremacy as hateful as their own, and then they find it easy to contest the matter with you, writing and speaking as they do chiefly to a Protestant audience. On this point there should be no possibility of mistake; and not only should the demand for equality be unequivocal, but it appears to me most desirable that some mode of attaining it should be distinctly pointed out. We may, perhaps, imagine an "equality" which would allow the Protestant Establishment to remain as it is, or, at least, to continue to be a State Church, building up at its side a Catholic Establishment; and, to complete the scheme, a Presbyterian Establishment also, having a batch of Catholic prelates and of Presbyterian divines in the House of Lords; but, in my opinion, any scheme of "equality" of this description would be, and must necessarily be, altogether impracticable.

Lord John Russell, I think in 1843, expressed an opinion that the Protestant Church in Ireland should not be subverted, " but that the Roman Catholic Church, with its bishops and clergy, should be placed by the State on a footing of equality with that Church." He adopted the term "equality," and said that any plan he should propose would be "to follow out that principle of equality with all its consequences." Lord Grey, in 1845, was, if possible, still more explicit, for he said, after expressing his opinion that "the Catholics have the first claim" on the funds applied to ecclesiastical purposes in Ireland, "you must give the Catholic clergy an equality also in social rank and position;" and he went even further than this, and said, "I carry my view on this subject as far as to wish to see the prelates of the Roman Catholic Church take their places in this House on the episcopal bench." From this it appears that Lord John Russell and Lord Grey, seeing the enormous evil of the existing system, were ready to justify almost any measure that promised political and ecclesiastical equality, to be obtained without the subversion of the Protestant Established Church in Ireland.

Of course, if all parties among the statesmen and the public of the United Kingdom were agreed, funds might be provided for the perpetual endowment and subjection to State control of the Irish Catholic and Presbyterian Churches, and some plan might be devised to secure them a representation in the House of Lords; but, happily for sound principles in civil government, and happily for religion itself, all parties are not agreed to do this, but are rather agreed that it shall not be done. The "equality" which Lord John Russell would "follow out with all its consequences" is a dream, and Lord Grey's bold idea of giving the Irish Catholics "the first claim to the funds" and of placing their bishops in the House of Lords is not less impracticable. To have two Established Churches in Ireland, the one Protestant and the other Catholic; to have in the House of Lords Protestant and Catholic bishops, elbowing each other on "the right reverend bench," guarding the temporal and spiritual interests of two Churches which denounce each other as idolatrous or heretical, would be an inconsistency so glaring, that it would go far to overthrow all reverence for Governments and Churches, if not for Christianity itself. The scheme is surely too absurd to be seriously thought of, and if there be a statesman bold enough to propose it, he will find no support in the opinion of the English public, except from that small section with whom religion goes for nothing, and churches and priests are tolerated as machinery in the pay and service of the Government.

But there is an "equality" which is attainable without inconsistency, which would meet with favour among large classes in every part of Great Britain, and which, I think, if fairly proposed, would be well received by many of the more enlightened and just Protestants in Ireland. It is an " equality" which must start from this point, that henceforth there must be no Church in Ireland in connection with the State. The whole body of English Dissenters, the United Presbyterian Church of Scotland, and the Catholic population of the United Kingdom, might be expected cordially to welcome such a proposition; and it is difficult to understand how the Presbyterians of the north of Ireland, or the Free Church of Scotland, or the adherents of the Wesleyan Conference in England, could, with any consistency or decency, oppose it; and I am confident that a large number of persons connected with the Established Churches in the three kingdoms, who are enlightened enough to see what is right, and just enough to wish it to be done, would give their support to any Minister who had the courage to make such a measure the great distinguishing act of his administration. But if this principle were adopted—that is, the principle that henceforth there must be no Church in Ireland in connection with the State —there would still be a question as to the appropriation of the large funds now in the hands of the Irish Established Church.

There are two modes of dealing with these funds, either of which may be defended, but one of them seems to offer facilities which do not belong to the other. The most simple plan would be to absorb the revenues of the Established Church, as the livings become vacant, and to apply them in some channel not ecclesiastical, in which the whole population of Ireland could participate. The objections to this plan are, that it would be hard upon the Protestant Episcopalians, after having pampered them so long with a munificent support, to throw them at once on their resources; and that to withdraw the *Regium Donum* from the Presbyterians of the North, when they have no other provision made for their religious wants, would be to create a just discontent among them. There is some force in this, inasmuch as upon one generation would be thrown the burden of the creation and support of a religious organization which, in voluntary churches, is commonly the work of successive generations of their adherents, and the argument may be considered almost irresistible when it is offered to a Government which does not repudiate, but rather cherishes, the principle of a State Church. But, whatever may be the inconveniencies of this plan, they are, in my estimation, infinitely less than those which are inseparable from a continuance of the present system.

There is, however, another mode of settlement which, though open to some objection, is probably more likely to obtain a general concurrence of opinion in its favour in Ireland, and to which, I think, a great amount of consent might be obtained in England and Scotland. Your present ecclesiastical arrangements are briefly these: The Protestant Episcopal

Church has 500,000*l.* per annum intrusted to it, or a principal sum, at twenty years' purchase, of 10,000,000*l.* sterling. The Presbyterian Church or Churches have 40,000*l.* per annum, or, estimated at the same rate, a principal sum of 800,000*l.* The Roman Catholic Church has 26,000*l.* per annum, or a principal sum of 520,000*l.* I will say nothing about the exact proportions of population belonging to each Church, for I do not wish to give opportunity for dispute about figures. It is sufficient to say, what everybody knows to be true, that the Irish population is Catholic, and that the Protestants, whether of the Episcopalian or Presbyterian Church, or of both united, are a small minority of the Irish people. I will admit the temporary hardship of at once withdrawing from the Protestant sects all the resources which the State has hitherto provided for them; but, at the same time, no one can deny, and I cannot forget, the hardship to which the Catholics have been subjected, inasmuch as they, the poorest portion of the people, and by many times the most numerous, have been shut out from almost all participation in the public funds applied to ecclesiastical purposes in Ireland. Is it not possible to make an arrangement by which the menaced hardship to the Protestants may be avoided, and that so long endured by the Catholics, in part at least, redressed? And can this be done without departing from the principle, "that henceforth there must be no Church in Ireland in connection with the State?" Let an Act be passed to establish a "Church Property Commission" for Ireland, and let this Commission hold in trust, for certain purposes, all the tithes and other property now enjoyed by the Established Church; let it, in fact, become possessed of the 10,000,000*l.* sterling, the income from which now forms the revenues of that Church, as the livings and benefices become vacant. It would be desirable to offer facilities to the landed proprietors to purchase the tithes at an easy rate, in order that funds might be in hand to carry out the other arrangements of the scheme.

I have estimated the total value at 10,000,000*l.*; it might not reach that sum if the tithes were sold at a low rate; but whether it were 10,000,000*l.* or only 8,000,000*l.* would not affect the practicability or the justice of this proposition. Let this Commission be empowered and directed to appropriate certain portions of this fund as a free gift to each of the three Churches in Ireland—to the Protestant Episcopalian, the Presbyterian, and the Roman Catholic Church. Whatever is thus given must be a free gift, and become as much the private property of the respective sects or Churches as is the property of the Free Church in Scotland, or that of the Wesleyan Methodists in England. It must no longer be a trust from the State, liable to interference or recall by the State, or the "equality" and independence of the Irish sects will not be secured.

There comes now the question of the amounts to be thus given. From some inquiries I have made I have arrived at the conclusion that if in each parish in Ireland there was a house and a small piece of land, say from ten to twenty acres, in the possession of the Roman Catholic Church, that would be all the provision that would be required or wished for, as the general support of its ministers would be derived, as at present, from the voluntary contributions their flocks. There are, in round numbers, about 1000 parishes in Ireland. In many of them there is now a provision up to the standard above stated in the possession of the Roman Catholic Church, but I will assume that in all of them such provision would have to be made. One thousand pounds for each parish, taking one parish with another, would amply make up any deficiency, and this amount throughout the parishes of Ireland would require the sum of 1,000,000*l.* sterling to be appropriated from the general fund; and this should be made over absolutely and for ever to the Roman Catholics of Ireland, in such hands and in such manner as the funds of their Church raised by voluntary effort are usually secured.

Under an arrangement of this kind, of course, the special grant to the College of Maynooth would be withdrawn. The Presbyterians, under the operation of this Act, would lose their annual grant of 40,000*l.*; but, in place of it, assuming that they have an organization and a system of government which would enable them to hold and administer funds for the use of their Church, a portion of the general fund should be set apart for them, equal to the production of a revenue of like amount with that they now receive by grant from Parliament. This should also be given to them absolutely and for ever, and they should become henceforth a voluntary and independent Church.

The Protestant Episcopalians should be treated as liberally as the Presbyterians, with whom, it is estimated, they are about on a par in point of numbers. Assuming that they could and would form themselves into a Free Episcopal Church, the Commission would be empowered to grant them a sum equal to that granted to the Presbyterians, and which would be about the same in amount as that granted to the Catholics. And further, so long as they undertook to keep the churches in repair, they might be permitted to retain possession of them at a nominal rent, for their own use only; and that when or where they had no congregation sufficient to maintain the church, then the buildings should be at the disposal of the Commission to let or sell, as might be thought best. In the case of the Protestant Episcopalians, as with the Presbyterians and the Catholics, whatever sum is given to them must be given absolutely and for ever, that henceforth they may rely on their own resources and become a voluntary and independent Church.

The State would thus have distributed about 3,000,000*l.* of the original fund, and would have relinquished all claims upon it for ever; and it would be the duty of the Commission to take care that those grants were applied, in the first instance, for the purposes and in the manner intended by the Act. The remaining 5,000,000*l.* or 7,000,000*l.*, as the case might be, might, and in my opinion ought, to be reserved for purposes strictly Irish, and directed to the educational and moral improvement of the people, without respect to class or creed. This fund would extend and perfect the educational institutions of the country; it would establish and endow free libraries in all the chief towns of Ireland, and would dispense blessings in many channels for the free and equal enjoyment of the whole population. Of course there will be objections started to this scheme, as there will be to any scheme which attempts to remedy an injustice which has lasted for centuries. The "Church party" may, and probably will, denounce it as a plan of spoliation most cruel and unholy; but no man who proposes to remedy Irish ecclesiastical wrongs can expect to find favour with the sect whose supremacy he is compelled to assail. We must hope that State patronage has not so entirely demoralized the members of the Protestant Episcopalian sect, either in England or Ireland, as to leave none among them who are able to see what is just on this question, and who are willing that what is just should be done. I believe there are many intelligent and earnest Churchmen, and some eminent politicians connected with the Established Church, who would welcome almost any proposition which afforded a hope of a final settlement of this question.

From Scotland, and probably from certain quarters in England, we may hear of the great crime of handing over 1,000,000*l.* sterling to the Roman Catholics of Ireland. It will, perhaps, be insisted upon that to add to the means of a Church whose teaching is held to be "erroneous" is a grievous national sin; and many will honestly doubt the wisdom of a scheme which proposes such an appropriation of a portion of the public fund. Now, there is not a man in the United Kingdom more averse to religious endowments by the State than I am. I object to the compulsory levying of a tax from any man to teach any religion, and still more to teach a religion in which he does not believe; and I am of opinion that, to take a Church into the pay of the State, and to place it under the control of the State, is to deaden and corrupt the Church, and to enlist its influence on the side of all that is evil in the civil government. But in the plan now suggested the Irish sects or Churches would be left entirely free, as is the Free Church in Scotland, or the Wesleyan Methodist Church in England. The grants once made, each Church would possess absolutely its own funds, just as much as if they were the accumulations of the voluntary contributions and liberality of past generations of its members, and thus would be avoided the damage to religion and to civil government which is inseparable from what is called the union of Church and State; whilst the sum granted to each Church, being equal to a provision of about 40,000*l.* per

annum, would be too small to create any
important corporate influence adverse to the
public interest.

As to the complaint that the sum of
1,000,000*l.* is proposed to be given to the Irish
Catholics, I will ask any man with a head to
comprehend, and a heart to feel, to read the
history of Ireland, not from the time of Henry
VIII., but from the accession of William III.,
and if he insists upon a settlement of this question
by grants to the Protestant sects, and by
the refusal of any corresponding grant to the
Roman Catholics, I can only say that his statesmanship
is as wanting in wisdom as his Protestantism
lacks the spirit of Christianity. If,
for generations, a portion of the Protestants of
Ireland, few in number, but possessing much
wealth, have enjoyed the large ecclesiastical
revenues of a whole kingdom; and if, during
the same period, the Roman Catholics, the bulk
of the population, but possessing little wealth,
have been thrown entirely on their own limited
resources, and under circumstances of political
and social inferiority, can it be possible, when
an attempt shall be made to remedy some of
the manifold injustice of past times, that any
Englishman or any Scotchman will be found to
complain of the impartiality of the Government,
and in his zeal for Protestantism to forget the
simple obligations of justice?

But it may be objected that it is contrary to
sound policy to make grants of public money
to any public body, or corporation, or sect, not
submitting to State control—that, in fact, a

Church receiving anything from the State should be a State Church. No one is more sensible of the weight and soundness of this argument than I am; but observe the peculiarities of this case. I start from the point that "henceforth there shall be no Church in Ireland in connection with the State." I have to free the Protestant Episcopalian sect and the Presbyterians from their State connection; and to make the Irish sects voluntary Churches for the future. I propose an appropriation of about one-third of existing ecclesiastical property in Ireland, with a view to soften the apparent severity of the change to the sects heretofore paid by the State, and to make some amends to that majority of the Irish population, the injustice of whose past treatment is admitted by all the world. The Protestants of Ireland have done hitherto little for themselves, because the bounty of the State has paralysed their exertions, or made exertion unnecessary. The Catholics have done much for themselves; but they are in great poverty, and our existing ecclesiastical legislation has been felt, and is now felt, by them to be grievously unjust. Would it not be worth the concession of the sum I have suggested, and of the deviation from ordinary rule which I venture to recommend, to obtain the grand result which is contemplated by the change now proposed? I have said that there will be objections to this scheme and to every scheme. The grievance is centuries old, and around it are entwined interests, prejudices, fanaticism, animosities, and convictions. It is a desperate evil, and whoever waits till the remedy is pleasant to everybody may and will wait for ever. The object in view is the tranquillity of Ireland. The means are simple, but altogether novel in that unhappy country—to do full and impartial justice to her whole population. I propose to leave the Presbyterians as well circumstanced as they are now, with this exception, that all future extension of their organization must be made at their own cost; and I would place the Protestant Episcopalians in as good a position as the Presbyterians. The Catholics only could have any ground of complaint, owing to their numbers so far exceeding those of the Protestant sects; but in the application of the remainder, and much the largest portion of the funds, for educational or other purposes, they would participate exactly in proportion to their numbers; and I have a strong belief that, so far as they are concerned, such an arrangement as is now suggested would be accepted as a final settlement of a most difficult and irritating question.

As you know, I am neither Roman Catholic, Protestant Episcopalian, nor Presbyterian, nor am I an Irishman. My interest in this matter is not local or sectarian. I have endeavoured to study it, and to regard it as becomes an Englishman loving justice and freedom, anxious for the tranquillity of Ireland, the welfare of the empire, and the honour of the imperial government. I believe that statesmanship does not consist merely in preserving institutions, but rather in adapting them to the wants of nations, and that it is possible so to adapt the institutions of Ireland to the wants and circumstances of Ireland, that her people may become as content as the people of England and Scotland are with the mild monarchy under which we live. Some experience and much reflection have convinced me that all efforts on behalf of industry and peace in Ireland will be in great part unavailing until we eradicate the sentiment which is universal among her Catholic population—that the Imperial Government is partial, and that to belong to the Roman Catholic Church is to incur the suspicion or the hostility of the law. A true "equality" established among the Irish sects would put an end to this pernicious but all-pervading sentiment; and Catholics, whether priests or laymen, would feel that the last link of their fetters was at length broken. Supremacy on the one hand, and a degrading inferiority on the other, would be abolished, and the whole atmosphere of Irish social and political life would be purified. Then, too, Christianity would appeal to the population, not as a persecuting or a persecuted faith, with her features disfigured by the violence of political conflict, but radiant with the divine beauty which belongs to her, and speaking with irresistible force to the hearts and consciences of men.

I know not if the statesman be among us who is destined to settle this great question, but whoever he may be he will strengthen the monarchy, earn the gratitude of three kingdoms,

and build up for himself a lasting renown. I
am sensible that in writing this letter, and in
expressing the views it contains, I run the risk
of being misunderstood by some honest men,
and may subject myself to misrepresentation
and abuse. It is under a solemn sense of duty
to my country, and to the interests of justice
and religion, that I have ventured to write it.
I have endeavoured to divest myself of all feeling of preference for, or hostility to, any of the
Churches or sects in Ireland, and to form my
judgment in this matter upon principles
admitted by all true statesmanship, and based
on the foundations of Christian justice. If I
should succeed in directing the attention of any
portion of those most deeply interested to some
mode of escape from the difficulties with which
this question is surrounded, I shall willingly
submit to the suspicions or condemnation of
those who cannot concur with me in opinion.
I wish this long letter were more worthy of its
purpose. As it is, I send it to you, and you
may make whatever use of it you think will be
likely to serve the cause of "religious equality"
in Ireland.

    Believe me to be, very truly yours,

                             JOHN BRIGHT.

ON THE WAR WITH RUSSIA.

Written to Mr. David Urquhart, and read at a
public meeting convened by that gentleman at
the Corn Exchange, Manchester, on April 19th,
1854, to discuss the question, "With whom are

we at war?" In opening the meeting Mr. Urquhart said it was his sense of alarm that had prompted his audacity in calling the meeting, and he thanked them for approving of that audacity by their attendance.

Rochdale, April 18, 1854.

DEAR SIR,—I have to thank you for your note of the 15th inst., inviting me to a meeting to be held in Manchester to-morrow. I am not astounded at your audacity in calling the meeting; on the contrary, I believe in your sincerity. I regard your resolution to appeal openly to your countrymen as courageous and proper. If I agreed with you on this Eastern question; if we had one starting-point—if our sentiments in regard to it were in harmony—I should feel it my duty to be at your side. But the fact is that we differ widely on almost every point, except in the condemnation of this war; and I do not think I should do anything for the cause of peace by appearing to go with you, when, in truth, there is little agreement between us. I believe the war to be altogether unnecessary, and that nothing can be said either for its justice or its expediency. I believe, further, that after having permitted the country by a series of blunders to drift into war, the ministers who have chiefly spoken on the subject, with the exception of Lord Aberdeen, have misrepresented the facts of the case, and have thereby misled public opinion.

With regard to the professed objects of the war, I believe them to be impossible of attainment, and that Russia, in her wildest dreams of ambition, never imagined so many calamities to Turkey as have been brought upon that devoted country, in a single year, by the friendship which our Government has professed towards her. It is a melancholy circumstance that the English public—not examining, and not reflecting, accepting, with a childlike simplicity, the declarations of statesmen, whose only present bond of union is a partnership in the guilt of this war, and relying on the assertions of a press more anxious for a trade in newspapers than for truth—should give their sanction to proceedings as much opposed to their own interests as they are to every principle of morality. Our countrymen fancy they are fighting for freedom because the Russian Government is a despotism: they forget that the object of their solicitude is no less a despot; that their chief ally but the other day overthrew a republic, and imprisoned or expatriated the members of a freely-elected parliament; that they are alternately coaxing and bullying Austria, whose regard for freedom and justice Hungary and Italy can attest, to join them in this holy war, and that the chief result of their success, if success be possible, will be to perpetuate the domination of a handful of the followers of Mahomet over many millions of Christians throughout the provinces of European Turkey.

There was a time when it was fashionable to have sympathy for Greece. Now, Athens is to be occupied by English and French troops if a strong anti-Turkish feeling is manifested there. Five years ago English Liberals wished success to the insurrections in Italy and to the war for independence in Hungary; now, the efforts of the Greeks for freedom are pronounced ill-timed, as if we, who are sending our fleets and armies to perfect their subjugation to the Turks, were the best judges of the moment when their fetters should be struck off. The people, or a portion of them, are drunk with a confused notion of fighting with Russia; they confound the blowing up of ships and the slaughter of thousands with the cause of freedom, as if there were any connection in matters wholly apart.

I cannot hope to change this feeling, and fear you cannot. Time and experience alone will convince them, perhaps when too late, that a great national crime lies at their door. The time will come when history will record what English treasure was expended, and what English blood was shed, for an object in which England had no real interest, and for an object, too, which the very statesmen who advised it knew could not possibly succeed. I have spoken my sentiments on this painful question in the House of Commons—my constituents are generally acquainted with them—and therefore I feel it the less needful for me to take part in the meeting to-morrow.

I am, with great respect,
Yours, &c.,
JOHN BRIGHT.

David Urquhart, Esq., Manchester.

LETTER TO MR. ABSALOM WATKIN.

Mr. Absalom Watkin, of Manchester, having invited Mr. Bright to a meeting for the Patriotic Fund about to be held in that city, and having stated that in his opinion the present war was justified by the authority of *Vattel*, Mr. Bright replied in the subjoined letter.

Rhyl, North Wales, October 29, 1854.

MY DEAR SIR,—I think, on further consideration, you will perceive that the meeting on Thursday would be a most improper occasion for a discussion as to the justice of the war. Just or unjust, the war is a fact, and the men whose lives are miserably thrown away in it have clearly a claim upon the country, and especially upon those who, by the expression of opinions favourable to the war, have made themselves responsible for it. I cannot, therefore, for a moment, appear to discourage the liberality of those who believe the war to be just, and whose utmost generosity, in my opinion, will make but a wretched return for the ruin they have brought upon hundreds of families.

With regard to the war itself, I am not surprised at the difference between your opinion and mine, if you decide a question of this nature by an appeal to *Vattel*. The "law of nations" is not my law, and at best it is a code full of confusion and contradictions, having its foundation on custom, and not on a higher morality; and on custom which has always been determined by the will of the strongest. It may be a question of some interest whether the first crusade was in accordance with the law and principles of *Vattel;* but whether the first crusade was just, and whether the policy of the crusades was a wise policy, is a totally different question. I have no doubt that the American war was a just war according to the principles laid down by writers on the " law of nations," and yet no man in his senses in this country will now say that the policy of George III. towards the American colonies was a wise policy, or that war a righteous war. The French war, too, was doubtless just according to the same authorities; for there were fears and anticipated dangers to be combatted, and law and order to be sustained in Europe; and yet few intelligent men now believe the French war to have been either necessary or just. You must excuse me if I refuse altogether to pin my faith upon *Vattel.* There have been writers on international law, who have attempted to show that private assassination and the poisoning of wells were justifiable in war; and perhaps it would be difficult to demonstrate wherein these horrors differ from some of the practices which are now in vogue. I will not ask you to mould your opinion on these points by such writers, nor shall I submit my judgment to that of *Vattel.*

The question of this present war is in two parts—first, was it necessary for us to interfere by arms in a dispute between the Russians and the Turks? and secondly, having determined to

interfere, under certain circumstances, why was
not the whole question terminated when Russia
accepted the Vienna note? The seat of war is
3000 miles away from us. We had not been
attacked—not even insulted in any way. Two
independent Governments had a dispute, and
we thrust ourselves into the quarrel. That
there was some ground for the dispute is admitted by the four powers in the proposition of
the Vienna note. But for the English Minister
at Constantinople and the Cabinet at home the
dispute would have settled itself, and the last
note of Prince Menschikoff would have been
accepted, and no human being can point out any
material difference between that note and the
Vienna note, afterwards agreed upon and recommended by the Governments of England,
France, Austria, and Prussia. But our Government would not allow the dispute to be settled.
Lord Stratford de Redcliffe held private inter-
views with the Sultan—did his utmost to alarm
him—insisted on his rejection of all terms of
accommodation with Russia, and promised him
the armed assistance of England if war should
arise.

The Turks rejected the Russian note, and
the Russians crossed the Pruth, occupying the
Principalities as a " material guarantee." I do
not defend this act of Russia: it has always
appeared to me impolitic and immoral; but I
think it likely it could be well defended out of
Vattel, and it is at least as justifiable as the
conduct of Lord John Russell and Lord Palmerston in 1850, when they sent ten or twelve

ships of war to the Piræus, menacing the town with a bombardment if the dishonest pecuniary claim made by Don Pacifico were not at once satisfied.

But the passage of the Pruth was declared by England and France and Turkey not to be a *casus belli*. Negotiations were commenced at Vienna, and the celebrated Vienna note was drawn up. This note had its origin in Paris, was agreed to by the Conference at Vienna, ratified and approved by the Cabinets of Paris and London, and pronounced by all these authorities to be such as would satisfy the honour of Russia, and at the same time be compatible with the "independence and integrity" of Turkey and the honour of the Sultan. Russia accepted this note at once,—accepted it, I believe, by telegraph, even before the precise words of it had been received in St. Petersburg. Everybody thought the question now settled; a Cabinet Minister assured me we should never hear another word about it; "the whole thing is at an end," he said, and so it appeared for a moment. But the Turk refused the note which had been drawn up by his own arbitrators, and which Russia had accepted. And what did the Ministers say then, and what did their organ, the *Times*, say? They said it was merely a difference about words; it was a pity the Turk made any difficulty, but it would soon be settled. But it was not settled, and why not? It is said that the Russian Government put an improper construction on the Vienna note. But it is unfortunate for those who say this, that the Turk placed precisely the same construction upon it; and further it is upon record that the French Government advised the Russian Government to accept it, on the ground that "its general sense differed in nothing from the sense of the proposition of Prince Menschikoff." It is, however, easy to see why the Russian Government should, when the Turks refused the award of their own arbitrators, re-state its original claim, that it might not be damaged by whatever concession it had made in accepting the award; and this is evidently the explanation of the document issued by Count Nesselrode, and about which so much has been said. But, after this, the Emperor of Russia spoke to Lord Westmoreland on the subject at Olmutz, and expressed his readiness to accept the Vienna note, with any clause which the Conference might add to it, explaining and restricting its meaning; and he urged that this should be done at once, as he was anxious that his troops should re-cross the Pruth before winter. It was in this very week that the Turks summoned a grand council, and, contrary to the advice of England and France, determined on a declaration of war.

Now, observe the course taken by our Government. They agreed to the Vienna note; not fewer than five members of this Cabinet have filled the office of Foreign Secretary, and therefore may be supposed capable of comprehending its meaning: it was a note drawn up by the friends of Turkey, and by arbitrators self-constituted on behalf of Turkey; they urged its acceptance on the Russian Government, and the Russian Government accepted it; there was then a dispute about its precise meaning, and Russia agreed, and even proposed that the arbitrators at Vienna should amend it, by explaining it, and limiting its meaning, so that no question of its intention should henceforth exist. But, the Turks having rejected it, our Government turned round, and declared the Vienna note, their own note, entirely inadmissible, and defended the conduct of the Turks in having rejected it. The Turks declared war, against the advice of the English and French Governments—so, at least, it appears from the blue-books; but the moment war was declared by Turkey, our Government openly applauded it. England, then, was committed to the war. She had promised armed assistance to Turkey—a country without government, and whose administration was at the mercy of contending factions; and incapable of fixing a policy for herself, she allowed herself to be dragged on by the current of events at Constantinople. She "drifted," as Lord Clarendon said, exactly describing his own position, into the war, apparently without rudder and without compass.

The whole policy of our Government in this matter is marked with an imbecility perhaps without example. I will not say they intended a war from the first, though there are not wanting many evidences that war was the object of at least a section of the Cabinet. A distinguished member of the House of Commons said to a friend of mine, immediately after the accession of the present Government to office, "You have a war Ministry, and you will have a war." But I leave this question to point out the disgraceful feebleness of the Cabinet, if I am to absolve them from the guilt of having sought occasion for war. They promised the Turk armed assistance on conditions, or without conditions. They, in concert with France, Austria, and Prussia, took the original dispute out of the hands of Russia and Turkey, and formed themselves into a court of arbitration in the interests of Turkey; they made an award, which they declared to be safe and honourable for both parties; this award was accepted by Russia and rejected by Turkey; and they then turned round upon their own award, declared it to be "totally inadmissible," and made war upon the very country whose Government, at their suggestion and urgent recommendation, had frankly accepted it. At this moment England is engaged in a murderous warfare with Russia, although the Russian Government accepted her own terms of peace, and has been willing to accept them in the sense of England's own interpretation of them ever since they were offered; and at the same time England is allied with Turkey, whose Government rejected the award of England, and who entered into the war in opposition to the advice of England. Surely, when the Vienna note was accepted by Russia, the Turks should have been prevented from going to war, or should have been allowed to go to war at their own risk.

I have said nothing here of the fact that all these troubles have sprung out of the demands made by France upon the Turkish Government, and urged in language more insulting than any which has been shown to have been used by Prince Menschikoff. I have said nothing of the diplomatic war which has been raging for many years past in Constantinople, and in which England has been behind no other Power in attempting to subject the Porte to foreign influences. I have said nothing of the abundant evidences there is that we are not only at war with Russia, but with all the Christian population of the Turkish empire, and that we are building up our Eastern Policy on a false foundation—namely, on the perpetual maintenance of the most immoral and filthy of all despotisms over one of the fairest portions of the earth which it has desolated, and over a population it has degraded but has not been able to destroy. I have said nothing of the wretched delusion that we are fighting for civilization in supporting the Turk against the Russian and against the subject Christian population of Turkey. I have said nothing about our pretended sacrifices for freedom in this war, in which our great and now dominant ally is a monarch who, last in Europe, struck down a free constitution, and dispersed by military violence a national Representative Assembly.

My doctrine would have been non-intervention in this case. The danger of the Russian power was a phantom; the necessity of permanently upholding the Mahometan rule in Europe is an absurdity. Our love for civilization, when we subject the Greeks and Christians to the Turks, is a sham; and our sacrifices for freedom, when working out the behests of the Emperor of the French and coaxing Austria to help us, is a pitiful imposture. The evils of non-intervention were remote and vague, and could neither be weighed nor described in any accurate terms. The good we can judge something of already, by estimating the cost of a contrary policy. And what is that cost? War in the north and south of Europe, threatening to involve every country of Europe. Many, perhaps fifty millions sterling, in the course of expenditure by this country alone, to be raised from the taxes of a people whose extrication from ignorance and poverty can only be hoped for from the continuance of peace. The disturbance of trade throughout the world, the derangement of monetary affairs, and difficulties and ruin to thousands of families. Another year of high prices of food, notwithstanding a full harvest in England, chiefly because war interferes with imports, and we have declared our principal foreign food-growers to be our enemies. The loss of human life to an enormous extent. Many thousands of our own countrymen have already perished of pestilence and in the field; and hundreds, perhaps thousands, of English families will be plunged into sorrow, as a part of the penalty to be paid for the folly of the nation and its rulers.

When the time comes for the "inquisition for blood," who shall answer for these things? You have read the tidings from the Crimea; you have, perhaps, shuddered at the slaughter; you remember the terrific picture—I speak not of the battle, and the charge, and the tumultuous excitement of the conflict, but of the field after the battle—Russians in their frenzy or their terror, shooting Englishmen who would have offered them water to quench their agony of thirst; Englishmen, in crowds, rifling the pockets of the men they had slain or wounded, taking their few shillings or roubles, and discovering among the plunder of the stiffening corpses images of the "Virgin and the Child." You have read this, and your imagination has followed the fearful details. This is war,—every crime which human nature can commit or imagine, every horror it can perpetrate or suffer; and this it is which our Christian Government recklessly plunges into, and which so many of our countrymen at this moment think it patriotic to applaud! You must excuse me if I cannot go with you. I will have no part in this terrible crime. My hands shall be unstained with the blood which is being shed. The necessity of maintaining themselves in office may influence an administration; delusions may mislead a people; *Vattel* may afford you a law and a defence; but no respect for men who form a Government, no regard I have for "going with the stream," and no fear of being deemed wanting in patriotism, shall influence me in favour of a policy which, in my conscience, I believe to be as criminal before God as it is destructive of the true interest of my country.

I have only to ask you to forgive me for writing so long a letter. You have forced it from me, and I would not have written it did I not so much appreciate your sincerity and your good intentions towards me.

Believe me to be very sincerely yours,
JOHN BRIGHT.

Absalom Watkin, Esq., Manchester.

ON HIS REPRESENTATION OF MANCHESTER.

Read at a public meeting in the Free Trade Hall, Manchester, on Thursday evening, the 29th of January, 1857. The meeting was held to support the cause of Free Trade and Reform, Mr. George Wilson being in the chair. The letter was received with applause, and a resolution was afterwards enthusiastically passed, expressing sympathy with, and unabated confidence in, Mr. Bright, and requesting him to allow the continuance of his parliamentary connection with that city.

Mr. Bright had represented Manchester since July, 1847, when he was elected along with Mr. Milner Gibson. From 1843 up to that time he had represented the City of Durham.

Rochdale, November 5, 1856.

MY DEAR WILSON,—I mentioned to you a few days ago that I was about to leave England for a considerable time, probably for several months. My health, as you know, is greatly improved during the past six months—so much so as to afford strong reason for the belief that a further period of relaxation, and change of objects and interests, will so far restore me as to enable me again to attend to public business. I have consulted physicians of extensive practice, and eminent in the profession, and their opinions all concur in this—that a complete rest from public labour, for a longer period, is necessary; and that this, it may be hoped and believed, will give me renewed health and strength. Acting upon this advice, which my own judgment entirely approves, I am about to leave home for some months, and I shall, therefore, in all probability, not be able to attend the House of Commons during the next session of Parliament.

I think it my duty, under these circumstances, to write to you in your capacity of chairman of the committee which undertook the management of my election in 1852. I am very sensible of the kindness shown to me by my constituents, inasmuch as I believe they freely consented to my absence from Parliament during the past session. In absenting myself for another session, however, I feel that I am bound to enter into a more public and definite explanation with them.

Incapable as I am at present, of performing any of the duties of their representative, it would seem to be my duty to resign my seat in Parliament, and to give them the opportuity of electing my successor. I feel, however, that the wishes and convenience of the constituency ought to be consulted before I decide. If we were at the beginning, instead of being, as we are, very near the end of a Parliament, the interests of all concerned would probably be best promoted by my immediate resignation; but as a general election is likely to take place during the year 1857, it may not be thought desirable to have two elections for Manchester during the same year. This is a point which I am anxious to refer to my friends in Manchester before I do anything which would make an immediate election unavoidable.

You will greatly oblige me, therefore, if you will take such steps as appear to you best, to ascertain the wishes of my constituents as to the course I should take. I shall be guided by their decision, either to vacate my seat in Parliament on the opening of the coming session, or to retain it till the dissolution of the Parliament, which may come in the spring, and is almost certain to come in the autumn, of 1857.

I hope I am not too sanguine in believing that a few months more of rest—rest of the faculties which have had almost no rest during the past fifteen years,—will restore to me the power, as I still have the will, to labour in that field in which so much of my life has been spent. If I am permitted to recover my former strength before the occurrence of a general election, I shall then hope for a continuance of the confidence which the electors of Manchester have so long placed in me; if renewed health be not granted to me, I shall then withdraw from public life, remembering, as long as I live, how much I owe to the kindness and forbearance of those in whose name, and on whose behalf, I have acted for nine years past in the House of Commons.

Believe me very sincerely yours,
JOHN BRIGHT.

ON LOSING HIS SEAT FOR MANCHESTER.

At the general election, in March, 1857, a strong effort was made by the leading Whig politicians in the city to secure the defeat of Mr. Bright and his colleague, Mr. Milner Gibson, the members for Manchester, on account of their opposition to the Russian war. Mr. Bright was seeking health on the Continent at the time, and he was represented in the election contest by his friend, Mr. Cobden. The result of the polling was that Mr. Bright and Mr. Gibson were defeated, Sir John Potter and Mr. J. Aspinall Turner being returned to Parliament in their stead.

Upon receiving, by telegram, the result of the election, Mr. Bright wrote the following farewell address to the electors of Manchester, which appeared in the *Examiner and Times* of the 8th of April, 1857:—

TO THE ELECTORS OF THE CITY OF MANCHESTER.

GENTLEMEN,—I have received a telegraphic

despatch, informing me of the result of the election contest in which you have just been engaged. That result has not greatly surprised me, and, so far as I am personally concerned—inasmuch as it liberates me from public life in a manner which involves on my part no shrinking from any duty—I cannot earnestly regret it. I lament it on public grounds, because it tells the world that many amongst you have abandoned the opinions you professed to hold in the year 1847, and even so recently as the year 1852. I believe that slander itself has not dared to charge me with having forsaken any of the principles on the honest support of which I offered myself twice, and was twice accepted as your representative. The charge against me has rather been, that I have too warmly and too faithfully defended the political views which found so much favour with you at the two previous elections.

If the change in your opinion of me has arisen from my course on the question of the war with Russia, I can only say that, on a calm review of all the circumstances of the case,—and during the past twelve months I have had ample time for such a review,—I would not unsay or retract any one of the speeches I have spoken, or erase from the records of Parliament any one of the votes I have given upon it, if I could thereby reverse the decision to which you have come, or secure any other distinction which it is in the power of my countrymen to confer. I am free, and will remain free, from any share in the needless and guilty bloodshed of that melancholy chapter in the annals of my country. I cannot, however, forget that the leaders of the opposition in the recent contest have not been influenced by my conduct on this question. They were less successful, but not less bitter, in their hostility in 1852, and even in 1847, when my only public merit or demerit consisted in my labours in the cause of Free Trade. On each occasion, calling themselves Liberals, and calling their candidates Liberals also, they have coalesced with the Conservatives, whilst now, doubtless, they have assailed Mr. Gibson and myself on the ground of a pretended coalition with the Conservatives in the House of Commons.

I have esteemed it a high honour to be one of your representatives, and have given more of mental and physical labour to your service than was just to myself; I feel it scarcely less an honour to suffer in the cause of peace, and on behalf of what I believe to be the true interests of my country—though I could have wished that the blow had come from other hands, at a time when I could have been present to meet face to face those who dealt it.

In taking my leave of you and of public life, let me assure you that I can never forget the many—the innumerable kindnesses I have received from my friends amongst you. No one will rejoice more than I shall in all that brings you prosperity and honour; and I am not without a hope that, when a calmer hour shall come, you will say of Mr. Gibson and of me, that, as colleagues in your representation for ten years, we have not sacrificed our principles to gain popularity, or bartered our independence for the emoluments of office, or the favours of the great. I feel that we have stood for the rights, and interests, and freedom of the people, and that we have not tarnished the honour or lessened the renown of your eminent city.

I am now, as I have hitherto been,

Very faithfully yours,
JOHN BRIGHT.

Florence, March 31, 1857.

ON REFORM.

Written in reply to a letter enclosing resolutions passed at a public meeting at Hawick, expressing sympathy with Messrs. Cobden, Bright, and Gibson, in losing their seats in Parliament.

Geneva, May 17, 1857.

DEAR SIR,—Your kind note, enclosing a copy of the resolutions passed at a public meeting of the inhabitants of Hawick, reached me only last evening. I lose no time in writing to say that I am very glad to find that in your town the cause of Reform, Free Trade, and Retrenchment has so many warm friends, and that you have understood and approved the policy which Mr. Cobden, Mr. Gibson, and myself have supported in the House of Commons. In the question of Free Trade little progress has been made for some years past. As to Retrenchment, the word has become almost obsolete, and the military expenditure of the country is now nearly double the amount which the Duke of Wellington and Sir Robert Peel thought necessary in 1835, although we have no more territory to defend, and although a large army is no longer necessary to maintain tranquillity in Ireland. As to Reform, whilst almost everybody professes to be in favour of it in some shape, the preparation of the particular bill to be brought forward next year is left in the hands of a minister whose hostility to every proposition for Reform since the year 1832 is notorious and undeniable. Whether on these three points, to which your resolutions refer, the country is in a satisfactory condition, I must leave the friends of Free Trade, Reform, and Retrenchment to decide.

With regard to the promised Reform, let me warn you to look not more to the question of the franchise than to the other arrangements of the measure. It would be easy to double the number of electors, and at the same time to increase the aristocratic influence in Parliament. To give votes without giving representatives in some fair degree in proportion to the votes, is but to cheat the people; and to give a large increase of votes without the security of the ballot will subject increased numbers of our countrymen to the degrading influences which wealth and power now exercise so unscrupulously upon the existing electoral body. A moderate measure, and an honest one as far as it goes, is far more to be desired than one of great pretensions with some fraudulent scheme for defeating the wishes of the nation.

A dishonest apportionment of members may effectually destroy a representation, and any trick to obstruct the free action of majorities, such as that proposed in Lord John Russell's last Bill, should be strenuously resisted as calculated to undermine the very basis of representative institutions, and designed only to cheat the people of that increased power which the Bill would profess to confer upon them.

Whether I shall ever again in Parliament support the policy you approve is extremely uncertain, but I shall always retain a grateful sense of the kindness which I have received in past times, and at the present time, from the intelligent community on whose behalf you have written to me.

Believe me to be very sincerely yours,

JOHN BRIGHT.

To Alex. Laing, Esq., Hawick.

ON HIS BEING ELECTED A MEMBER FOR BIRMINGHAM.

A vacancy having occurred, through the death of Mr. Muntz, in the representation of Birmingham, it was resolved at a public meeting held on the 4th of August, 1857, to put forward Mr. Bright as a candidate, and on being asked he consented to stand. He was elected on the 10th of August, in his absence—his health not having yet been thoroughly re-established—and without opposition. On the receipt of the news of his election, Mr. Bright sent the following address to the electors :—

TO THE ELECTORS OF BIRMINGHAM.

Gentlemen,—Your respected chief magistrate has informed me by telegraph that he has this day declared me to be duly elected one of your representatives in Parliament; and I have learned from other sources that such was the feeling manifested in my favour, that no other candidate was presented to you at the hustings, and that, therefore, my election has been without contest or opposition from any quarter.

When I addressed you two days ago, I had no expectation of a result so speedy and so tranquil of the then impending struggle. I accept it as a conclusive proof of the bias of your political views, and of a confidence in me which I shall strive to maintain undiminished.

It is a matter of real regret to me that I have not been able to be with you during the past week, and at the hustings this day. I shall hope, however, that on some not distant occasion, I may be permitted to meet you in your noble Town Hall, and to become more intimately acquainted with a constituency from whom I have received an honour as signal as it was unexpected, and towards whom I can never entertain other feelings than those of respect and gratitude.

With heartfelt thanks for your kindness, which I trust I may have the health and the opportunity in some measure to repay, I subscribe myself,

Very faithfully yours,
John Bright.

Rochdale, August 10, 1857.

ON BEING ASKED TO SUBSCRIBE TO A BAZAAR.

A gentleman connected with a bazaar which was opened in Birmingham on the 10th of August, 1857, thinking that as the occurrence of Mr. Bright's election on that day had interfered with the probable profits, the honourable member might be induced from this circumstance to assist their funds, wrote him to that effect. Mr. Bright sent him the following reply:—

August, 1857.

SIR,—I am sorry if the occurrence of the election should have made your bazaar less productive; but if it has done so, I can hardly be held in any way responsible for it. I cannot undertake to subscribe to public objects in Birmingham, on account of my political connection with it. Since I have been in Parliament I have always abstained from subscriptions for objects connected with the constituency I represented, and I intend to continue that course. A contrary course would lead me to an expenditure which I could not consent to with any prudence, and might lead to an endeavour to secure public favour by means which I cannot practise or approve. I hope, therefore, you will excuse me, if I find myself unable to add to your funds, and that you will rightly interpret the grounds upon which I act in this matter.

I am, very respectfully,
JOHN BRIGHT.

ON THE GOVERNMENT OF INDIA.

Written to Mr. Alderman Lloyd, of Birmingham, the day before the opening of Parliament in December, 1857. The terrible struggle for the suppression of the mutiny in India was at that time taking place.

Rochdale, December 2, 1857.

MY DEAR SIR,—As Parliament, contrary to expectation, is about to meet before the usual time, I fear the electors of Birmingham will feel some disappointment if I do not make my appearance in the House during the present week, and the more so, from the circumstance that my colleague, Mr. Scholefield, will also be absent.

It is not necessary for me to explain to you, or to the gentlemen who communicated with me at the time of the election, why I am not likely to begin my parliamentary duties before Christmas. It was then understood that, for six months, that is, until the time when Parliament usually assembles, I was not to be expected to undertake any labour connected with the position in which I was then placed by the good opinion of the electors of Birmingham. My own judgment, and the urgent advice of my friends and medical advisers, compelled me to make a resolution to that effect, and those of my Birmingham friends with whom I had any communication granted me a dispensation for that period. I do not suppose that any real business will be transacted before February, and therefore I hope that nothing which is entrusted to me will suffer from my temporary absence from the House.

It is because I wished to abstain as much as possible from public affairs, that I have not troubled my constituents with any views I may entertain on the great subjects which have been so much discussed during the past three months. On the question of India, indeed, I feel that it is almost rashness to utter a decided opinion, and I know not whether one ought to regard with admiration or with pity many of those who have written and spoken so confidently upon it since the occurrence of the insurrection. Judging from the writings of the newspapers, and from the speeches of public men, I fear the country is by no means sufficiently aware of the crisis which has arisen, whether we regard the difficulty of restoring order in India, or the obstacles which oppose themselves to the future government of that country. Five years ago, when the India Bill was about to come under discussion, I thought I knew something of India, and felt that I could give advice on the subject. But the scene has totally changed, and that which was easy to be done in fair weather, may be impossible, or of little avail, when the storm rages. I presume, however, that the days of the Leadenhall Street rulers of India are numbered. Without character and without power, it requires but a vote of Parliament to give legal effect to that which, I believe, the public opinion of England has already decreed.

If the coming session shall establish the Government of India on a secure and wide basis, so far as that is possible in the unnatural position in which we stand to that country, I shall feel that Parliament has not laboured in vain; and if the threatened postponement of a Reform Bill be a disappointment to me and to many others, I shall endeavour to console myself with the hope that the improvement of our representation will hereafter be entrusted to more friendly hands than those which now administer the affairs of the country.

Excuse me for troubling you with this letter, and believe me very sincerely yours,

JOHN BRIGHT.

Thomas Lloyd, Esq., Birmingham.

ON REFORM.

THE NECESSITY OF A REDISTRIBUTION OF SEATS AND THE BALLOT.

Read at a meeting held in the Town Hall, Birmingham, on the 2nd of February, 1858, in support of Parliamentary Reform.

The London circular, referred to in the letter, was an address on the subject of Reform, issued in London in January, 1858. It was signed by over thirty Liberal Members of Parliament of advanced views, and urged upon the people the desirability of insisting upon the following points :—

1. (*a*) The extension of the borough franchise in England and Wales to every male person of full age and not subject to any legal

incapacity, who shall occupy, as owner or tenant in part or whole, any premises within the borough which are rated for the relief of the poor.

(*b*) The extension of the county franchise in England and Wales to all 10*l.* occupiers at least.

(*c*) The assimilation, as far as possible, of the franchises in Scotland and Ireland to those of England and Wales.

2. Protection to the voter by the ballot, on a plan similar to that adopted in the Australian colonies.

3. A reapportionment of seats that shall make such an approach to an equalization of constituencies as shall give in the United Kingdom a majority of members to a majority of electors.

4. Abolition of property qualification for members.

5. The calling of a new Parliament every three years.

Rochdale, February 1, 1858.

My dear Sir,—Although I am unable to be upon your platform to-morrow, be assured that I shall be with you in spirit, and that I wish every success to your Reform movement. May I intrude upon you with a few lines on the great topic you are about to discuss?

I observe that in the first paragraph in your circular you ask the aid of your townsmen in the endeavour to obtain an "extension of the suffrage." Afterwards you insert the propositions of the London Committee, which I am very glad to see you have adopted. But you are probably looking to the extension of the suffrage as the main point and principal demand of the new agitation. I am as much for this extension as you can be, and therefore I can, without suspicion as to my wishes with regard to it, the more frankly warn you of a danger which I see before us. Twenty-five years ago, the Tory party, and the Whigs almost as much so, were greatly afraid of an extension of the suffrage. Now very few persons of any intelligence, even among the Conservatives, are afraid of it. The propositions made some time ago by the government of Lord John Russell and Lord Aberdeen, showed clearly that the franchise is no longer the dread of the aristocratic and ruling classes, and it is not unlikely that Lord Palmerston, if he produces a Reform Bill, will go a long way in the direction we wish to go, so far as the franchise is concerned. We can easily understand this. The franchise itself gives no real power, unless accompanied by the right on the part of all the possessors of it to elect something like an equal number of representatives. I could easily frame a bill which would give "universal suffrage" in its widest sense, and which would confirm more strongly than ever the supremacy of the English oligarchy over the English people. If your great city, with its great constituency, is only to send two men to Parliament, whilst an equal population and property in some other part of the kingdom is to send twenty men to Parliament, then, I say, your franchise is of little avail. The man who can merely shout at the hustings, or contribute to the show of hands, is, in reality, in almost as good a position as the man who votes, if the value of votes is rendered so unequal, or is nearly destroyed, by the unequal distribution of representatives among the whole body of electors. The Government and the Parliament, even the House of Lords, will consent to a large increase of electors; and men who have not considered the subject fully will imagine they have gained much by the concession. Lord John Russell, in his many speeches on a further measure of Reform, generally, if not always, confines himself to an extension of the franchise; and his last bill, although it would have added to the number of electors throughout the kingdom, would have done absolutely nothing to lessen the power of the order to which he belongs, or to increase that of the nation as distinguished from its privileged and aristocratic class.

It is not a matter of opinion, or of any doubt, that I am discussing. It is a question of fact and of arithmetic; and therefore I wish to urge it strongly upon your attention. The contest on the question of Reform will be on the distribution of seats. Will the great borough of the Tower Hamlets, with its half a million of population, be content to return only two members to Parliament? Will Finsbury, will Marylebone, will Lambeth, and the other London boroughs? Will Glasgow, and Manchester, and Liverpool, and Birmingham, and the other leading cities of the United Kingdom, be content to dwarf themselves politically to the size of boroughs whose whole population would scarcely people one of the inferior streets? Shall it be admitted that the more men come together, the more they are industrious, skilful, intelligent, and powerful in every other respect, the less shall be their influence in the government of their country? This is the great question, and it rests with the people of Birmingham to do much to solve it.

Any Reform Bill which is worth a moment's thought, or the smallest effort to carry it, must at least double, and it ought to do much more than double, the representation of the metropolitan boroughs and of all the great cities of the United Kingdom. The United States of America, and Belgium, and Sardinia, comprehend this simple question. A year ago I was in the city of Genoa, and I found that it returned seven representatives to the Sardinian Parliament at Turin, seven being its fair share, calculated according to the population of the various cities and districts of the Sardinian kingdom. In this country, throughout Great Britain and Ireland, you will find that property rated to the relief of the poor follows very closely the course of population; and the only just principle of representation is that the industry, property, intelligence, and population of the country should be, as nearly as may be, equally represented, wherever they are to be found. I am not arguing for any mathematical precision in this matter, but for such a change as shall really give the House of Commons to the nation.

The third proposition in your list adopts this principle; and I only dwell upon it because I know that reformers are too much accustomed to look upon the suffrage as if it were the all-important one, the only important point in their creed.

With regard to the ballot, it is worthy of remark that no meeting has been held in favour of Reform at which the ballot has not been strongly insisted upon. If Reform is to be granted to gratify and content reformers; if their judgment and unanimity are sufficient to justify or to force its concession, then surely the ballot cannot be denied to us, and I feel certain it will not long be refused. The ballot is not so much a principle as a convenience. It does not bestow the franchise, it guarantees that which the law has already conferred. A voter goes to the poll in a cab, because it is easier and sometimes safer for him than to struggle through an excited crowd on foot. Why should he not be allowed to vote by ballot to shelter him from the more serious annoyance he may be, and is now often subjected to, from the importunity of the threats of his landlord, his creditor, or his customer? When the 200 men in the House of Commons, who are pledged to support the ballot, or when 100 of them, or when fifty of them are in earnest, and tell the Government they are resolved to have it, and that they will leave any government that will not grant it in the hands of the Philistines on the opposite side of the House, then, and probably not till then, the ballot will be conceded. I dread to think of the consequences of a wide extension of the suffrage in our manufacturing districts should it be obtained without the ballot. It will tempt employers of labour to a hateful tyranny, and it will doom multitudes of the employed, I fear, to a not less hateful condition of political degradation.

I write this letter chiefly that I may warn you against the pitfalls that are in your path. Your cause is not in the hands of friends. Your forces in the parliamentary field are commanded by men taken from, or chosen from, your constant and natural opponents, and they lead them, not for your purposes, but for their own. I beseech you to watch well what is proposed and what is done. Be the measure great or small, let it be honest in every part. Include as many as you can in the right of the franchise, insist upon such a distribution of seats as shall give the House of Commons fairly to the industry, the property, the intelligence, and the population of the country. Demand the ballot as the undeniable right of every man who is called to the poll, and take special care that the old constitutional rule and principle, by which majorities alone shall decide in Parliamentary elections, shall not be violated.

I give my hearty support, as I have heretofore done, to the proposition contained in your circular. I lament that I cannot join in your meeting to-morrow, for I esteem it a great honour to be permitted to act with the inhabitants of Birmingham on that question which, a quarter of a century ago, they did so much to advance, and on which their potent voice is once more about to be heard.

I am, very sincerely yours,
JOHN BRIGHT.

ON MR. MILNER GIBSON.

The Right Hon. T. Milner Gibson, who along with Mr. Bright was defeated at Manchester at the general election in 1857, was subsequently returned for Ashton-under-Lyne, and on the 28th of January, 1858, a *soirée* was given at the Ashton Town Hall to celebrate his election. At the meeting, the following letter was read from Mr. Bright :—

Rochdale, January 20, 1858.

DEAR SIR,—I regret very much that I cannot avail myself of the invitation to your approaching public *soirée*, so kindly forwarded to me by your committee. I need hardly say that it would have given me extreme pleasure to have seen my friend and late colleague—and may I not say still my colleague—among his new constituency. That you have filled up the vacancy which occurred in the representation of your borough by the return of Mr. Milner Gibson has been a subject of rejoicing in every house in the kingdom which is the house of an honest and intelligent reformer.

To me it has given greater satisfaction than I have words to express; for I, who for fourteen years have worked incessantly with him, may perhaps be more capable than almost any other man of appreciating his worth in the House of Commons. To refer only to one subject of legislation—the freedom of the press from taxes intended to crush or to cripple it—I would ask, to whom is the country so much indebted as to your member? And what services can be greater in a nation pretending or aspiring to be free than to give it a free and cheap press, whereby the whole population may be informed from day to day of all questions affecting the public interests? I am deeply grateful to you for the course you have taken, and hope I may still be able, though it may be with diminished force, to work with Mr. Gibson in behalf of the true interests of our country. I desire to thank the gentlemen of your committee for their kindness in inviting me, and yourself also for the kindly expressions contained in your letter.

I am, &c.,
JOHN BRIGHT.

Mr. William Hill, Ashton-under-Lyne.

ON THE CONSPIRACY BILL.

ON the 14th of January, 1858, an attempt was made to assassinate the Emperor of the French, and as it was found that the assassins had prepared their plot whilst in England, much feeling was excited in France against this country, and a despatch was sent from the French Government to their ambassador in London, instructing him to ask the English Government to take such measures as they saw fit with regard to it. The British Government did not reply to the despatch; but Lord Palmerston brought a bill into the House of Commons on the 8th of February, 1858, to amend the law of conspiracy to murder. Hitherto conspiracy to murder was a simple misdemeanour in this country, punishable in the same manner as a conspiracy to commit any other act which was in violation of the law. Lord Palmerston proposed to make it punishable by penal servitude for such term of years as the Court should award up to penal servitude for life.

The bill was unpopular in the country, and caused a good deal of discussion. On the 15th of February, 1858, a meeting was held at the Freemasons' Tavern, London, in opposition to the bill, and " to protest against the surrender of English liberties at the dictation of a foreign power." The following letter from Mr. Bright was read at the meeting :—

London, February 12, 1858.

DEAR SIR,—I am not able to attend any public meeting, but I go heartily with the opposition to the Conspiracy Bill. I am very anxious, however, that any opposition to it should be conducted, so as not needlessly to cause any irritation between this country and the people or government of France. Our business is simply with our Government. We have to condemn them for their total want of dignity in this matter; for their shrinking from their duty in giving a proper and respectful but firm reply to the French despatch; and because they have brought forward a bill which can have no influence in adding to the security of the emperor or of any other person, and can only be pointed to as a hasty and humiliating concession to a hasty and needless demand. We have for years past been judging the government of other nations; it is now time for us to examine the condition of our own.

I am, yours, &c.,
JOHN BRIGHT.

ON THE CONSPIRACY BILL.

The second reading of the Conspiracy to Murder Bill was moved by Lord Palmerston on the 19th of February, 1858. Mr. Milner Gibson moved the following amendment:—" That this House hears with much concern that it is alleged that recent attempts upon the life of the Emperor of the French have been devised in England, and expresses its detestation of such guilty enterprises. That this House is ready at all times to assist in remedying any defects in the criminal law which, after due investigation, are proved to exist; yet it cannot but regret that her Majesty's Government, previous to inviting the House to amend the law of conspiracy at the present time, have not felt it their duty to make some reply to the important despatch received from the French Government, dated Paris, the 20th of January, 1858, and which has been laid before Parliament."

The amendment was seconded by Mr. Bright, supported by Mr. Gladstone and others, and carried, 234 voting for it, and 215 against, the Government thus being defeated by 19 votes.

In consequence of this vote Lord Palmerston resigned office, and Lord Derby was entrusted with the formation of a government.

For opposing the bill Mr. Bright received a vote of thanks from a public meeting held in Newcastle-upon-Tyne, and he acknowledged the compliment in the following letter to Mr. Joseph Cowen, Jun. :—

House of Commons, March 1, 1858.

DEAR SIR,—I have received with much pleasure the announcement contained in your letter of the 27th ult., that a vote of thanks has been passed to Mr. Gibson and myself for the part we have taken in opposing the "Conspiracy Bill," by a large and enthusiastic public meeting of the inhabitants of Newcastle. I am greatly obliged to your townsmen for their kindness to me.

I must say, however, that I took no part in the recent debate. I seconded the resolution proposed by my friend Mr. Gibson, and entirely approved of it, and rejoice at the result which has followed. I congratulate you and the country on the downfall of the very worst Ministry that I have known. The Ministry which has succeeded to it may be deemed a transition Ministry, to be followed, I trust, by one more entitled to the confidence of the great Liberal party in the country, a party which includes a vast majority of the nation.

I beg to thank you for the kind expressions towards myself which are contained in your letter.

I am, yours respectfully,
JOHN BRIGHT.

Joseph Cowen, Esq.

ON THE CONDITION OF THE COUNTRY.

At a meeting in March, 1858, of the unemployed workpeople in Birmingham, a memorial to the Queen was passed, praying for an extensive system of free emigration. The chairman of the meeting was requested to ask Mr. Bright to present the memorial, and to his communication received the following reply:—

London, March 25, 1858.

DEAR SIR,—When your memorial reaches me or Mr. Scholefield, we will at once take the usual course with respect to its presentation to the Queen.

I am sorry to find that the "unemployed" should be so numerous in Birmingham as to induce them to unite, with a view to some public measure for their relief. At this moment the unfavourable condition of the markets of the United States, and of the continent of Europe, will account for much of the suffering which is being endured by the working men of England. I confess, however, that I can see no remedy for a large portion of the mischief complained of, so long as we find our taxes constantly on the increase, and our national expenditure augmenting.

We are now spending twenty millions a year more than we were spending only a few years back, and our military expenses have doubled since the year 1835, when the Duke of Wellington and Sir Robert Peel were in power.

This year I suppose we shall raise in taxes at least fifty millions sterling more than will require to be raised by an equal population, living, not in England, but in the United States of America. Surely this will account for much of the evils which you, and the memorialists, and the working classes generally, suffer; and I am not surprised that sensible men should wish to quit a country where the burdens are so heavy, and the political privileges of three-fourths of them are so few. Every man who is not prepared to compel a better and more economical government at home should emigrate, or the pauperism of his day will be deeper, and more without remedy, in the days of his children. I wish I was able to come to Birmingham and talk to you about these questions.

Yours very respectfully,

JOHN BRIGHT.

ON THE REPRESENTATION OF BIRMINGHAM.

Before the election of Mr. Bright to represent Birmingham in Parliament, the report was industriously circulated that, even if elected, he would make the seat a mere temporary convenience, to be relinquished as soon as the constituency of Manchester regained its senses, and asked him to represent it once more. The rumour turned up again in 1858, and became so commonly talked of as to induce a gentleman connected with the Liberal party in the borough to write to Mr. Bright for an explanation. Mr. Bright replied as follows:—

Rochdale, May 26, 1858.

DEAR SIR,—I know nothing of the report to which you allude, and certainly I have said nothing to justify it. Remembering the circumstances under which I was returned for Birmingham, it is strange that any one should imagine I could prefer any other constituency so long as I remain in the House of Commons, and so long as my opinions and course in Parliament are not opposed to the views of those I have now the honour to represent. I know no nobler constituency than that of Birmingham, and no member of the House of Commons owes more to a constituency than I owe to that on whose behalf I now speak and vote in Parliament.

I am, very respectfully yours,
JOHN BRIGHT.

ON THE NECESSITY FOR EMIGRATION AND ITS CAUSES.

Read at a meeting held in Glasgow, on the 16th of September, 1858, for the purpose of considering some scheme to enable the working classes to emigrate to the colonies. The special object of the meeting was for the adoption of resolutions and of a memorial to her Majesty in favour of such a scheme, and for the enrolment of a band of pioneers for British Columbia.

Rochdale, September 1, 1858.

SIR,—I have to thank the council of your association for the invitation to your approaching meeting. I cannot be present at it, but I hope your discussions will do good to those most interested in them. I have read your resolutions, and I am not surprised that great numbers of the working men are anxious to emigrate; and if I were younger and in their position, I should strain every nerve to enable me to find a home in the United States or in one of the British colonies.

I do not think you are quite correct in the assertions of the resolutions. Generally, the waste lands in the colonies belong to the colonies. Canada belongs to the people of Canada, and Australia to the people of Australia—and I think any other arrangement would work badly. Any interference by the Home Government would do mischief, and would certainly breed disputes between the Colonial Governments and populations.

Again, I do not know that it is the "bounden duty" of the Government to adopt measures to enable a portion of our population to emigrate; for if such a duty is laid upon it, I know not where it must end. Every man who thinks he can improve his position abroad may ask to be sent abroad, and, all men having an equal claim upon the Government, the difficulty may become, and soon will become, insurmountable.

I do not believe that it is the duty of the Government to provide means of emigration for the people, and therefore I could not support the main point in your resolutions. What I have long told the working men is this:—Here you have no political power, for the arrangements of the Reform Bill purposely excluded you. Here you are mixed up with the wretched confusion of European politics, and your sweat is pawned by the crimes of past generations. So thoroughly are you involved in European complications, that in any year you may have your taxes raised, and the demand for your labour destroyed, in pursuit of some phantom in which your rulers persuade you that you are interested; your want of information unfortunately renders you easy victims to the delusion practised upon you. Not five years ago you rejoiced in peace, and there was a growing prosperity evident in every part of the country. Since that time we have sacrificed forty thousand English lives, and have spent one hundred millions of pounds sterling in one short war. You were consenting parties to that war; your comrades shed their blood in its worthless contests, and you have paid a portion of your day's labour and day's wages ever since, to defray the cost of it; and your voice, so far as it was heard at all, was in favour of the war. What is gained by it? Who has gained, except the military class and the eaters of taxes? To working men, these wars with Russia, with Persia, with China, bring only taxes, want of employment, precarious and diminished wages, and that pressure upon the means of living which urges them to look to emigration as a remedy for the evils they endure. And it is a remedy, and the only remedy, until great changes take place in public opinion, and in the law and policy of this country.

If you emigrate you may reach a country where land is accessible to you, where there are no great hereditary proprietors, as in Scotland, who dare to outrage heaven and mankind by keeping 20,000, or 50,000, or 100,000 acres of land depopulated, that a handful of men may enjoy the pleasures of the chase. You may flee to a land where laws of primogeniture are unknown, or known only to be abhorred, and where the soil is left free to the industry and enterprise of the whole people. You may find a home where such destructive delusions as the "balance of power" are unheard of, and where the toil of the nation of which you have become a part is not absorbed to the amount of fifty millions sterling a year to pay for wars that are past, and for preparations of wars that are to come. You may become a part of some youthful and growing people, with whom a feudal proprietorship of lands, national debts, great armaments, oppressive taxes, and a sham representation, are but traditions of a melancholy past, to be studied only as rocks to be avoided in its new and more prosperous career.

If I do not see how the Government can be called upon to provide the means of emigration, do not suppose I think emigration unwise; on the contrary, I feel assured that, with the past and present policy of England, labour will find its best reward in Canada, in the States, or in Australia. I would prefer that Englishmen should stay at home—that our country should be well governed, that its foreign policy should be just and rational, that its burden of taxes should be light; but, seeing small chance of such a state of things, I not only cannot blame, but I must applaud the resolution of every man who is determined, by his industry and his economy, to provide the means of conveying himself and his family to another, and to him and them, a more happy country.

Government cannot enable you to emigrate. Many of you can, by severe effort and saving, obtain the means to cross the ocean; to many, I fear, this is not possible. I can only hope, for them, that our countrymen may become wiser, and that, under the influence of a more sensible policy and a greater economy in the national expenditure, we may be entering on a period of prolonged peace, during which even the poorest and most suffering of our population, may make some progress in the way of comfort and independence.

I must ask your excuse for writing so long a

letter, and the more, as it is opposed in some degree to your view.

I am, very respectfully yours,
JOHN BRIGHT.

Mr. Andrew Cumming, 414, Argyle Street, Glasgow.

ON THE CURRENCY.

A number of the inhabitants of Birmingham, under the auspices of Mr Edmund Taunton, having addressed a memorial to Mr. Bright, soliciting his " advocacy in Parliament in behalf of the interest of labour against that of money," Mr. Bright sent the following reply :—

Rochdale, January 12, 1859.

SIR,—I have received a memorial with many signatures, of which yours is the first, requesting me to endeavour to procure " the abolition of the monopoly in money." It might be deemed a sufficient answer to say that my time and thoughts are just now so fully occupied with a great public question, that I cannot undertake anything further; that is certainly the position in which I am placed, but I will not confine myself to such a reply.

To tell you the truth, I do not comprehend what you complain of, or what you wish to be done, for in the many conversations I have had with persons who thought themselves well informed on what is called " Our Monetary System," I have never had the good fortune to find any two of them agreeing upon the exact grievance, or the precise remedy. I have always thought this a great misfortune, because until I could see clearly where the wrong was, or is, I could have small hope of discovering a remedy. I do not defend what exists in connection with the Bank of England—much of it seems to be at variance with the laws of political economy; but I find many of the propositions made by those who wish for a change are even less in accordance with that science, and long discussion with those who most loudly denounce the present system only leaves me more puzzled than before. I confess, therefore, that I am not the most suitable person to undertake the great change which I presume you are looking for. I will willingly support any inquiry by Parliament, in the hope that the truth may at last be discovered; but I do not feel competent to teach Parliament and the country on the abstruse question to which you have drawn my attention. When it comes before the House of Commons, I will give it all the consideration in my power. I wish I could send you a more satisfactory reply.

I am, very respectfully yours,
JOHN BRIGHT.

ON REFORM.

MR. BRIGHT'S REFORM BILL.

In 1859, Mr. Disraeli, on behalf of Lord Derby's Government, introduced a Reform Bill in the House of Commons. It consisted mainly of a string of ridiculous clauses, artfully designed to give the measure an appearance of extending the franchise; but with the real object of continuing the exclusion of the working classes from the suffrage. The Bill was exceedingly unpopular in the country, and on the 31st of March, at the close of the debate on the second reading in the House of Commons, it was rejected, and a dissolution of Parliament ensued. At the end of 1858 Mr. Bright, in response to a request from some of the friends of Reform, had drawn up a scheme for a Reform Bill, and his proposals became again, at this crisis, the subject of discussion. Reform was now the all-engrossing question of the hour, and the following letter from Mr. Samuel Morley shows how Reformers were looking to Mr. Bright for guidance :—

> Parliamentary Reform Committee,
> 15, King Street, Cheapside,
> April 7, 1859.

DEAR SIR,—At a conference of friends of Reform, in November last, convened by this Committee, at the Guildhall Coffee House, you were earnestly and unanimously requested to prepare a bill intended to meet the wishes of earnest reformers. You have already explained the principles of your measure to the country, but no formal declaration has been made of its exact contents. On the eve of a general election, it is most important that the main provisions of your bill should be distinctly laid before the country. On behalf of this committee I venture therefore to request you that you will, in the manner you think most advisable, enable us to carry out this view. We shall be glad of your reply at the earliest convenience.

I am, dear sir, yours truly,
S. MORLEY.

John Bright, Esq., M.P.

To this letter Mr. Bright sent the following reply:—

Reform Club, April 9, 1859.

MY DEAR SIR,—It seems scarcely needful, after the explanations I have publicly given of the principles of my bill, to enter into any long statement as to its exact provisions. I will endeavour, however, in a few words, to place before you what I intended to propose to Parliament, if the session had not been suddenly interrupted by the dissolution which is impending.

With regard to the franchise, I propose, in counties, to extend the right of voting to all occupiers of the value of 10*l*. and upwards, with the proviso that, in every such occupancy, not less than 6*l*. of the value shall be in a dwelling-house. The object of this is to prevent the fabrication of fictitious votes by pretended lettings of land where no real tenancy may exist. I propose to extend the right of voting (possessed by freeholders of the value of 40*s*. and upwards) in England and Wales, to Scotland, and to place the elective rights of freeholders in Scotland upon the same footing as in England and Wales in every respect.

With regard to the borough franchise, I propose the present municipal franchise with two variations. The municipal franchise is now possessed by every man who is a ratepayer, whether his rates are paid by himself or by his landlord, and without regard to the value of the property he occupies, or the amount of his rating. I propose to adopt the same arrangement down to a certain point: that is, I would give the vote to all persons rated at not less than 3*l*., or occupying to the value of not less than 4*l*. per annum, whether the rates are paid by the tenant or by the landlord. Below that point, in order not to exclude any industrious and frugal man, wishful to have a vote, I would allow any person being a rated occupier, to secure his vote by undertaking to pay and by paying his own rates. This is the only test I would apply, and I think its effect would be to exclude none but such as are not likely to have any independence, and such as are utterly careless as to the possession of a vote.

The Municipal Act requires a residence of two years and eight months before a person can be placed upon the burgess roll. This is done by a clause inserted in the House of Lords, and was a concession of the House of Commons to the apprehensions of the Peers. It assumes to be directed specially against the poor, and to be conservative in its character; whilst, in fact, it acts almost equally upon every class, lessening the number of burgesses, without being a guarantee for their independent character, or for their superiority in any respect. I propose to adhere to the present term of residence for parliamentary electors—that is, to have a twelve months' residence. This is, in fact, a sixteen months' residence, for no person can now be placed on the register, which comes into force on the 1st of December in any year, who was not in occupation of his premises on the 31st of July of the year preceding; and if his occupation began on the 1st of August, his residence must be two years and four months before he can give a vote. Under the present law, the occupation of every person who becomes entitled to vote will vary from sixteen months to twenty-eight months, or an average of twenty-two months. Surely this is long enough, and nothing but ignorance of the law and the facts, or a dread of numbers, can induce any man to wish for any longer period of residence.

In addition to this general proposition to extend the right of voting in boroughs, I propose to give the franchise to occupiers of apartments; that is, to lodgers, paying a rent of not less than 10*l*. per annum, subject to the same period of residence as in the case of rated occupiers, and whether the rent be paid half-yearly or at any shorter period.

To all voters, whether in counties or in boroughs, I would give the ballot, and my bill provides for the appointment of a commission to decide upon the best means of securing secrecy, and expedition, and order in the taking of votes at elections; that is, to discover the best means of voting by ballot.

I need not now enter into any details about the disfranchisement of small boroughs, and the redistribution of seats; my schedules have been and are before the public. They who regard them as extreme and hurtful are they who wish the House of Commons to be the coadjutor of the House of Lords, rather than a fair representation of the people. I believe the time will come when my propositions on this point will be considered as moderate as I now believe them to be just.

I regret very much that I have been unable to introduce my bill to the House of Commons. I feel certain that I could have removed some misapprehensions with regard to it, created chiefly by the untruthful criticisms of the newspapers in the interest of the two aristocratic parties. I could not bring in my bill before the Government brought in theirs, and I could not with advantage have asked the House to consider it whilst that of the Government was under discussion. The ground was cleared when the great division was announced; but on the very evening when I intended to give notice of the introduction of my bill, we were informed of the impending dissolution of Parliament, and thus all chance of proceeding with any important business was at an end.

The question of Reform is now before the constituencies. The quality and extent of the measure to be passed in the new Parliament will depend on the earnestness of the existing body of electors. I hope they may act up to the occasion.

I am, truly yours,
JOHN BRIGHT.

Samuel Morley, Esq.

ON THE GOVERNMENT OF INDIA.
WRITTEN TO A GENTLEMAN IN INDIA.

Rochdale, January 14, 1860.

Dear Sir,—I have received your letter on the subject of your next meeting, and informing me of the petitions which have been forwarded to my friend, Mr. John Dickenson, jun. I shall have great pleasure in presenting the petitions to the House of Commons, and in giving such help as may be in my power to your views. I am not sanguine that we shall easily produce any change in the Indian government. The whole concern is one of patronage—and those who now hold the good things will not willingly give them up. The English people, too, are very slow, and very careless about everything that does not immediately affect them. They cannot be excited to any effort for India except under the pressure of some great calamity, and when that pressure is removed they fall back into their usual state of apathy.

The English Government has always too much on its hands. To keep itself in power is considered its first duty, and there is little force or leisure to do anything else. It hands over India to Sir John Hobhouse, or Mr. Herries, or Sir C. Wood, or Lord Stanley, and takes no further interest in it until an insurrection is announced, or a loan in England is necessary; and the Indian minister is expected never to trouble his colleagues except in the last extremity. Parliament cares about India little more than the Cabinet; and thus the interests of your vast population are left to the tender mercies of an exclusive service whose main object of adoration is patronage. I almost despair of anything being done here, but you may rely on my honest assistance whenever there seems a chance of doing anything.

I am much obliged to Mr. Norton and to others of your friends for their too kind mention of me at the meetings, the report of which you have sent me.

I am, with great respect,
Yours sincerely,
JOHN BRIGHT.

H. Nelson, Esq.

ON STRIKES, AND THE EXCLUSION OF THE WORKING CLASSES FROM THE SUFFRAGE.

Written in answer to a letter Mr. Bright had received from a spinner and manufacturer in Blackburn, in which a complaint was made that education, literary and religious, had failed to teach the working classes wisdom in relation to their own interests.

Rochdale, November 3, 1860.

MY DEAR SIR,—I am glad to hear from you, and to learn that your health is better. I am, however, very sorry for the cause of your writing to me, and can understand the disappointment you feel at the small result of so many efforts to instruct the working population around you. It is not to be expected that the workmen in our population should be wiser than other classes, and we know well that other classes have, whenever able to do it, enforced combination prices, and endeavoured to make a scarcity in the articles in which they have dealt. The fact is, that among all classes there is a lamentable ignorance of the laws which ought to regulate labour and trade, and that the study of political economy is totally neglected in the education of the whole people. At this moment the views of a large portion of the highest class—I mean highest in position, in wealth, and in scholarship,—are wholly unsound on these subjects, and, making allowance for difference of circumstances, they support precisely the same principles as those contended for by trades' unions. At first sight, nothing appears more clear to a workman than that it is a great advantage to him to be able to force his employer to give him higher wages; and for this end, an end apparently so desirable, almost everything will appear to the mind of the workman proper and justifiable. He considers the whole matter to be a struggle between capital and labour, and that anything is fair in his fight with the claims of capital. Hence the folly and injustice of many of the proceedings of the trades' unions, and the discord which arises between the class of workmen and the class of employers.

Along with the mischief which springs from

ignorance on these questions, there is another source of evil, to which I think employers ought to turn their attention. The whole body of workmen, speaking in general terms, are excluded—purposely excluded—from the franchise. They have no political position, and therefore, practically, they have no politics. In this respect they are no more free than the labourers in Austria or in Russia, and consequently they have no inducement to consider political questions, and to examine or to suspect how far their condition is affected by the policy and acts of the Government of the country. They are shut out from the political world; they are told that they ought to have, and shall have, no opinion and no voice in the direction of public affairs; that they are an ignorant and a dangerous class; and that what are called the institutions of their country would not be safe if they were permitted to take any part in them. The inevitable result is that these men, growing every day in information, and in restlessness and discontent, rather it may be with their social than their political condition, and growing also in numbers and in the means of organization, maintain a contest with the only authority they see and feel, namely, with their employers, who are to them almost all they know and comprehend of superior power and of Governmental control.

The fact is, our system of political exclusion has this effect, it makes of the working classes a nation, separated by a gulf, passable only by few of them, from that other nation to which the existing constitution pretends to give, though it does not honestly give, political power. There is thus no real amalgamation of classes. The class receiving wages is shut out from the questions and the interests which occupy the minds and engage the energies of the employing class. Its members are limited to the consideration of their own individual, and local, and class interests; and their mental activity is devoted to something like a servile war, because everything that is broader and greater is excluded from their view. So long as the employers of this county, and of the neighbouring counties, are content to allow the governing class to refuse the rights of citizenship to the industrious men, without whose skill and toil our national greatness could have no existence, so long will these men, whose general intelligence and whose energies are acknowledged by all, concentrate that intelligence and that energy on efforts to amend their condition within those limits of action which are open to them. If the capitalists practically assert that the workman is born only to labour, and that he is incompetent to take any part in those great discussions on public affairs which are so deeply interesting to the more fortunate and privileged of his countrymen, and so important to all—and if, unhappily, the workman should practically acquiesce in this view, and should abstain from efforts to invest himself with the rights of citizenship,—let us be assured that his activity will not cease—that his energies will not slumber. He may not read and think politics; he may not canvass for and conduct elections; he may not strive to influence the deliberations of Parliament, and to urge on or to check the action of the administration; but he will not be idle, and his own condition and that of his class will not have lost all interest in his eyes. He will ignore the obstacles to his well-being which arise from violations of economic principles by the Government; he will take no strong interest in the taxation of the country, or in the expenditure of the State; he will conclude that the only mode of bettering his condition is in an advance of wages, forced from capital, it may be, at the risk of its destruction, and gained and secured only by combinations which in the long-run must be as injurious to himself as to the employer against whom he is contending.

I have never denied the legal or the moral right of workmen or employers to combine; but I believe there is not one case in a hundred where it is wise to exercise this right. And, looking at the consequences of the strikes we have seen in this country, it is amazing that so many men of sense, so many men competent to works of skill and ingenuity, should take any part in them. I do not expect in our time that these deplorable transactions will come to an end, but I am persuaded that they would occur much more rarely, and be attended with less of bitterness and of that obstinate folly which now so often distinguishes them, if the wall of partition between classes were broken down by the admission of the great "labour interest" into the rights of citizenship. Then the same questions would interest us all; the same grievances, where grievances exist, would be seen to affect us all; the same great public objects would stimulate us all; and instead of being, as we now are, two nations in one country, having different ends and adverse sympathies, we should have objects and purposes in common, to the incalculable and permanent gain of the whole people.

I am not now propounding a new doctrine. I have held this opinion ever since I have considered social and political questions. I have as much interest in the harmonious working of our industrial organization, and in the welfare of my country, as any other man has, and I give it as my deliberate judgment, that it is the interest and the duty of all the employers of labour amongst us to confer upon the workman, whose labour we purchase, and whose wages we provide, those rights of franchise and of citizenship which we ourselves possess. Some men imagine that the existing exclusion can be perpetuated, and that it is safer to repress and exclude than to admit. This is the common delusion of those who shut their eyes to all that is passing around them, and who, in their timidity, adhere to a course which, more than any other, is dangerous and untenable.

The workmen are great in numbers, growing in intelligence, and their power of combination is without limit. They will contend *for* themselves, by themselves, if condemned to remain a separate and suspected order in our social system; and this contest has in it the seeds of future and tremendous evil to them and to the great industrial interests of the country. I wish to unite all, to have no separate interests; to blend all in a common sense of common rights, and thus to give peace and strength where now discord and weakness too much prevail.

I do not write this to you as though you differed from me in opinion on this subject, but I take the opportunity which your letter affords me of expressing to you the views I honestly hold, earnestly hoping they may one day become those of all the employers of labour in the manufacturing counties of England.

I am, very sincerely yours,
JOHN BRIGHT.

ON THE INCOME-TAX, AND ON TAXATION AND REPRESENTATION.

Written to the chairman of an anti-income-tax meeting at Birmingham.

4, Hanover Street, London,
March 11, 1862.

DEAR SIR,—I have received your letter and a copy of the resolution on the subject of the income-tax, and thank you for them. I am not surprised at the hostility which you describe as existing in the minds of many persons in Birmingham against this tax; in truth, I am only surprised at the patience—I think I may say the culpable patience—with which it has been so long endured. At the same time I regret to say that I cannot see the wisdom of the course you recommend with a view to procure the repeal or alteration of the tax, and it does not appear to me to offer any prospect of success. I cannot, therefore, pledge myself to act as you wish; that is, to undertake to "divide the House against the present income-tax laws on every possible occasion."

The evil of which you complain is not to be got rid of through the direct action of Parliament, and the course you recommend to my colleague and to myself would, I fear, only subject you to disappointment and us to ridicule. The House of Commons, and, I may say, Parliament as a whole, including both Houses, finds no special grievance in heavy expenditure and heavy taxation; and the inequalities of which you justly complain tell in favour of the rich, and especially in favour of the owners of what is called real property. It is not from Parliament, therefore, in the first instance that you are to look for redress.

The income-tax was imposed in the year 1842, to enable Sir Robert Peel to begin the reform of the tariff. The tariff has been to a great extent reformed; and, although the custom duties produce more now than they did in 1842, the income-tax remains with a heavier pressure and a wider field. The cause is on the surface. Parliament consents now to an annual expenditure about twenty millions in excess of that of 1842, and the income-tax raises one-half of the increased taxation required by this increased expenditure. If I complain to Government or to Parliament that this expenditure is unnecessary, and this taxation burdensome, Government and Parliament tell me that the nation is not of my opinion, and that the people do not blame the one, or suffer sensibly under the other.

I believe a very heavy taxation can rarely, perhaps never, be levied with much regard to justice. In this country, where the rich only govern, equality and fairness in taxation are impossible. The rich may spend the public revenues with a careless prodigality, but they will fight with a desperate unity of purpose to place the burden on the whole people, with little regard to the means of those who are to bear it. In the United Kingdom there are seven millions of men who pay taxes, and of these about six millions are never consulted as to the amount which shall be spent, or the mode in which it shall be raised. Of the one million who are apparently consulted, it may be said that political power is so unequally apportioned among them, that less than one-fourth of them nominally elect a majority of the members of the House of Commons, by which seventy millions of taxes are annually collected from seven millions of men, which determines the mode in which this vast sum of money shall be raised, and how it shall be expended.

I have now had an experience of nearly twenty years in the House of Commons, and during that time I have given such assistance as I could to every attempt to keep down expenditure, and to make taxation more equal and more just. The expenditure is now twenty millions more than it was when I entered Parliament. Since 1853-4, when Lord Palmerston and Lord John Russell led the nation into war with Russia, the public exchequer has been open to the rapacity of the military services, and they have revelled, without check, in the wealth which industry has created. These old statesmen, steeped in the traditions of the last generation, conceive the grandeur of a country to consist in the vastness of its taxation and the extent of its military preparations, and they have succeeded in so exciting the fears and imposing upon the understanding of the middle classes of the people, as to induce them to tolerate a constantly-growing extravagance in the executive government, and a burden of taxation which in a time of peace would have driven their forefathers into revolt.

The English middle class believes itself to be represented, while its representation is mainly a fraud. The great mass of the people are purposely excluded from all representation. Force is no longer used as the instrument of tyranny amongst us; but fraud, and delusion, and alarm, and panic are found in our day more profitable than force. I write to you, who, in respect to the subject of our correspondence, are a representative of the middle class; and I say that until that great class, in many things so intelligent, so moral, and, when it rises to any great duty, so powerful, shall examine public affairs for itself, and shall shake itself free from the impositions which are so impudently practised upon it, I see no hope of any sensible diminution of the burden of taxation, or of any more just apportionment of that taxation, from which it is impossible to escape. If the middle class prefer an alliance with the aristocratic or ruling party, to the cordial co-operation and help of the great nation now excluded from the franchise and from all political power, they must be content with a profligate government expenditure, and a taxation burdensome from its amount, and insulting from its inequality and injustice.

I hope I need not tell you how glad I shall be to witness an expression of public opinion in favour of economy. The old watchwords of the Liberal party were "Peace, Retrenchment, and Reform." Of late years, under the leadership of statesmen who care for none of these things, the party has become feeble, debauched, and humiliated, and has trampled in the dust the only principles on which it had any pretence to become a party.

I cannot give you any hope of diminished or more equal taxation from the House of Commons. I should only add another to the many delusions practised on the people, if I were to tell them, after nearly twenty years' experience, that anything can be done there, in your direction, except under a pressure which cannot be resisted, and which can only come from without. I shall rejoice if that pressure be created, and it will give me infinite satisfaction to assist it and to obey it.

I am, with great respect, yours sincerely,
JOHN BRIGHT.

To J. S. Manton, Esq., Regent Works, Birmingham.

THE INCOME-TAX.

In a further letter on the subject Mr. Bright wrote:—

Rochdale, March 21, 1862.

DEAR SIR,—I have to thank you for your second letter. I do not know that I can add much to what I have already written to you.

If Birmingham is in earnest in a movement against the income-tax, and if other towns will join in the movement, the tax can be overthrown; and I am not sure that it will not be overthrown more easily than made more equal and just. I can vote against the income-tax with a clear conscience, because I believe the whole sum annually raised by it might be saved by a Government anxious to do its duty to the people. But I must tell you plainly, that so long as there is an apparent popular acquiescence in the present expenditure, and particularly in that branch of it which is connected with the military services, I do not believe that the tax will either be overthrown, or its pressure sensibly mitigated.

I am prepared to vote for any honest attempt to make the tax more equal, as I am prepared to vote for its abolition. With regard to the precise course to be taken in the House of Commons in dealing with the subject, I must be left at liberty to do that which at the time may seem most judicious.

I think you should correspond with all the principal towns in the kingdom, if you wish your views on the income-tax to prevail.

I am, very truly yours,
JOHN BRIGHT.

J. S. Manton, Esq., Regent Works, Birmingham.

ON THE UNITED STATES.

From the beginning of the terrible struggle between the Northern and Southern States of America, Mr. Bright was the friend and champion of the North and their cause, and many enthusiastic acknowledgments have since been made to him by the American people of the services he rendered to their country at that time. The first public recognition he received was from the Chamber of Commerce of the State of New York, the members of which, at a meeting on Thursday, the 6th of March, 1862, unanimously adopted a resolution recording their gratitude for his eloquent and fearless advocacy of "the principles of constitutional liberty and international justice for which the American people were contending."

This resolution having been forwarded to Mr. Bright, he replied as follows :—

London, April 4, 1862.

DEAR SIR,—I have received through the hands of the Hon. Mr. Adams, the Minister of the

United States, your letter of the 8th of March, and the resolution unanimously adopted by the Chamber of Commerce of the State of New York on the 6th of March.

I wish you to convey to the eminent body of gentlemen over whom you preside the expression of my sense of the honour they have conferred upon me, and of the pleasure which it gives me to know that the course I have taken in reference to the events which are now passing in your country has met with the warm approval of those whom they represent. I accept their most kind resolution, not only as honourable to myself, but as a manifestation of friendly feeling to the great majority of my countrymen, whose true sentiments I believe I have not mistaken or misrepresented, when I have spoken on the side of your government and people.

I believe there is no other country in which men have been so free and so prosperous as in yours, and that there is no other political constitution now in existence, in the preservation of which the human race is so deeply interested, as in that under which you live. This is true, beyond all doubt, when applied to the Free States of your Union; I trust the time is not distant when it will be true all over your vast territory, from the St. Lawrence to the Gulf of Mexico.

Notwithstanding much misapprehension and some recent excitement, I am sure that an overwhelming majority of the people of the United Kingdom will rejoice at the success of your government, and at the complete restoration of your Union.

While asking you to convey the expression of my grateful feelings to the members of your chamber, I desire to tender to you my thanks for the very kind letter from yourself which accompanied the resolution.

I am, with great respect, very truly yours,
JOHN BRIGHT.

To P. Perit, Esq., President of the Chamber
of Commerce of the State of New York.

ON MR. RUBERY'S CASE.

In 1863 Mr. Bright, by his intercession with the American Government, obtained the pardon of a young Englishman from Birmingham, named Rubery, who had gone to America, and who, during the war, had been found guilty of the crime of treason, and sentenced to a term of imprisonment. An article containing some inaccuracies, purporting to give an account of the affair, was copied into several newspapers, and amongst others into the *Star*, to the editor of which Mr. Bright wrote the following letter:—

London, January 6, 1864.

SIR,—In the paragraph in your paper of this morning on the subject of the pardon of Mr. Rubery, copied from the *Birmingham Daily Post*, there are some mistakes which I will thank you to allow me to correct. It was Mr. Rubery's brother, Mr. John Rubery of Birmingham, who applied to me, and asked me to endeavour to procure his liberation. I have done nothing in the matter in consequence of any representation to me from Mr. Sturge, or from any member of his family, or from any other person. Mr. Rubery was arrested at San Francisco on the charge of being concerned in fitting out a vessel called the *Chapman*, for the purpose of privateering under the flag of the " Confederate States." When he was arrested and imprisoned, I wrote to a friend of mine in America with a view to obtain a lenient consideration of his case. The President very properly declined to interfere in the matter whilst it was in course of law. Rubery was tried and convicted with some of his associates. He was not sentenced to death—the Government of the United States, so far as I know, has never yet inflicted that punishment for treason—but he was sentenced to ten years' imprisonment and a fine of 10,000 dollars. When I saw the report of his conviction, I again wrote to my friend in Washington, and he brought the case before the President, and I am informed, in a letter dated the 15th of December, that the President has pardoned Rubery, and that the pardon will issue as soon as the papers can be prepared. I know nothing of the previous character or conduct of Mr. Rubery, but I believe the statements in the paragraph in question are much exaggerated. Mrs. Rubery, the mother of the misguided young man, is a widow lady well known and much esteemed in Birmingham, and I need not tell you that it has given me much pleasure to have been able, in part, to relieve her great anxiety as to the fate of her son.

I am, respectfully yours,
JOHN BRIGHT.

ON THE MALT-TAX.

Read at a public meeting held in the Town Hall, Birmingham, on Thursday evening, the 14th of April, 1864, to discuss the question of the total repeal of the tax.

London, April 11, 1864.

DEAR SIR,—I must ask your committee to excuse me, if I am unable to be present and to take part in the meeting to be held on Thursday next. I cannot, without the greatest inconvenience, leave town during this week. I may say, however, that I could not, if present at the meeting, undertake the part you wish to assign to me, for I am not sufficiently informed on the matter to be able to assert what is contained in the resolution you wish me to move. In taking off taxes, as in putting them on, it is the duty of Parliament to consult the interests of the people. With my present information I would prefer to return to the people the six millions raised from tea or sugar, rather than that sum raised from malt. If I joined in a vote against the malt-tax, it would be with a view to force a reduction of expenditure, and not because I thought the malt-tax so bad as the tea or the sugar tax. For the present session, however, there will be no reductions

of taxation beyond those already proposed by
the Chancellor of the Exchequer, and there will
be time enough for tea, sugar, and beer to fight
their battle in public discussion before any one
of them is likely to be further interfered with.
I think a moderate attention to economy would
enable Parliament to repeal any one of the four
great taxes—on income, tea, sugar, or beer—
and the diminution of the public expenditure
by the amount of one of these taxes would be
felt to be a great relief to the public. I shall
read the report of your proceedings with much
interest.

I am, very respectfully yours,
JOHN BRIGHT.

ON THE LICENSING SYSTEM.

Written in reply to an inquiry respecting
Mr. Bright's speech in a recent debate on Mr.
Lawson's (now Sir Wilfrid Lawson) Bill, as to
whether he had advocated the investing of Town
Councils with the power to suppress licensing.

London, June 13, 1864.

DEAR SIR,—If it is desired to put the
licensing power into the hands of the residents
of any town or district, I think the municipal
corporations are the proper channels for exer-
cising that power, and they would give licences
freely or not, as public opinion directed them.
I did not propose to give them the power to
shut up all the public-houses and beershops,
but only for the future to restrict the granting

of licences; they would also have the power to suspend or withdraw licences in cases where there were just grounds of complaint against those to whom they have already been granted. I do not urge this proposition with much confidence—there is something to be said against it; but I think it better than the schemes of the friends of the Permissive Bill. I cannot consent to the rough-and-ready way of dealing with the question which many friends of temperance in their zeal seem disposed to advocate. I think they would inflict a great injustice in many cases, and might create a strong reactionary feeling against their own principles. The case is full of difficulty, and I speak with hesitation upon it.

I am, very respectfully yours,
JOHN BRIGHT.

Robert Martin, Esq., Warrington.

ON IRISH QUESTIONS.

Read at a meeting held on Thursday, the 29th of December, 1864, at the Rotunda, Dublin, for the purpose of promoting an association for the following objects:—

1. A reform of the law of landlord and tenant, securing to the tenant full compensation for valuable improvements.

2. The abolition of the Irish Church Establishment.

3. The perfect freedom of education in all its branches.

The meeting was convened by the Lord

Mayor of Dublin, and was addressed by the Archbishops of Dublin and Cashel, and other Roman Catholic prelates.

Rochdale, December 22, 1864.

My dear Lord Mayor,—I have to thank your committee for their friendly invitation to your approaching meeting, although I shall not be able to avail myself of it. It is difficult for me to leave home at this season, and I have an engagement to be in Birmingham about the time when your meeting is to be held.

I am glad to see that an effort is to be made to force on some political advance in your country. The objects you aim at are good, and I hope you may succeed. On the question of landlord and tenant I think you should go farther, and seek to do more. What you want in Ireland is to break down the laws of primogeniture and entail, so that in course of time, by a gradual and just process, the Irish people may become the possessors of the soil of Ireland. A legal security for tenants' improvements will be of great value, but the true remedy for your great grievances is to base the laws which affect the land upon sound principles of political economy.

With regard to the State Church, that is an institution so evil and so odious, under the circumstances of your country, that it makes one almost hopeless of Irish freedom from it that Irishmen have borne it so long. The whole Liberal party in Great Britain will, doubtless, join with you in demanding the removal of a wrong which has no equal in the character of a national insult in any other civilized and Christian country in the world.

If the popular party in Ireland would adopt as its policy "Free Land" and "Free Church," and would unite with the popular party in England and Scotland for the advance of Liberal measures, and especially for the promotion of an honest amendment of the representation, I am confident that great and beneficial changes might be made within a few years. We have on our side numbers and opinion, but we want a more distinct policy, and a better organization; and these I hope, to some extent, your meeting may supply.

I thank you for your very kind invitation to the Mansion House, and am, my dear Lord Mayor,

Yours very truly,
JOHN BRIGHT.

The Right Hon. the Lord Mayor of Dublin.

ON REFORM.

At a private meeting of Radical electors held in Carlisle early in May, 1865, it was decided to solicit the opinion of Mr. Bright respecting the position to be assumed by the party at the ensuing election, which was then imminent. In reply to the appeal addressed to him, Mr. Bright wrote the following letter. The members for Carlisle at this time were Mr. Wilfrid (now Sir Wilfrid) Lawson, and Mr. Edmund Potter.

Rochdale, May 15, 1865.

Dear Sir,—My opinion is that the proper course for the Liberal members is to withdraw their support from any Government which will not bring in and carry a good measure for the extension of the suffrage.

Fortunately your members are well disposed on the Reform question, and would do anything that was thought wise in the matter.

Lord Palmerston is the real difficulty. He is not a Liberal, and the failure of the Bill of 1860 was owing entirely to him. When he is out of the way, no Government can exist on our side of the House which will not deal with the question of Reform.

I hope, at the coming election, the Radical electors will endeavour to bring their members up to the point of refusing to support a Government not willing to fulfil the pledges of 1859 and 1860. When it is a question of Reform or expulsion from office, the Whig statesmen will decide in favour of Reform. This is the only effectual mode of dealing with them, and I hope it will be adopted.

I hope the electors of your city will not think it needful to make any change in your representation.

I am, very respectfully yours,
John Bright.

ON THE UNITED STATES AND CANADA.

Read at the sitting of a commercial convention held at Detroit on the 12th of July, 1865.

London, June 10, 1865.

DEAR SIR,—I am much obliged to you for the invitation to your approaching commercial convention, to be held in the month of July. If I were on your continent I should avail myself of your friendly offer to be present at your deliberations, and if I could not add much to their usefulness, I could learn much from them; but to me Detroit seems a long way from England, and, unfortunately for me, I seem never to be able to steal three months from my many engagements here, to enable me to pay a long-hoped-for visit to the United States, and now I find it quite out of my power to avail myself of your tempting invitation. The project of your convention gives me great pleasure. I hope it will lead to a renewal of commercial intercourse with the British North-American provinces, for it will be a miserable thing if, because they are in connection with the British crown, and you acknowledge as your chief magistrate your President at Washington, there should not be a commercial intercourse between them and you, as free as if you were one people, and living under one government. I have faith that when your people, so free and so instructed, apply their minds to any question of commerce, they will soon discern what is true and adopt it, and in this faith I shall look with confidence for the most beneficial results from the discussions into which you are about to enter. Whatever tends to promote harmony and commercial dealings between the United States and the Canadas will be favourably regarded by every intelligent statesman in this country.

Wishing you the happiest results from the convention, and thanking you for your letter,

I am, with great respect,
Very sincerely yours,
JOHN BRIGHT.

Joseph Aspinall, Esq.

ON REFORM.

LORD PALMERSTON AND REFORM.

Written in reply to an invitation to attend a Reform meeting in Glasgow.

Pitnacree, Dunkeld, September 10, 1865.

DEAR SIR,—Mr. Dalglish has forwarded your letter to me. I thank you for your invitation, although I do not feel myself able to accept it. If I come to Glasgow, I must go to other places. I cannot bear the weight of an agitation for Reform, and spend the winter in attending great meetings, as I did in the years 1858-9, and, therefore, I feel compelled to shun engagements which I know I should find too heavy for me. I have as much interest in the question as I have had at any time, and believe, and indeed I know, that it is advancing with most certain steps. When the present Prime Minister[1] leaves office, no ministry will be possible of the Liberal party which will not deal with the Reform question. I am not

[1] Lord Palmerston.

anxious that it should be dealt with during his official life, for he is the only man connected with the Liberal party who is at once both able and willing to betray it. One sentence from his lips would have passed the Bill of 1860, and that sentence he refused to utter. His colleagues preferred their places to their honour as public men, and they consented to the greatest political fraud of our times rather than leave the treasury bench even for a season. Happily the question does not depend on the Prime Minister. He has never promoted its growth, and he cannot prevent its success. There is at work a steady and a silent force which all who are not blind may mark, and every day's delay will but add to the certainty and fulness of our triumph. I hope every Liberal constituency will so act through its representatives as to make a sham Liberal Government henceforth impossible. For what can be more degrading to a Liberal member of the House of Commons than to sit as a supporter of an administration which repudiates and has betrayed the first and greatest question or cause upon which the whole policy of the Liberal party is founded?

I am, very truly yours,
JOHN BRIGHT.

Mr. George Newton, Glasgow.

ON THE GAME LAWS.

Read at a meeting of the Midland Farmers' Club, held in Birmingham on Thursday, the 5th of October, 1865.

Rochdale, September 30, 1865.

DEAR SIR,—I am glad to hear that you are about to read a paper on the subject of the Game Laws. I do not think much good would be done by holding a meeting in Birmingham. The towns are known to be against the Game Laws, but so long as the county constituencies send game preservers to Parliament, the members for the towns can do nothing for the farmers.

It is about twenty years since I gave much time and labour with a view to relieve the farmers from the evil of the Game Laws; and I spent at least 300*l*. in bringing before them and the public some of the facts of this great grievance. Up to this time nothing has been done in the way of relief, but, on the contrary, the laws which favour the preservation of game have been made more strict. I fear the evil has become, not less, but greater, and I see only one way in which any real improvement can be made. It can only be done by having in Parliament a larger number of representatives of the people, and fewer representatives of a class and of the prejudices and usurpations of a class. How can this be brought about and secured? By the admission of another million of the people to the elective franchise, so that the House of Commons may become truly representative of the true interests and wishes of the nation.

But there is one thing which the farmers may do for themselves whenever an election for a county takes place. At present *they* are not asked who shall pretend to represent them, but the lords and squires of the county name the candidate, and, as a rule, the tenant farmers vote for him, and he enters the House to do the work of the lords and squires who selected him. A main part of that work is to keep guard over the laws which favour the preservation of game. I know how many reasons there are why a tenant should be disposed to support the nominee of his landlord. He feels in many ways his landlord or his landlord's agents can annoy and injure him, and he submits to a power which he has not learned to resist. But the time is coming when tenants will dare to believe and act for themselves in the performance of their political duties. They can combine with great ease, and, when combined, their power is irresistible. I hope the day may soon come when they will take the elections of members for the counties in some degree into their own hands; and when this is done, their political and social deliverance will be secured.

You will see at once how easy it is for you to combine. Every farmer has a horse and gig, or dog-cart, or conveyance of some kind, so that he can go to the poll without any cost to himself. Farmers meet almost every week at their market town, and they can know the feelings of their class without difficulty. In every county they should select a "farmers' candidate." If a good tenant farmer can be selected, bring him forward; if not, then some other respectable and intelligent man. If you can find a landlord who is willing to be just to the tenant farmers, both in his private conduct and in respect of legislation which affects them, take him as your candidate, and give him a zealous support. You can contest a county almost at no expense. A subscription of one pound from each tenant will raise a sum large enough to pay for all the printing you require; and you can take yourselves and your neighbours to the poll at a trifling expense. The farmers' candidate will be the popular candidate. The Liberals in the towns will give him their support, and you will carry him into Parliament to do the work of the farmers and of the people, instead of that of the lords and of the squires.

Some will say I am advising you to work a revolution; and so I am. It will be a revolution that will transfer the county representation from a dozen rich men or families to the real people of the counties. It will send men to Parliament who will care more for the rights and interests of the population than for the semi-barbarous sports of a class. When the tenant farmers see their power, and arouse themselves to exert it, the days of the Game Laws are ended, and there will not be wanting just and good men among the landlords themselves who will give them a hearty co-operation in the good work.

As to changes in the Game Laws, I see no great good in them. What you want is the repeal of all laws which are made with the object of favouring the preservation of game. The fundamental principle of the tenant farmers should be this: That they shall have absolute and undisputed ownership of, and control over, all animals which live upon the produce of the land. They occupy land, and pay rent for it; they risk all they have—their money, their time, their labour, their hopes, their present and their future—in the cultivation of their farms; the horses, cows, sheep, and swine are theirs; and the hares and rabbits, and game of every kind living upon their farms, should also be theirs. Till this is the settled law, and also the practice of the country, the tenant farmers will never hold the position to which they have a just claim, and the evils of game laws and game preservation will never be wholly removed.

At present it is impossible for your friends in Parliament to do anything for you. You can do much—I think you can do everything for yourselves. Let it be a rule that no tenant farmer will support a candidate who is not in favour of full justice to tenant farmers, and the whole character of county representatives will be changed.

I would advise your committee to correspond with farmers in every county in the kingdom, and to exhort them everywhere seriously to consider this great question, and to prepare to act when another general election shall take place. Your deliverance from the insulting grievance of which you complain rests mainly with yourselves.

I am, very respectfully yours,
JOHN BRIGHT.

Mr. A. Robotham, The Oak Farm,
   Drayton Basset, near Tamworth.

ON IRISH AFFAIRS.

The following letter, written during the outbreak of Fenianism in Ireland, was read at a meeting of the National Association in Dublin, on Tuesday, the 6th of March, 1866. The speech to which it alludes was delivered by Mr. Bright on the 18th of February, 1866, in the House of Commons on the occasion of the introduction of a Bill by Sir G. Grey, on behalf of Earl Russell's Government, for the suspensions of the Habeas Corpus Act in Ireland. Mr. Bright did not oppose the Bill, believing, he said, that the course which was about to be pursued, was the most merciful course for Ireland under the circumstances; but he made a powerful appeal for the removal of some of the evils under which the Irish people groaned, and denounced the way in which Ireland had been governed by this country for the previous 100 years.

London, March 3, 1866.

MY DEAR SIR,—I have received the copy of the resolution of thanks voted to me by the Committee of the National Association of Ireland. I value it very much, and ask that you will convey to the committee my gratitude for the approval they have expressed of my recent speech on the affairs and conditions of Ireland. I think there is a better prospect for your unfortunate country, and I shall gladly do all in my power to assist her own representatives and the Government in such legislation as may be required for her good. From the present administration [1] I am sure you will receive sympathy, and I cannot but hope that at an early period there will be a resolute attempt to conquer the malady which, from time to time, brings so much suffering to Ireland and so much discredit to England. I believe it is in the power of Parliament to remove all just causes of discontent with you, and I shall heartily co-operate in every effort tending to that result.

Believe me, always sincerely yours,
JOHN BRIGHT.

Peter Paul M'Swiney, Esq.

ON REFORM.

THE REFORM BILL OF 1866.

Read at a town's meeting held at Birmingham on the 26th of March, 1866, to consider the Reform Bill introduced in the House of Commons by Mr. Gladstone on behalf of Earl Russell's Government on the 13th of March. The last sentence but one in this letter furnishes a proof that Mr. Bright at this time sanctioned the separation of franchise and redistribution.

Rochdale, March 25, 1866.

MY DEAR MR. LLOYD,—I feel sorry that I cannot be at your meeting to-morrow night, to witness and to help the expression of the sentiments of Birmingham upon the question which is now exciting so much interest throughout

[1] Earl Russell's.

the country. I cannot write as I could speak, but I must write a few lines to you.

The Franchise Bill now before Parliament is a perfectly honest Bill. It will, if it becomes law, give votes extensively to the middle classes, both in counties and boroughs, and it will overthrow the principle of working-class exclusion which was established by the Reform Bill of 1832. It will admit to the franchise so many of the working men in all important and populous boroughs, that they, as a class, will no longer feel themselves intentionally excluded and insulted by the law.

In the counties it will enfranchise 200,000 men; and it may be expected in some counties to make the representation less that of the class of landlords and more that of the great body of the occupiers of houses and land within the county.

It will enfranchise, in London and in all the great cities, a considerable number of young men and of artisans who live in lodgings or in parts of houses, and it will thus extend the franchise to many not included in the suffrage granted by the Reform Act.

I say the Bill is an honest Bill; and if it is the least the Government could offer, it may be that it is the greatest which the Government could carry through Parliament.

Parliament is never hearty for Reform, or for any good measure. It hated the Reform Bill of 1831-2. It hated the Bill which repealed the Corn Law in 1846. It does not like the Franchise Bill now upon its table. It is to a large extent the offspring of landlord power in the counties, and of tumult and corruption in the boroughs; and it would be strange if such a Parliament were in favour of freedom and of an honest representation of the people. But, notwithstanding such a Parliament, this Bill will pass, if Birmingham and other towns will do their duty.

There is opposed to it the Tory party, of whose blindness and folly we have abundant proofs in all history. We have no reason now to expect for it a wiser course, and we have a small section of men who do not accept the name of Tory, but zealously do its work. These combined to form a conspiracy on which all the hopes of Mr. Disraeli and the Opposition are based. I think a more dirty conspiracy has not been seen in the House of Commons for many generations. It is directed against this Bill, and not less against Lord Russell, by whom the Liberal and popular policy of the Government has been determined.

What should be done, and what must be done under these circumstances? You know what your fathers did thirty-four years ago, and you know the result. The men who in every speech they utter insult working men, describing them as a multitude given up to ignorance and vice, will be the first to yield when the popular will is loudly and resolutely expressed. If Parliament Street, from Charing Cross to the venerable abbey, were filled with men seeking a reform bill, as it was two years ago with men come to do honour to an illustrious Italian, these slanderers of their country would learn to be civil, if they did not learn to love freedom.

This Bill appeals to the middle and working classes alike. It is a measure of enfranchisement to both of them, and they should heartily unite in an effort to make it a law. That which the Tories and "dirty conspiracy" oppose cannot but deserve the support of every Liberal man in the kingdom. If the population of the Birmingham district would set apart a day, not for "humiliation," but for a firm assertion of their rights in great meetings or in one vast gathering, they might sustain their Franchise Bill, and beat down, as by one blow, the power that threatens to bolt the door of Parliament against the people.

I hope we shall see in all the towns of Great Britain, during the coming fortnight, a great support of the Government and the Bill. If the vote of want of confidence is carried against the Government, there will be a change of ministers or a dissolution of Parliament. If the towns do their duty, the Government will be safe, because the Bill will be safe, and the suffrage once more established on a more rational basis. The country can then turn its attention to the arrangement and distribution of seats, which is just as needful as a wider suffrage to give us a fair representation of the nation.

Great meetings and great petitions will not only be useful but effectual.

I am, very truly yours,
JOHN BRIGHT.

Thomas Lloyd, Esq.

THE REFORM BILL OF 1866.

An open-air meeting, convened by the Reform League, was held on Monday afternoon, the 21st of May, 1866, on Primrose Hill, London. Mr. E. Beales was called to the chair, and read the following letter from Mr. Bright. The Distribution of Seats Bill mentioned in it was a Bill introduced by Mr. Gladstone after the second reading of the Franchise Bill. It proposed, by the partial disfranchisement of some boroughs and the grouping of others, to distribute forty-nine seats amongst the counties and larger boroughs.

Rochdale, May 19, 1866.

Dear Sir,—I thank you for your invitation to the meeting to be held on Monday, but I am not able to be present at it. I hope all your friends will understand the exact position of the Reform question. The main portion of the objections to the Franchise Bill on the second reading were mere pretences; there was no truth in them. The only real objection was against the admission of any portion of the working men to the suffrage. The same game will be played hereafter. There will be resolutions saying one thing and meaning another. Everything will be criticized; but the thing really hated and feared will be the extension of the franchise to the working men. The Government Distribution of Seats Bill, I fear, is not good enough to excite the hostility of the Conservatives or those from the Liberal ranks who have joined them, as it has little in it to excite enthusiasm or favour among the people. It will be opposed chiefly because it is henceforth a part of the Bill which offers the franchise to working men, and because a rejection of any considerable or important part of the Bill will be the rejection of the whole. The Tory party, and those from the Liberal ranks who join it, are animated by an unchangeable hostility to any Bill which gives the franchise to the working men. They object to any transfer of power from those who now possess it, and they object to share their power with any increased number of their countrymen who form the working class. They regard the workmen here as the southern planter regards the negroes who were so lately his slaves. They can no longer be bought or sold; so far they are free men. They may work and pay taxes; but they must not vote. They must obey the laws, but must have no share in selecting the men who are to make them. The future position of the millions of working men in the United Kingdom is now determined, if the opposition of the Tory party is to prevail—it is precisely that fixed by the southern planter for the negro. Millions of workmen will bear this in mind; they will now know the point or the gulf which separates one party from the other in the House of Commons.

There will be great efforts made to induce the Government to abandon the line of 14*l.* for the county, and 7*l.* for the borough franchise. If the Government yields, it will probably destroy itself, and it will leave the question open for the next Parliament—for no man can suppose the suffrage question settled for the term of a single Parliament, on the basis of a departure from the figures of the present Bill. Lord Derby's Bill of 1859 proposed a 10*l.* franchise for counties, and Lord Palmerston's Bill of 1860 offered the same county franchise, and a 6*l.* franchise for boroughs. If anything less or worse than a 14*l.* and 7*l.* franchise be now carried, there will not be a single reformer in the kingdom who will not be at liberty, when the Bill is passed, to petition or to move the House for a further extension of the suffrage. I hope you may have a good meeting, but I shall regard it only as a preliminary to the meetings you will hold, if the moderate measure now before Parliament should be mutilated or rejected. Working men everywhere should feel that the real position and future of their class are now in suspense, and that they depend mainly on themselves.

I am, sir, &c.,
JOHN BRIGHT.

ON REFORM.

THE HYDE PARK DEMONSTRATION IN 1866.

The following letter has reference to the celebrated Reform meeting, when the railings of Hyde Park were pulled down. The Reform League had made arrangements to hold a meeting in Hyde Park on Monday, the 24th of July, 1866, but the Government (that of Lord Derby) refused to allow the meeting to be held there. At five o'clock on Monday afternoon the park entrances were all closed, 1500 policemen were placed inside, and the Foot and Life Guards were held in readiness. About seven o'clock the Reform League processions arrived at the gates and were refused admission, whereupon, after protest being made, the League went to Trafalgar Square and held a great meeting there. A large crowd, however, remained at the gates, and after attempting, without success, to effect an entrance there, they attacked the railings and pulled them down for several yards. The police then charged the crowd, and a fight ensued, in which several policemen were wounded and some inspectors unhorsed. The people poured into the park by thousands, and although the police charged again and again they were unable to drive them out. The police would have been utterly routed, if it had not been for the intervention of the military. The Foot Guards with loaded guns and fixed bayonets were drawn up near the Marble Arch, and a Horse Guards' troop patrolled the avenues. Eventually a meeting was held, and resolutions condemning the Government were passed.

Rochdale, July 19, 1866.

DEAR SIR,—I thank your council for the invitation to the meeting intended to be held in Hyde Park on Monday next. I cannot leave home for some days to come, and therefore cannot be in London on the 23rd instant.

I see that the chief of the metropolitan police force has announced his intention to prevent the holding of the meeting. It appears from this that the people may meet in the parks for every purpose but that which ought to be most important and most dear to them. To meet in the streets is inconvenient, and to meet in the parks is unlawful—this is the theory of the police authorities of the metropolis. You have asserted your right to meet on Primrose Hill and in Trafalgar Square. I hope after Monday next no one will doubt your right to meet in Hyde Park. If a public meeting in a public park is denied you, and if millions of intelligent and honest men are denied the franchise, on what foundation does our liberty rest?—or is there in the country any liberty but the toleration of the ruling class? This is a serious question, but it is necessary to ask it, and some answer must be given to it.

I am, very respectfully yours,
JOHN BRIGHT.

Mr. George Howell,
Secretary to the Reform League,
8, Adelphi Terrace, Strand.

ON RECEIVING AN INVITATION TO A BANQUET IN DUBLIN.

Written in reply to the following invitation, signed by over twenty Irish Members of Parliament, which was sent to Mr. Bright in August, 1866:—

Sir,—We, the undersigned, admiring your public character and grateful for your eloquent advocacy of the rights of our country, respectfully request your acceptance of a public banquet at Dublin on as early a day as your convenience will permit.

Rochdale, September 1, 1866.

My dear Mr. Dillon,—I am afraid you will think me long in answering your letter of the 21st ult., and in replying to the invitation to the proposed banquet, which has duly reached me. The invitation is a very remarkable one, and I cannot doubt it represents an important amount of public opinion in Ireland. To myself it is a testimony of approval and kind feeling which I estimate most highly, although it involves me in no small difficulty, for I have been hoping for a quiet autumn, with an absence of public meetings and of public labour. I am not confident that my coming to Ireland will be of any service, but as so many among you are of opinion that something may be done to make a more perfect union between the Liberals of Ireland and the Liberal party here, with a view to wiser legislation for your country and for ours, I have not felt myself at liberty to refuse the invitation which has been sent to me. I accept it with much gratitude to those from whom it comes, and with a hope that in doing so I may not be stepping beyond the bounds of what seems to be my duty. Some time during the month of October will, I hope, be convenient to all concerned, but I must ask you to leave the precise day to be fixed two or three weeks hence. About the middle of the month will probably be the best time for me, if there be no objection to it on the part of my friends in Dublin.

With many thanks to you and to those on whose behalf you have written to me,

I am, very sincerely yours,
JOHN BRIGHT.

Mr. John B. Dillon, M.P., Dublin.

ON AN ANTICIPATED VISIT TO IRELAND.

In reply to a communication from Mr. John M'Corry on behalf of the working classes of Dublin, requesting that Mr. Bright would afford them an opportunity, when in that city, of expressing their gratitude to him for his warm advocacy of the cause of Ireland. Being in Dublin in October and November, Mr. Bright, after attending the banquet given to him by Irish Liberals on the 30th of October, addressed a meeting of working men in the theatre of the Mechanics' Institute on the 2nd of November, and was enthusiastically received.

Rochdale, September 27, 1866.

DEAR SIR,—I have to thank you for your kind letter. My stay in Dublin will be short, and I cannot now promise to attend any public meeting; but if your friends will allow the matter to stand over till nearer the time, perhaps some arrangement may be made which may not be inconvenient to them. I am much obliged to Mr. James Haughton for his kind offer. I think I was at his house when in Dublin more than twenty years ago. May I request you to convey my thanks to those on whose behalf you have written to me, for their friendly sentiments towards me?

I am, very truly yours,
JOHN BRIGHT.

ON MR. GARTH'S LIBELS.

The following correspondence between Mr. Bright and Mr. Richard Garth, elected member for Guildford in December, 1866, gives an illustration of the kind of weapons with which Mr. Bright has at times been attacked.

Rochdale, December 24, 1866.

SIR,—Through the courtesy of an elector of Guildford, I have received a handbill printed by Mr. Stent, printer, stationer, &c., Guildford, purporting to contain a report of a speech delivered by you to an "enthusiastic meeting of Mr. Garth's supporters, held at the 'White Hart Hotel,' Friday evening, the 14th of December, 1866." I wish to call your attention to some passages in this speech. I pass by much which is open to criticism, and confine myself to certain exact statements to which you appear to have committed yourself.

1. You ask, "What has Mr. Bright done for his own people? Has he ever stood for his own place? Dare he ever stand for it? Not he! He has been hooted away from his own premises—his own people distrust him."

2. You ask, "What did he do in the cotton famine, when thousands of men were out of employment, when people down here, who had no direct interest in the matter, subscribed so liberally? Why, he did not subscribe a half-penny."

3. You say, "I will tell you what he did. He wanted to give them a loan which was to be repaid in so many years, so that during those years he would have these people as his serfs at his beck and call, to do what he pleased with, and to prevent their rising when he chose to put wages at whatever rate he liked."

You state that I have not answered charges of a similar kind made against me, and you therefore assume that they are true. I cannot stoop to reply to the folly and the slander of every poor Tory partisan who assails me, and I should not have noticed you but for the fact that you are a member of the House of Commons. I am quite sure you will not venture to say on the floor of Parliament, where I could meet you, what you have had the courage to say at the "White Hart," in Guildford; and therefore I address this letter to you, rather than wait till the opening of Parliament.

With regard to the paragraph which I have marked No. 1, I beg to tell you that the only part of it which is not false is that which assumes or asserts that I have not stood as a candidate for the borough of Rochdale. I have not been a candidate for this borough, though on several occasions I have been asked to stand by the most eminent men of the Liberal party, which has a large majority in the borough. I believe there is not a respectable man in Rochdale, of your own party, who will not admit that, if I had wished it, and had consented to leave the great constituency which has for nine years past honoured me with its confidence, I might at this moment have been the Parliamentary representative of this borough.

The rest of the paragraph marked No. 1 is simply a falsehood in every part of it. Of the assertion in paragraph No. 2 I may say the same. It is a falsehood in every part of it. I am not in the habit of boasting of what I give, and I shall not now enter into particulars that I may confute you. I may say that, after we had subscribed as largely as any firm in the town, my only complaint against the relief committee in this district was that it did not make further calls upon the mill-owners here before it applied for assistance from the general fund at the disposal of the committee in Manchester. I may say further that, according to my means, I believe I did not fall short of what was done by any other contributor to the fund, whether in or out of this country. Possibly you are not aware of the fact that the largest sum given by any contributor to the fund is but a trifle when compared with the losses suffered by nearly all the firms in the cotton trade during the disastrous years of the American war. In paragraph No. 3 you make a strange assertion, both as to fact and motive. I am obliged to tell you that the whole paragraph is false from beginning to end. You must be singularly ignorant of the condition and temper of the working men of this district, to imagine that any employer can have them "as his serfs at his beck and call, to do what he pleases with, and to prevent their rising when he chooses to put wages at whatever rate he likes."

I have now called your attention to some statements of your speech. I say that these statements are false—wholly and absolutely false. If you knew them to be false when you made them, I need not write the word which would properly describe you. If you made them, not knowing whether they were true or false, I can only pity your disregard of all honourable feeling and caution when dealing with the character of your opponents.

I do not expect you will deny the accuracy of the report of your speech, for I find that you repeated the substance of the slanders in your speech at the nomination for Guildford. I do not expect that you will attempt to prove the charges you have made, for I know that to be impossible. Whether you will retract what you have said, and express sorrow for having said it, will depend on whether, being a Queen's Counsel and a member of Parliament, you possess the qualities which are never found wanting in the character of a gentleman.

I am, respectfully,

JOHN BRIGHT.

R. Garth, Esq., M.P., 3, Paper Buildings, Temple.

The foregoing letter produced the following reply from Mr. Garth :—

Temple, January 3, 1867.

Sir,—I have already explained to you my reasons for not replying earlier to your letter of the 24th of last month.

I was anxious, in justice to you, as well as to myself, to put you in possession, as far as I could, of the sources of information upon which the statements I made at Guildford, and of which you complain, were founded. I have no personal knowledge either of yourself or of Rochdale, and my impressions have been derived partly from your own speeches, and partly from correspondence and other statements which have appeared from time to time in the public prints.

I have not yet been able to lay my hand upon some of these, but I would call your attention to two speeches, which I had recently read, and which, no doubt, were fresh in my memory at the time when I addressed my friends at Guildford.

The first of these is a speech of Mr. Pope Hennessy, addressed to the electors of the county of Wexford, and reported in the *Times* of the 6th of November last, from which the following is an extract:—

"He is a great manufacturer, and he employs what he calls a good many hands; .. he employs a large number of human beings—men, women, and children. Now, no man stands up so stoutly for his own strong class as against the weak instruments they employ as Mr. Bright; he was a leader in the defence of the cruel old system of slavery, of disease, of ignorance, of shortened, unhappy lives which the Factory Acts have successfully attacked. Hardly two years have passed since, at a meeting of the magnates of Manchester, he boasted of his former opposition to the Factory Acts, and said he should be prepared to do the same again. He kept his word; for when the Lace Factories Bill was before the House, and the Bleach Works Bill, and a Bill to give some protection to the poor girls who work in the Bradford warehouses, he was not only present, but violent in his opposition to those salutary and benevolent Acts. He fought, and the other Radical manufacturers with him, for what he deemed to be a sort of property of his—the right of doing what he liked with his own workpeople. He carried his class-feelings even below the surface of the earth, and when the Mines Regulation Bill was before Parliament, he and his class would not give the smallest help to the miner to get better ventilation or greater safety from accidents, simply because better ventilation and greater safety means additional expense to the mine-owner.... In 1861 a deputation from the miners came to London, and presented me with an address of thanks for some little services I tried to render them, and from those men I heard an unanimous condemnation of Mr. Bright."

The other speech to which I allude (and of which printed copies have, I believe, been widely circulated) was delivered by Mr. Ferrand to the Working Men's Conservative Association at Bradford on the 20th of November last. In this speech Mr. Ferrand says:—

"I have watched Mr. Bright for years, and although, as I have told you, he is possessed of marvellous powers of eloquence, a greater political coward never entered the House of Commons. . . . I never heard him make a speech which inculcated peace and goodwill amongst men; but, on the contrary, he has always tried to set the different classes of the community against each other, and thereby to encourage bloodshed. For twenty-five years I have worked with you working men of Bradford in obtaining many great and conciliating measures from Parliament, while he has opposed them all. During that time, I never heard him speak a word in favour of working men in the House of Commons. You have been reminded of what his conduct was in Lancashire during the cotton famine. He took no part, either in purse or person, to relieve the distress in his native county; but when I met, at Manchester, a great assembly of delegates from the cotton districts of Cheshire, Lancashire, Staffordshire, and Yorkshire, they unanimously declared that England had no more bitter enemy than Mr. Bright, and that he was detested by all the working men in Lancashire."

I can hardly suppose that your attention as a public man has not been directed to these passages; and I am not aware that they have ever been contradicted. I had seen other public statements, and I had heard reports, evincing your unpopularity amongst the working classes at Rochdale and in Lancashire generally; and I certainly did believe that you

were unpopular there. You admit that you
never stood for Rochdale, although you have
been invited to do so by your friends, and it
was therefore surely not unreasonable that I
should form an opinion, which I believe I share
in common with many others, that if you had
stood for Rochdale you would not have been
successful. My views in this respect may have
been erroneous, but I consider that I had a
perfect right to entertain those views, and to
express them.

I also most firmly believed, from statements
and reports which I had seen and heard, that
you had been hooted from your own premises,
and were distrusted by your own workpeople;
but, as you tell me that what I said in this
respect was wholly without foundation, I, of
course, take it for granted that I was misin-
formed, and I beg, not only to retract my statement, but to express my sincere regret for
having made it.

With regard to the other paragraphs of which
you complain, I must observe that the report of
my speech is in some respects inaccurate. I
disclaim having ever said, or intended to say,
that "you had not subscribed a halfpenny" in
aid of the distress which prevailed during the
cotton famine. I sincerely hope and trust that
there was no manufacturer in any of the cotton
districts against whom such a charge could
justly be made. But I believe that I am quite
correct in supposing that at Rochdale, in the
month of January, 1862, you did propose, or
suggest, that, instead of raising further sub-

scriptions, the Poor-Law Guardians, or the mill-owners, or both, should lend sums of money to the distressed operatives, upon the understanding that such loans should be repaid out of their earnings as soon as they should be restored to work.

It was this proposition of yours to which I alluded, and upon which I animadverted in my speech at Guildford; and I certainly was of opinion then, and I am so still, that the effect of such a scheme as you proposed would have been to entail a very heavy load of obligation upon the working men, which would have placed them, possibly for years, in great measure under the control of their employers, who might have exercised that control, either in regulating the amount of wages, or in other ways; and I was, and am still further of opinion, that to have carried out your proposition at such a time, and under such circumstances, would have been by no means a liberal or generous policy towards the distressed operatives.

It is almost unnecessary to add, that you are quite at liberty to make any use you please of this letter.

I am, sir, your obedient servant,
RICHARD GARTH.

John Bright, Esq.

Mr. Bright replied to this letter as follows:—

Rochdale, January 4, 1867.

SIR,—Your letter of yesterday has just

arrived, and I find it almost precisely what I expected. After a week's search, you have not found a single fact to establish the gross charges brought against me in your speech at Guildford. Instead of facts and proofs, you fill three pages of your letter with extracts from speeches of Mr. Ferrand and Mr. Hennessy, which speeches have doubtless been spoken, but which I have never read.

. . . . . .

You made three charges of the most distinct character: that I had been hooted from my own premises; that I had not given "a half-penny" to the relief of the distress in these districts; and that I wished to support the suffering workmen by loans, that I might have them at my "beck and call," "to do what I pleased with," and to prevent their rising when I chose "to put wages at whatever rate I liked."

Your authority for the first charge is evidently such that you dare not produce it; it is not even equal to the authority of Mr. Ferrand and Mr. Hennessy, and therefore you retract it. The second charge you escape from by denying the accuracy of the report, without saying what you actually did say in place of what you are reported to have said. With regard to the third charge, you seek to avoid it by expressing an opinion that if money were lent to families in distress, it would be burdensome to repay it, which nobody doubts; but you express no regret that you charged me with recommending a system of loans *in order that I might use them as a means of oppressing the workmen during the* period that would be required for the repayment of the loans.

My object in suggesting loans was to give relief in such a manner, to a large number of persons, as would not bring them into the list of ordinary paupers, and would not wound their honourable pride; and if the distress had lasted only for a few months, as was then hoped would be the case, the plan would have been practicable, and might have been adopted with great advantage.

On a review of your speech and your letter, I come to this conclusion—that you wished to get into Parliament, and were not particular as to the path which might lead to it. You threw dirt during your canvass, doubtless knowing that, if needful, you could eat it afterwards. There are many men who go "through dirt to dignities," and I suspect you have no objection to be one of them.

I am, with whatever respect is due to you,
Yours, &c.,
JOHN BRIGHT.

Richard Garth, Esq., M.P., Temple, London.

[The Editor has omitted from the above letter an anecdote which was related to Mr. Cobden by Mr. Byng, one of the oldest members of the House of Commons, and which was quoted by Mr. Bright. While regarding the introduction of this anecdote as perfectly justifiable under the circumstances under which it was written, the Editor has left it out, under the impression that Mr. Bright would prefer that it should not, after this lapse of time, be repeated. As regards the opposition to the Factory Act, it may be here stated that Mr. Bright has always been in favour of legislation to protect children from overwork. He has been opposed to any restriction of the labour of adults, whether of men or women.]

ON REFORM.

THE REFORM RESOLUTIONS OF 1867.

On Lord Dunkellin's amendment being carried in Committee on the Reform Bill of 1866, Earl Russell resigned office, and Lord Derby was asked to form a ministry. As soon as the Conservatives were in office they reopened the question of Reform. The course they proposed to take was to pass a series of resolutions, and Mr. Disraeli arranged to move them on the 25th of February. They were as follows:—

"This House having, in the last session of Parliament, assented to the second reading of a Bill, entitled, 'A Bill to extend the Right of Voting at Elections of Members of Parliament in England and Wales,' is of opinion:—

"1. That the number of electors for counties and boroughs in England and Wales ought to be increased.

"2. That such increase may best be effected by both reducing the value of the qualifying tenement in counties and boroughs, and by adding other franchises not dependent on such value.

"3. That while it is desirable that a more direct representation should be given to the labouring class, it is contrary to the constitution of this realm to give to any one class or interest a predominating power over the rest of the community.

"4. That the occupation franchise in counties and boroughs shall be based upon the principle of rating.

"5. That the principle of plurality of votes, if adopted by Parliament, would facilitate the settlement of the borough franchise on an extensive basis.

"6. That it is expedient to revise the existing distribution of seats.

"7. That in such a revision it is not expedient that any borough now represented in Parliament should be wholly disfranchised.

"8. That in revising the existing distribution of seats, this House will acknowledge as its main consideration the expediency of supplying representation to places not at present represented, and which may be considered entitled to that privilege.

"9. That it is expedient that provision should be made for the better prevention of bribery and corruption at elections.

"10. That it is expedient that the system of registration of voters in counties should be assimilated, as far as possible, to that which prevails in boroughs.

"11. That it shall be open to every Parliamentary elector, if he thinks fit, to record his vote by means of a polling paper duly signed and authenticated.

"12. That provision be made for diminishing the distance which voters have to travel for the purpose of recording their votes, so that no expenditure for such purpose shall hereafter be legal.

"13. That a humble address be presented to her Majesty, praying her Majesty to issue a Royal Commission to form and submit to the consideration of Parliament a scheme for new and enlarged boundaries of the existing Parliamentary boroughs, where the population extends beyond the limits now assigned to such boroughs, and to fix, subject to the decision of Parliament, the boundaries of such other boroughs as Parliament may deem fit to be represented in this House."

These resolutions were very distasteful to the Reform party in the country, and at public meetings held to consider them they were generally condemned. Amongst others the Bradford branch of the National Reform Union declared them to be unsatisfactory and delusive, and a report of the meeting's proceedings having been sent to Mr. Bright, he wrote the following letter in reply :—

Rochdale, February 16, 1867.

DEAR SIR,—I think your resolutions very good. The course taken by the Government is an insult to the House, and a gross offence to the whole body of Reformers in the country. I cannot say what the House will do till after the meeting which is called for Thursday next.

The Administration is bitterly hostile to Reform. When in Opposition this was abundantly proved, and it is confirmed by its course since its accession to office. It has not the honesty or the courage to pronounce boldly against Reform, but it seeks to murder the cause and the question by a course contrary to Parliamentary usage and odious in the sight of all honest men. If the House joins in the guilt of this odious proceeding, it will only add to the distrust with which it is now regarded by vast multitudes of the people in all parts of the country.

You are right in holding meetings, and in every town and village meetings should be held. Already they have been held more generally, and more numerously attended than at any other time since 1832. Hitherto the effect seems little, so far as we may judge from the action of the Administration, and whether further meetings will produce any greater effect, I cannot undertake to say. But I will venture to say this, that a Government unmindful of the opinion expressed so clearly in the great centres of our population is running the country into great peril. If meetings have no effect—if the open and almost universal expression of opinion has no power on the Administration and the Legislature,—then, inevitably, the minds of the people will seek other channels with a view to obtain and secure the rights which are so contemptuously denied them. If I am wrong in believing this, then history is a lie from the beginning, and we have all been mistaken in our estimate of the causes out of which many of the great and deplorable transactions it has recorded have sprung.

I understand that in Birmingham a great demonstration of opinion is contemplated, and I suppose other parts of the country will have something to say to an Administration which abdicates its function, and is ready to betray both Queen and people, that it may remain in office for another session.

I am, with great respect, yours truly,

JOHN BRIGHT.

The Secretary of the Bradford Branch
of the Reform Union.

THE REFORM RESOLUTIONS OF 1867.

Written to the Secretary of the Birmingham branch of the Reform League.

Rochdale, February 18, 1867.

DEAR SIR,—I thank you for your note and the copy of the resolutions passed at the great meeting held on Tuesday last. I believe that all you say about the Government and the resolutions offered to the House is quite true, and I hope that no attempt at legislation will be founded upon the resolutions. The Reform question cannot be dealt with in a manner satisfactory to the people by the enemies of Reform, and it will be better for us to wait till we have a Government honestly favourable to Reform before anything further is sought to be done in the House of Commons. I hope all classes of Reformers in the country will combine to bring about such an expression of opinion as will induce the Legislature to deal honestly and generously with the question of representation. In Birmingham, I believe, the middle class is ready to work heartily with the "working class," and I hope a thorough union may take place with you and in all parts of the kingdom.

Yours, &c.,
JOHN BRIGHT.

Mr. Roger Bateson, 12, Ann Street, Birmingham.

THE REFORM BILL OF 1867.

Read at a public meeting held in Glasgow on Thursday, the 21st of March, 1867, under the auspices of the Scottish Reform League, at which the Bill introduced by Mr. Disraeli was unhesitatingly condemned. This measure at its introduction was regarded by the Reform party as a very unsatisfactory measure; but in its passage through Committee, it underwent, by the action of Liberals, a remarkable and beneficial change.

Reform Club, March 19, 1867.

DEAR SIR,—I cannot come to your meeting, for I cannot leave London just now. My own opinion is that Reform should be in the hands of its friends and not of its enemies. The present Government is not willing to deal with the question, and I think the interests of the country require that the Bill and its authors should be got rid of. I wish the question could have been fairly met and settled, but it seems to me impossible under the conduct of Lord Derby and Mr. Disraeli. It may be necessary to hold meetings, greater even than those of last year. I have no fear that the Reformers of Scotland will not do their part.

I am, &c.,
JOHN BRIGHT.

ON THREE-CORNERED CONSTITUENCIES.

Written to a leading member of the Liberal party in Birmingham in reference to Lord Cairns' Amendment in Committee of the Reform Bill of 1867 in the House of Lords, providing that in constituencies represented by three members, every elector should have only two votes.

Manchester, July 31, 1867.

My dear Sir,—You see the vote in the Lords. It partially disfranchises Birmingham. Instead of your having *three* voices, or *two*, in a great division on a great principle, you are now to have only *one*.

Your future Tory member will pair with me or with Mr. Dixon, and there will be left only one vote for your great community. Birmingham is now reduced to the position and weight of Arundel or Calne in a great Parliamentary division, and this in the year of Reform and extension of popular power.

You will see that certain of the Whig peers have joined this childish or nefarious scheme. It is not the less dangerous on that account. I hope you will take some steps to counteract this proposition. The great towns should send deputations up to London to urge the Government to maintain the integrity of the Bill. I do not think Mr. Disraeli wishes to injure the Bill. He spoke earnestly against this scheme in the House, and I hope he will adhere to his own view on so grave a matter.

You should not for a moment dream of consenting to the audacious proposal to destroy the political weight and force of your borough.

I am, sincerely yours,
JOHN BRIGHT.

THE BALLOT.

Written to Mr. Beales, the President of the Reform League, in reply to the announcement that the League would use its organization, consisting of 430 branches, for the purposes of registration, educating the people in the use of the vote, and promoting the return to the next Parliament of members pledged to advanced Liberal principles.

August 18, 1867.

MY DEAR MR. BEALES,—I am glad to see that it is not intended to discontinue the organization and labours of the Reform League, although so great a step has been gained in the extension of the suffrage. On that branch of the question of Reform I presume you will not feel it necessary now to agitate further, so far as the boroughs are concerned. But the concession of a wide franchise is most incomplete as long as the security of the ballot is denied. As a machinery for conducting elections without disorder the arrangement of the ballot is perfect, and, if on that ground only, it should be adopted. But there is a higher ground on which all Reformers should insist upon it. The more wide the suffrage, the more there are of men in humble circumstances who are admitted to the exercise of political rights, the more clearly is it necessary that the shelter of the ballot should be granted. I am confident it would lessen expenses at elections, greatly diminish corruption, and destroy the odious system of intimidation which now so extensively prevails, and that it would make the House of Commons a more complete representation of the opinions and wishes of the electoral body. I have a very strong conviction on this subject, and I hope all our friends throughout the country will accept the ballot as the next great question for which, in connection with Parliamentary Reform, they ought to contend. Without this safeguard there can be no escape from corruption and oppression at elections, and our political contests will still remain what they now are, a discredit to us as a free and intelligent people.

If the Reform League and Reform Union will make the ballot their next work, they must soon succeed. I need not tell you that I shall heartily join in their labours for this great end. I hope the friends of the ballot, those who care for freedom and morality in the working of our representative system, will provide the needful funds to enable you to move on with an increasing force to a complete success.

Believe me, always sincerely yours,
JOHN BRIGHT.

Mr. Edmond Beales, Lincoln's Inn, London.

ON REFORM.

REDISTRIBUTION AND THE BALLOT.

Read at a banquet held in connection with the Working Men's Reform Association at the Crystal Palace on the 30th of September, 1867, to celebrate the passing of the Reform Bill of 1867.

September 29, 1867.

Dear Sir,—I shall be very sorry to disappoint any of those who rejoice with us in the wide extension of the suffrage, but I cannot undertake to be present at the proposed great meeting and dinner at the Crystal Palace, to which you have kindly invited me. I have given what should have been the leisure of many autumns to the movement for Reform, and now, when one main part of the work is done, I do not feel disposed to give another autumn to platform labours to celebrate the victory we have won. I have already several invitations to dinners and meetings, and I shall have to send to each of them the answer I am compelled to send to you. I have fixed for myself a different kind of work for this Parliamentary recess, and I hope almost entirely to be able to escape from the labours of public meetings for the present.

It is quite natural and most just that the working men should rejoice at what has been gained, but I hope they will not forget that without a readjustment of members to population, and without the security of the ballot, the House of Commons will still be, for the most part, but a delegation from the rich, and not a real and free representation of the people. This should be borne in mind when preparing for the general election which must come at the end of next year. The destruction of the popular power of the great boroughs by the vote at the end of the session will show how little Parliament is now to be trusted on any question of Reform on which it may think it safe to go wrong. The Legislature has been driven in one direction by forces too strong for it, but its temper is not changed.

I am, with great respect, yours truly,
JOHN BRIGHT.

To Mr. George Potter.

ON THE IRISH LAND QUESTION.

Written to Mr. Henry Dix Hutton, who had recently published a pamphlet entitled "Prussia and Ireland."

Rochdale, November 11, 1867.

MY DEAR SIR,—I have read your "Prussia and Ireland" with much interest, and, as far as you go, I agree with you, but I think more requires to be done. Your plan is to help tenants to buy farms where owners are willing to sell, to lend them money on easy terms, and to take good security for the transaction. Owners are not very willing to sell, and the process of restoration, of creating an Irish proprietary, would be very slow. In my speech in Dublin a year ago I suggested another plan, not unlike yours, but more certainly operative, and with which yours might be combined. I proposed a Parliamentary Commission, empowered to buy large estates, particularly of English proprietors of Irish property, and to re-sell them in existing farms to existing tenants on terms something like those which you propose. A sum of 5,000,000*l*. thus at the disposal of the Commission would secure some large estates, and the process of creating "farmers, owners of farms," would begin at once and would go on rapidly. Your plan in fifty years would do much good, mine would do much in five years, and in twenty years or less would change the aspect of things in Ireland.

You want the change we are both in favour of, that is, we want to make the Irish farmer attached to the soil by the tie of ownership rather than by that which now exists, the necessity to have a holding in land that he may live. We want, further, to beget a new and national sentiment, to convince every Irishman now on the land that we do not intend to drive him across the Atlantic, but to remain a contented dweller on his own soil. I think my scheme would do this, would give hope and faith, and inspire him with a belief in the future, and stimulate him to effort and industry.

You will see the difference between your scheme and mine—mine is to grapple at once with the desperate malady which keeps your country in a state of chronic discontent and insurrection. Your plan may be more easily secured, but our children will only see much result from it—mine would, I think, restore confidence and banish speedily some of the despair and disloyalty which so extensively prevail. In some of our colonies, in Canada and in New Brunswick, I believe Government has bought off landlords' rights with great advantage to the people; why not try something in Ireland?

Thanking you for your excellent pamphlet,

I am, very truly yours,

JOHN BRIGHT.

Henry Dix Hutton, Esq., Dublin.

ON IRISH QUESTIONS.

THE CHURCH AND LAND.

On the 7th of October, 1880, a meeting of 105 of the leading landlords and agents of Ireland was held in Dublin for the purpose of considering the state of the country, which was at that time violently disturbed by agrarian agitations and outrages. After conferring together for some time, the meeting sent a deputation to the Lord-Lieutenant and Chief Secretary, to inform them in detail of the state of the country. The next day the following letter from a member of the deputation was sent to the Chief Secretary (Mr. Forster) and was subsequently published in the *Daily Express*:—

"Friday, October 8.—Sir,—The deputation who had the honour of an interview with his Excellency the Lord-Lieutenant and yourself yesterday did not require any assurance of his Excellency's and your entire and hearty disapproval of the programme of the Land League, their method of agitation, and its murderous accompaniments; but at the moment of your disapproval of any kind of sympathy, I held in my hand a MS. bearing the signature of one of the most prominent members of the Cabinet, declaring his hearty approval of a scheme embracing 'the abandonment of our territorial system,' and intimating in plain terms that the method to be pursued to obtain such a sweeping measure is that our rulers are to be 'sufficiently' intimidated by 'a United Ireland' demanding it, and menacing Great Britain if it should be refused. What, then, will avail your best conceived attempts to allay the storms thus invited, when we are aware that Mr. Parnell is acting in a parallel direction with the sympathies, and his movement travelling, if not in concert, yet at least in harmony with the ultimate designs of at least one member of the Cabinet? The people in Ireland require, therefore, more than the mere assurance of your personal intentions. They will not be satisfied until they see the Cabinet resolved to take energetic action. The document I refer to I shall make public in such manner and time as seem desirable, as the circumstances under which it came into my possession leave me free to utilize it for the public good."

The following is the document referred to in the preceding letter. It is in harmony with

Mr. Bright's other observations on the Irish land question, and to a calm observer does not offer the dark and terrible suggestions which the excited mind of an Irish landowner in 1880 gathered from it.

Rochdale, January 27, 1868.

MY DEAR SIR,—I have read the "proposals" over with great interest and care. They are wide, and embrace the whole Irish difficulty, and, if adopted, would at once apply a remedy to the two branches of the grand question. For twenty years I have always said that the only way to remedy the evils of Ireland is by legislation on the Church and land. But we are met still with this obstacle, even yet I fear insurmountable, that the legislation must come from and through a Parliament which is not Irish, and in which every principle essential for the regeneration of Ireland is repudiated. The knowledge of this makes me hesitate as to the wisdom of your "proposals" in their present shape. I fear the scheme is so broad, and so good, and so complete, that Parliament would stand aghast at it. To strike down an established Church and to abandon the theory of our territorial system by one Act of Parliament would be too much for Parliament, and would destroy any Government that suggested it. I can conceive a condition of things in Ireland under which such a great change might be accomplished—if Ireland were united in demanding it, and were menacing Great Britain if it should be refused; but now I suspect our rulers, though uncomfortable, are not sufficiently alarmed to yield. The Tories cannot deal with

Ireland. Their concession on Reform does not lead me to think they can give in on Irish affairs. The Whigs are almost as much afraid as the Tories are of questions affecting the Church and the land, and they seem to have almost no courage.

Lord Russell is old, and cannot grapple with a great question like this. Mr. Gladstone hesitates, and hardly knows how far to go. The material of his forces is not good, and I suspect he has not studied the land question, and knows little about it. The English people are in complete ignorance of Irish wrongs, and know little or nothing of the real condition of your country. This is a sad picture; but it is not coloured too darkly. There is no necessary connection between the Church and the land. To make a farmer proprietary would not involve the Government in any permanent expense, and it may be done without touching the Church question; and this, again, may be dealt with without meddling with the land. Now, the two schemes together and in one is a grand idea, Perhaps too grand for so slow a nation and parliament as ours. Many persons may be willing to get rid of the Church who are unwilling to depart from present theories with regard to the land, and some may go with you on the land and hold back on the Church. Is it supposed that for the whole scheme you can secure a larger support than for either of the two branches of it separately? This is the question you must answer. For myself, I should have no hesitation if I could persuade myself that others in sufficient numbers would follow; and, whether they follow or not, I am ready to state my general approval of your great plan, should it be brought before the public. If all the Liberal Protestants and all the Catholic population in Ireland will unite to support you, some impression may be made on English opinion and upon Parliament; but, looking to all past efforts among you, I am not very sanguine that you will succeed in bringing a strong and united pressure to bear upon our ruling class. I am expected to speak to-morrow week at Birmingham, and I intend to speak on Ireland. I am free from the trammels which fetter Mr. Gladstone, and I can speak without reserve and without fear. What I shall say will not increase your difficulties, but will, I trust, rather smooth your path with regard to English opinion. The Liberal party is not in a good position for undertaking any great measure of statesmanship. Some Whigs distrust Mr. Gladstone, and some, who call themselves Radicals, dislike him. He does not feel himself very secure as leader of a powerful and compact force. The Whig peers are generally feeble and timid, and shrink from anything out of the usual course. We want a strong man with a strong brain and convictions for a work of this kind, and I do not see him among our public men. I hope all that is wise and good in Ireland may support you, and that you may soon affect the opinion and conduct of Parliament.

I am, very sincerely yours,
JOHN BRIGHT.

ON THREE-CORNERED CONSTITUENCIES.

Read at a meeting of the Liberal electors of Birmingham, held on the 3rd of August, 1868, to impress upon the electors the duty of voting as they were requested by the Liberal Association at the following election, in order to secure the return of three Liberals.

Rochdale, August 1, 1868.

Dear Sir,—At the ward meeting the plan for returning three Liberals should be thoroughly explained, and every man who votes for two candidates, as recommended by the Committee, should feel that he has done his utmost to secure the return of all three. Without a good organization the return of three Liberals is impossible. With it you may succeed, and thus baffle the most offensive scheme ever devised for destroying the influence of the largest constituencies. I hope the candidates will be held to be on a perfect equality, and that the utmost effort will be made to return all three. Every man who votes for two of them in the manner proposed will most help to carry the three.

I am, very truly yours,
John Bright.

ON THE HOUSE OF LORDS.

Read at a meeting in Birmingham on the 14th of June, 1869. The peers were at that time threatening the Bill for the Disestablishment of the Irish Church, which had just passed the House of Commons; they, however, subsequently passed it. The expression, "a little childish tinkering about life peerages," in the letter, was an allusion to a Bill which was being considered by the House of Lords, on the introduction of Earl Russell, for the creation of life peerages.

This letter, coming from a member of the Government, gave great offence to some of the peers, and it was the subject of question and comment in the House of Lords.

London, June 9, 1869.

DEAR SIR,—I must ask my friends to excuse me if I am unable to accept their invitation for their meeting on Monday next.

The Lords are not very wise, but there is sometimes profit to the people even in their unwisdom. If they should delay the passing of the Irish Church Bill for three months, they will stimulate discussion on important questions, which, but for their infatuation, might have slumbered for many years. It is possible that a good many people may ask what is the special value of a Constitution which gives a majority of 100 in one House for a given policy, and a majority of 100 in another House against it. It may be asked also why the Crown, through its Ministers in the House of Commons, should be found in harmony with the nation, whilst the Lords are generally in direct opposition to it.

Instead of doing a little childish tinkering about life peerages, it would be well if the peers could bring themselves on a line with the opinions and necessities of our day. In harmony with the nation they may go on for a long time, but throwing themselves athwart its course, they may meet with accidents not pleasant for them to think of.

But there are not a few good and wise men among the peers, and we will hope their councils may prevail.

I am sure you will forgive me if I cannot come to your meeting.

Believe me always, very truly yours,
JOHN BRIGHT.
Mr. H. B. S. Thompson,
Secretary Birmingham Liberal Association.

ON BECOMING PRESIDENT OF THE BOARD OF TRADE.

On the formation of a Liberal Government in 1868, Mr. Gladstone offered Mr. Bright a seat in the Cabinet. It was expected in the country that Mr. Bright would be appointed Secretary of State for India, for which office he had shown himself to be qualified by his intimate acquaintance with Indian affairs; this office was indeed offered to him, but he declined it in preference for the more modest post of President of the Board of Trade. The following letter was written in reply to a note of congratulation sent him by a gentleman at Sheffield:—

London, December 9, 1868.

DEAR SIR,—I must send you a short note, to thank you for your very kind letter. It is a great pleasure to me to know that you and your friends in Sheffield are satisfied with the course I have taken in joining the new Administration. I have done it with extreme reluctance, but the pressure put upon me was more than I could withstand. I hope I have done what it seemed finally my duty to do. For your most friendly expressions and wishes accept my heartfelt thanks, and believe me always,

Very truly yours,
JOHN BRIGHT.

ON FREE TRADE AND TORY PAMPHLETEERS.

Written in acknowledgment of a Protectionist pamphlet which had been sent to Mr. Bright.

Rochdale, September 8, 1869.

DEAR SIR,—I thank you for the newspaper. There are knaves in the world, and there are simpletons, and the one class preys on the other.

The Tory party is always driven to these tricks; they cannot otherwise appeal to the multitude.

If they complain that too many customs' duties have been repealed, they will perhaps kindly tell the working men what duties they will put on again. Is it the duty on corn, or cattle, or do they wish a duty on imported cotton?

If a foreigner will not buy cheaply from us, will it mend the matter if we refuse to buy cheaply from him or from some other foreigner? If wages have risen from twenty to fifty per cent. since 1840, is this consistent with a wrong policy as to our foreign trade? The pamphlet to which you refer bears the marks of having been written in Bedlam; it is a mere confusion of figures, and is wholly without logic or sense.

The good harvest will tend to restore health to the general trade of the country, and when we have a sufficient supply of cotton, Lancashire will recover from its present distressed condition. It is more cotton we want, and not more taxes on imports. I suspect the people of Lancashire will not fail to understand this.

I am, respectfully yours,
JOHN BRIGHT.

Mr. Leonard Kaberry, jun.,
   46, Fenton Street, Rochdale.

ON HOME RULE.

Rochdale, January 20, 1872.

MY DEAR O'DONOGHUE,—It is said that some persons engaged in the canvass of the county of Kerry have spoken of me as an advocate of Home Rule for Ireland. I hope no one has ventured to say anything so absurd and untrue. If it has been said by any one of any authority in the county, I shall be glad if you will contradict it. To have two Legislative Assemblies in the United Kingdom would, in my opinion, be an intolerable mischief; and I think no sensible man can wish for two within the limits of the present United Kingdom who does not wish the United Kingdom to become two or more nations, entirely separate from each other.

Excuse me for troubling you with this. It is no duty of mine to interfere in your contest, but I do not wish to be misrepresented.

I am, yours very truly,
JOHN BRIGHT.

The O'Donoghue of the Glens, M.P.

ON THE REPRESENTATION OF BIR-MINGHAM.

Read at a meeting of electors in the Town Hall, Birmingham, the 29th of January, 1872, to hear the annual addresses of their representatives.

Rochdale, January 27, 1872.

MY DEAR MR. WRIGHT,—Your annual meeting is fixed for Monday next, and I regret very much that I am unable to be present at it. I am not sure that I ought not, two years ago, to have given up the office of your representative, when I found myself no longer capable of performing its duties—but I have trusted to the kindness of my friends, and have, I fear, trespassed somewhat too much upon it. Some months ago I thought I should have been able to be in Birmingham before the opening of the session, but I dare not yet attempt to take part in, or to be present at, one of your great Town Hall meetings. I expect, notwithstanding, that I shall be able to attend the House of Commons during some portion of the ensuing session.

I do not enter into political discussion, because I should require to write a pamphlet if I were only to touch upon the many questions now before the public which will soon come before Parliament. I hope the session will be fruitful in good measures, and that a determination to lessen the public expenditure may be manifested by the Administration and the House. I am very grateful to my friends for their long patience with me, and to my colleagues, Mr. Dixon and Mr. Muntz, that they have not permitted any matter specially affecting Birmingham to suffer from my absence.

Believe me, always sincerely yours,
JOHN BRIGHT.

ON THE INCOME-TAX.

Written in reply to an invitation sent him to join a deputation from the Birmingham Anti-Income-Tax Association to the Chancellor of the Exchequer on the 6th of March, 1872.

Rochdale, March 4, 1872.

DEAR SIR,—I regret to say that I shall not be able to be in town on Wednesday, and therefore cannot take part in the proposed deputation to the Chancellor of the Exchequer.

There is little difference of opinion as to the odious and unfair character of the income-tax: but it is not easy to see where the money is to be obtained which now comes from that tax. I see no chance of its abolition, except in a lessened expenditure, and at present there seems no probability of the creation of a political party resolved to lessen the public expenditure, and adopting that policy as the one great article of its creed. I do not believe in governments that cannot govern without taking seventy millions every year from the industry of the nation, and I hope the time will come when no such government will be permitted to exist.

For myself I should be ready to vote for such reduction of the expenditure as would enable the Chancellor of the Exchequer to remove the income-tax, or to abolish the taxes which add so greatly to the price of tea, coffee, and sugar.

I am, truly yours,

JOHN BRIGHT.

G. W. Plant, Esq., Birmingham.

ON REPUBLICANISM.

Written to a gentleman who had been told that the English Republicans would select Mr. Bright as their first President, and who wrote to ask the right hon. gentleman if he would accept the post.

Rochdale, April 7, 1872.

Dear Sir,—Your Republican friend must not be a very desperate character if he proposes to make me his first President, though I doubt if he can be a friend of mine. As to *opinions* on the question of Monarchy or Republicanism, I hope and believe it will be a long time before we are asked to give our opinion; our ancestors decided the matter a long time since, and I would suggest that you and I should leave any further decision to our posterity. Now, from your letter I conclude you are willing to do this, and I can assure you I am not less willing.

I am, truly yours,
John Bright.

ON FREE TRADE.

THE FRENCH COMMERCIAL TREATY OF 1872.

Written in reply to a letter from Mr. Nathaniel Poole, of Coventry, who enclosed a resolution passed at a public meeting at Coventry, and who said he was directed to ask whether there was any hope of the artisans of Coventry obtaining fair play in the fierce race of competition between France and England. If her Majesty's Ministers, he said, knew or considered "the vast amount of misery and wretchedness these continued one-sided and anti-free-trade treaties inflicted upon seven thousand industrious men and women in Coventry," he thought they would hesitate before they brought so great an evil upon them.

Llandudno, November 22, 1872.

Sir,—It is to be regretted that you and your friends should distress yourselves about the new treaty, and prefer, as I conclude you would prefer, to have no treaty at all. If there were no treaty, the French Government would not reduce their import duties, some of them they would probably raise, and the English Government would not impose new or higher duties on importations from France. The treaty, therefore, which fixes the limit of the French tariff, but which does not prevent its amendment in the direction of lower duties, and which in no degree affects the duties we impose on foreign goods, can inflict no injury on Coventry or on any other manufacturing town in the kingdom. The treaty may not be a wise treaty on the part of France, but it is impossible that it should be injurious to England, for under its provisions England does not bind herself to do anything which she would not willingly and wisely do if the treaty were not in existence. If, under the treaty, the French tariff is in any degree lower than it would be without the treaty, then by so much are we the gainers by it.

Our Government would have been delighted to have signed a treaty under which the French tariff would have been as liberal and as sensible as our own, but it can only act for England, and not for France. If I am not mistaken, you were against the treaty of 1860, and on the same grounds, doubtless, you are against the renewed treaty of 1872. You think the special interests of Coventry should have been cared for at the expense of the general population of the kingdom. But Lord Granville is not the Minister for Coventry only, but for the United Kingdom, and he and his colleagues must act for the general good, and not for any special interest or trade which clamours for protection at his hands.

In the protest you have sent me, you say that "while the French were fighting in 1871, the trade of Coventry was exceptionally good," that is, when you had no competition your trade was very good; and what you want now is, that our tariff should prevent foreign competition with you in this market, and give you the prosperity, at the cost of your customers, which you had last year, caused by the calamities of the French. I am sorry, if not surprised, that there are any working men in Coventry who still think duties for protection are just and good for English industry after the experience of the last twenty-five years. Surely it is something of a discredit to Coventry that, almost alone among all the towns of the United Kingdom, she should ask the Government to place her upon that "outdoor relief" which is intended by the system of special duties for the protection of special trades. I do not believe the workmen of Coventry are less able to fight the battle of competition than are the workmen of Bradford, or Birmingham, or Rochdale; and when the cry of protection is so thoroughly worn out in your ancient city that it can no longer serve a local political purpose, I suspect we shall hear no more of it even from you.

I am sorry to trouble you with so long a reply. In future I must ask you to forgive me if I am silent.

I am, respectfully yours,
JOHN BRIGHT.

Mr. Nathaniel Poole.

ON THE BIRMINGHAM CONSERVATIVE WORKING MEN'S MUTUAL IMPROVEMENT ASSOCIATION.

Addressed to the secretary of the above association, and read at their meeting on the 8th of March, 1873.

26, Dover Street, London,
February 28, 1873.

SIR,—I thank you for sending the copy of the speech to which your note refers. There are portions of it with which I entirely agree; there are others in regard to which I think the eyes of the speaker and the audience are but as yet partially open. They "see men as trees, walking;" by-and-by they will see more clearly.

It is pleasant to hear of a "Mutual Improvement Society" among any portion of the Conservative party. There is great room for improvement in the political department, and some progress is evidently being made. Your lecturer, Mr. Houghton, has some views of a very antiquated character, but with frequent discussion and an honest consideration of them, I cannot doubt that you will discover the truth and be able to correct him.

I shall be glad at any time to have reports of the discussions at your meetings, if you think it well to send them to me. I will not forget the resolution to which you have called my attention.

I am, very respectfully yours,
JOHN BRIGHT.

The following is a copy of the resolution to which Mr. Bright refers, and which was adopted at a meeting of the Birmingham Working Men's Conservative Association, held on the 15th of February, 1873 :—

"That, in the interests of the consumers, and as a great national question, this meeting is of opinion that all obstacles to the complete development of the agricultural resources of the country ought to be removed. That with this object the malt-duty, which operates indirectly as a tax on the people's food, should be repealed, its retention being in opposition to the principles advocated and enforced by Free-traders when applied to other interests. That tenant farmers, when required to quit, should have security for all expenditure which enhances the value of their holding, and for which they have not received an adequate return, especially during the last two years of their tenancy; and that such security should be binding on the successor to an entailed estate equally with the owner of an absolute freehold.

That compensation should be also given for damage done on arable land by the excessive preservation of ground game. And this meeting is further of opinion that by thus attracting the surplus capital of the country to the cultivation of the soil, the condition of the agricultural labourer would necessarily be improved and raised."

Mr. Houghton, the author of the speech referred to in the foregoing letter, subsequently wrote a letter to Mr. Bright, laying down certain propositions, and requesting him to indicate those that he agreed with and those that he disapproved of. Mr. Bright replied as follows:—

Rochdale, March 19, 1873.

DEAR SIR,—I thank you for your letter, which has been forwarded to me. If you refer to my letter, you will see that I recommended the working men to continue the discussion among themselves, not with me.

I find letter-writing the great burden of my life, and I avoid it, or try to avoid it, as much as I can. You alarm me by proposing to discuss with me the five paragraphs in your letter, and with a promise, if I agree with you upon them, to go more fully into the other paragraphs. I dare not enter into correspondence with you, as you suggest. I think nearly all the points you mention have been spoken to by me on various occasions, and I must leave them now without further comment.

I may, however, say that the malt-tax cannot be repealed without a great reduction of expenditure, and that in my opinion farmers ought to have an absolute ownership of all the animals bred, and reared, and living upon their farms. I cannot write further, but I hope you will still examine and discuss the questions which formed the matter of your address to the working men.

I am, respectfully yours,
JOHN BRIGHT.

Mr. John Houghton.

ON THE USE OF INDIAN CORN IN ENGLAND.

Written to a gentleman in Cincinnati, who had addressed a letter to Mr. Bright, urging the importance of introducing Indian corn as an article of food for the people of this country.

Rochdale, October 10, 1873.

DEAR SIR,—I duly received your interesting letter of the 28th of April last, and I have submitted it to Mr. Buckmaster, who has been giving lectures on cookery at South Kensington, and have asked him to consider how far anything can be done on the subject of the use of Indian corn in this country. Hitherto nothing has been done, and there are great difficulties in the way, which it will take time to overcome. The greatest difficulty is that which attends all new things—the indisposition of the people to give a favourable or even an impartial attention to what is new. The chief hindrance to the use of Indian corn has always been the want of knowledge as to the various modes of cooking it. I speak now of those who are favourably disposed towards it. There must be men and women in this country who are familiar with this branch of cookery as practised with you, or, if not, it would not be difficult to engage some American man or woman cook who would undertake to instruct in it. I shall probably see Mr. Buckmaster again when I go up to London, and I shall urge him and those with whom he is associated to arrange for some provision by which all that is known in the States with respect to Indian corn may also be known in this country. We have always to import a large portion of our food, and it seems very strange that an article of such great consumption with you should be so very little favoured or known among us.

I cannot say more on the subject now, but I will not forget it, or your letter upon it.

Yours respectfully,
JOHN BRIGHT.

Mr. John H. Osborne,
8, Merchants' Exchange, Cincinnati, U.S.A.

ON "FREE LAND."

Written to Mr. G. W. Sanders, of Stockton-on-Tees, in reply to an inquiry from that gentleman as to the meaning of the term "free land."

Rochdale, November 2, 1873.

DEAR SIR,—I have often explained in my speeches what is intended by the term "free land." It means the abolition of the law of primogeniture, and the limitation of the systems of entails and settlements, so that "life interests" may be for the most part got rid of, and a real ownership substituted for them. It means also that it shall be as easy to buy or sell land as to buy or sell a ship, or, at least, as easy as it is in Australia and in many or in all the states of the American Union. It means that no legal encouragement shall be given to great estates and great farms, and that the natural forces of accumulation and dispersion shall have free play, as they have with regard to ships, and shares, and machinery, and stock-in-trade, and money. It means, too, that while the lawyer shall be well paid for his work, unnecessary work shall not be made for him, involving an enormous tax on all transactions in connection with the purchase and sale of lands and houses.

A thorough reform in this matter would complete, with regard to land, the great work accomplished by the Anti-Corn-Law League in 1846. It would give an endless renown to the Minister who made it, and would bless to an incalculable extent all classes connected with and dependent on honest industry.

I am, respectfully yours,
JOHN BRIGHT.

Mr. G. W. Sanders, Stockton-on-Tees.

ON THE LICENSING SYSTEM.

A Liverpool working man wrote in November, 1873, to Mr. Bright, describing the deplorable poverty, degradation, vice, and drunkenness which characterized the condition of vast numbers in that town, and asked the right hon. gentleman " to lend his powerful aid in obtaining for every householder a direct personal voice or vote on spirit-vaults and beer-shops."

Mr. Bright replied as follows:—

London, November 27, 1873.

DEAR SIR,—Your letter is interesting, but it has made me sad to read it. The evils you describe seem too vast for any known remedy, and I know not who has courage to attempt to deal with them. To your concluding paragraph I must offer one remark by way of explanation. I cannot support the Permissive Bill, for reasons which I have given in the House of Commons, and to those who have sent me there. I do not approve of our present licensing system, for I think the magistrates are not the best authority to determine the number of houses that should be licensed, or to what houses licences should be granted or refused.

I am in favour of municipal control even in this matter—that is, of the ratepayers, through the local parliament which they elect. This, to my mind, would be much better than to invite the vote of the whole town; and I am satisfied that it would work better and more justly. The town council represents the town, and to its wisdom I would entrust the power to grant or refuse licences, subject, it may be, to such limits as Parliament might properly determine.

I think a licensing committee of the town

council would be a better authority than the magistrates, and through it the opinion of the ratepayers would be expressed and enforced. I am in favour of adding to the authority and dignity of our municipal government, and with that view I should have been glad to see the management of our elementary schools placed in their hands, and partly for the same reason, I would give them control over the licensing system, as closely connected with the good order of our towns and cities.

As we are moving now, we shall soon have little to do but to fight elections, which at best are but necessary evils. Parliamentary elections, municipal elections, school-board elections are surely enough; do not ask us to add to them Permissive Bill contests as often as a fluctuating public opinion may demand them. I have no objection to give opinion fair play, but I wish it to act through a recognized and constitutional channel.

I am, yours, &c.,
JOHN BRIGHT.

ON THE "RESIDUUM."

On the 6th of December, 1873, Mr. James Thornely, of Godley, near Manchester, wrote to Mr. Bright concerning a passage in a speech delivered by the Rev. A. Read, of St. George's, Hyde, the leading clergyman of the Church of England in the neighbourhood. The speech was reported in the *Hyde and Denton Chronicle* of that date, a copy of which Mr. Thornely forwarded with his letter. The following is the passage referred to :—

"There was another great Liberal leader, a most prominent member of the Government, who, in speaking of the poor working men of England, called them—he gave it a Latin name because he supposed he was ashamed to put it in English—the *residuum* of the population—that is, in plain English, the dregs of the population. That was a friend of the working people of England, that was one of their great men, a leading Liberal, Mr. John Bright, the Member of Parliament for Birmingham, one who had the presumption and impudence to call the working men of England the dregs of the population."

Mr. Bright replied as follows :—

Rochdale, December 9, 1873.

DEAR SIR,—I thank you for sending me a copy of the *Hyde and Denton Chronicle* of Saturday last, where I find a passage in a speech of the Rev. A. Read, of St. George's, Hyde, to which you have called my attention. I need hardly tell you that the statement of this slanderous clergyman is false, and that if he is not a singularly ignorant person, he must know it to be false.

If I had applied the word "residuum" to the "working men of England"—if I had deemed or called them "the dregs of the population"—should I have given much time, and labour, and many years of my life to procure for them the right to live by the free exchange of their industry, and the right to vote that they might share in the government of their country?

I do not remember the time when or the speech in which I used the word "residuum," or I would refer you to the passage. You would at once see how utterly unjust and false is the construction which Mr. Read has put upon it.

I do not know what Mr. Read is in his pulpit, but I would advise him to stay there, where he cannot be contradicted. On the platform he is, what is not uncommon in the hot, partisan priest, ignorant and scurrilous, and a guide whom no sensible man would wish to follow. His congregation should pray for him.

I am, very truly yours,
JOHN BRIGHT.

ON THE AMERICAN JUBILEE SINGERS.

Written on behalf of the Jubilee Singers in anticipation of their visit to Birmingham in 1873.

Rochdale, December 23, 1873.

DEAR SIR,—I have heard the Jubilee Singers, and they have been in this town, where they have met with great success. I believe they intend to pay us another visit. I hope Birmingham will receive them kindly, for your great city showed a wise and hearty sympathy with the United States during the great struggle which delivered the slaves from their bondage. The mission of these singers is one deserving of all support, and I feel very certain it will find a multitude of friends in Birmingham.

I am, truly yours,
JOHN BRIGHT.

ON EXTEMPORE SPEAKING AND PREACHING.

The following letter, which was published in the *Evangelical Magazine* of January, 1874, was written to a student in a Nonconformist college, who had asked Mr. Bright's opinions on the art of public speaking and on reading sermons:—

DEAR SIR,—Your letter, written in May last, only met my eye a few days ago; it has been at the Reform Club, and was not forwarded to me till quite recently. You ask me two questions, to one of which I can give a ready answer. I have never been in the habit of writing out my speeches, certainly not for more than thirty years past. The labour of writing is bad enough, and the labour of committing to memory would be intolerable; and speeches *read* to a meeting are not likely to be received with much favour. It is enough to think over what is to be said, and to form an outline in a few brief notes. But, first of all, a real knowledge of the subject to be spoken of is required; with that, practice should make speaking easy.

As to what is best for the pulpit, I may not venture to say much. It would seem that rules applicable to other speaking will be equally applicable to the pulpit. But in a pulpit a man is expected to speak for a given time, on a great theme, and with less of exact material than is obtainable on other occasions and on ordinary subjects. And further, a majority of preachers are not good speakers, and perhaps could not be made such. They have no natural gift for good speaking; they are not logical in mind, nor full of ideas, nor free of speech; and they have none of that natural readiness which is essential to a powerful and interesting speaker. It is possible, nay, perhaps very probable, that if reading sermons were abolished, while some sermons would be better than they now are, the majority of them would be simply chaos, and utterly unendurable to the most patient congregation. Given a man with knowledge of his subject, and a gift for public speaking, then I think reading a mischief; but given a man who knows little, and who has no gift of speaking, then reading seems to be inevitable, because speaking, as I deem it, is impossible. But it must be a terrible thing to have to read or speak a sermon every week, on the same topic, to the same people; terrible to the speaker, and hardly less so to the hearers. Only men of great mind, great knowledge, and great power, can do this with success. I wonder that any man can do it! I often doubt if any man has ever done it. I forbear, therefore, from giving a strong opinion on the point you submit to me. Where a man can speak, let him speak—it is no doubt most effective; but where a man cannot speak, he must read. Is not this the sum of the whole matter?

I thank you for the good wishes expressed in your friendly letter. My health is greatly improved, and I hope to be able to give some time to the House of Commons during the coming session.

I am,. truly yours,
JOHN BRIGHT.

ON THE LIBERAL PARTY.

Read at a Liberal demonstration held in the Temperance Hall, Bolton, on the 3rd of March, 1874.

March 2, 1874.

MY DEAR SIR,—I cannot come to your meeting, though I am very glad you have so much to congratulate yourselves upon. I dare not venture upon public meetings, and am forced to avoid them. If I came to Bolton, I should soon have a score of invitations, and the usual correspondence and difficulties about them. The Liberal party has failed mainly through want of organization, arising from the security caused by its great victory five years ago. It still lives, and may soon recover its supremacy. Meanwhile the party which has triumphed must march in its path. I am sorry I cannot come, but I feel sure my friends will excuse me.

Always sincerely yours,
JOHN BRIGHT.

ON MR. CHARLES SUMNER.

Addressed to a gentleman in Boston who had sent Mr. Bright a photograph of Mr. Sumner.

Charles Sumner, the distinguished orator and statesman alluded to in this letter, was born at Boston on the 6th of January, 1811. He began to practise as a lawyer at Boston in 1834, and in 1851 succeeded Daniel Webster as United States Senator. He took an active part as a public speaker in opposition to the annexation of Texas, and was identified with the peace and anti-slavery movements of the day. In the Senate he opposed the Fugitive-slave Act in a speech, in which he declared, "Freedom is national, and slavery sectional." After the delivery of his famous speech, "The Crime against Kansas," on the 19th and 20th of May, 1856, he was assaulted, while in his seat, by a member from South Carolina, and was so severely injured as to be unable to resume his public duties for three or four years. On resuming his seat in the Senate, his first speech was on "The Barbarism of Slavery," on the 4th of June, 1860. He early proposed emancipation as the speediest method of ending the Rebellion; and from 1861 to 1870 was chairman of the Senate Committee on Foreign Affairs. He died suddenly on the 11th of March, 1874.

Rochdale, April 4, 1874.

DEAR MR. KINSLEY,—I am much indebted to you for your letter, and for the photograph you have sent me. The portrait is admirable, and does justice to the great subject of it. Mr. Sumner spent his last night in England under this roof, and left us for Liverpool on the morning of the day on which he sailed. His health was very much shaken, and I was sorry his voyage was in the winter. The news of your great loss has made me very sad. I can imagine the feelings of sorrow it will have caused in the hearts of your countrymen. In this country the press has done justice to your great senator. His unblemished life, his noble aims, and his great services to freedom and humanity are freely admitted and greatly honoured by our public writers.

Very sincerely yours,
JOHN BRIGHT.

ON THE CIVIL SERVICE.

Written to Mr. Dorman B. Eaton, Chairman of the "Civil Service Commission" in the United States.

London, April 29, 1874.

DEAR SIR,—I am sorry I have been so long in replying to your letter, and now I do not feel that I can say much that will be of use to you. The working of our Civil Service has met with general approval, and, after the experience of some years, it would be now impossible to go back to the old system. The present plan is one which is felt to be more just to all classes, and it is calculated to supply more capable men for the various departments of the public service.

You are doubtless aware that appointments with us are, to a large extent, of a permanent character. No changes in persons employed in Government offices, in the Customs, Excise, Post-Office, and Telegraph Departments take place on a change of Government, and thus we avoid a vast source of disturbance and corruption which would be opened if the contrary plan were adopted. In these days, when so much is done by the Governments, and when so many persons are employed by them, it seems absolutely necessary to take precautions against the selection of incompetent men, and against the corruption which under the purest Administrations is always a menacing evil.

Your proposed reform is a great undertaking. I hope the good sense of your people will enable you to complete it. All the friends of your country in other nations will congratulate you on your success. I have directed to be forwarded to you some of our Parliamentary publications, that you may know the latest facts connected with what is doing here in the matter of our Civil Service.

I am, with great respect, yours sincerely,
JOHN BRIGHT.

ON TEMPERANCE.

Addressed to a gentleman at Bradford.

London, June 5, 1874.

DEAR SIR,—I cannot write you a long letter on the temperance question and my views upon it I am sorely troubled with letters, and am obliged to omit answers to very many of them. I mas say, however, that in my opinion appeals should be made to all members of Christian Churches, in the hope of creating a great public opinion among the thoughtful and religious classes in favour of temperance, and of offering through them to the view of the nation a grand example of abstinence from the use of articles which are so seldom useful and so often pernicious. If the professing Christian people would take this matter in hand, the great work would go on prosperously. Their example would tell rapidly upon public opinion and upon the customs of the nation, and a great reform would be in process of certain achievement; and as this more rational opinion was created, it would enable the Legislature to assist in it by such reasonable restrictions as the case may require, and as the constituencies would be able to sustain.

At present a few persons clamour for legislation which the country is not prepared for, and which it will not bear. The consequence of this is failure—there being much contention and no result.

The friends of temperance should leave Parliament, and form *opinion*, trusting that when opinion is formed whatsoever is judicious in legislation will naturally and easily follow. In a great reform of this kind Parliament can do little—but that portion of our people which cares for religion can do much—it can, indeed, do all. The ministers of religion and the multitudes of good men and women who listen to them from week to week can make the reform you seek. Without their zeal and co-operation it is impossible, and a dream. If I had time and opportunity, I could say much more, but this may be sufficient for the moment as a reply to your note.

I am, very truly yours,
JOHN BRIGHT.

Mr. W. H. Gregory, Bradford, Yorkshire.

ON TEMPERANCE.

Written in answer to a question as to what Mr. Bright had said with reference to his having had no intoxicating drinks in his house since he commenced housekeeping.

40, Clarges Street, London,
June 6, 1874.

DEAR SIR,—I have seen no report of what I said, but I have seen some extracts from newspapers, but all more or less inaccurate. There may have been times when I have doubted if I should have adopted the same course—not that I now doubt, or that I regret what was done thirty-five years ago. There is a great movement just now on the temperance question. The public conscience, even the Parliamentary conscience, seems shocked at what was done at the late election. There is a sense of humiliation at the thought that the publicans and beer-sellers destroyed a Government and installed another in its place, and that distillers and brewers were the best candidates for the Church and Conservative party, as most likely to secure the votes of publicans and beer-sellers. If the Christian Churches would move and speak, a great reform might be effected; but without a revival among them, I fear not much can be done. The Scottish Churches might banish whisky; Christian zeal and self-denial can work wonders.

Yours truly,
JOHN BRIGHT.

ON VACCINATION.

Read at a Conference of Anti-vaccinators held at Birmingham, on the 26th of October, 1874.

Dalguise, N.B., October 6, 1874.

DEAR SIR,—I cannot take any part in your Conference, nor will I express any opinion on the question in which you are interesting yourself except so far as to say that the facts which have come before me seem to be against you; but I have no objection to express my doubts as to the wisdom of compulsion, and I have always felt that the law which inflicts penalty after penalty on a parent who is unwilling to have his child vaccinated is monstrous, and ought to be repealed.

I am, truly yours,
JOHN BRIGHT.

Mr. Henry Pitman, Manchester.

ON FREE TRADE.

FREE TRADE IN RELATION TO THE PRICE OF FOOD.

At a ward meeting in Leeds in October, 1874, a Conservative speaker said " the people were no better off now relative to the price of bread than they were before the repeal of the Corn Laws and other protective laws." This statement was forwarded to Mr. Bright, and elicited the following reply:—

Corriebruck House, Pitlochry,
October 12, 1874.

DEAR SIR,—Your letter has been sent on to me, and I have only time to acknowledge the receipt of it. Your opponent must be a man profoundly ignorant or strangely perverse, or he would have a different opinion of the effects of Free Trade in corn. He, perhaps, does not know that last year, 12,000,000 quarters of wheat were imported, worth in this market last year nearly 40,000,000*l.* sterling, and that great quantities of other grain were also imported; that not less than 500,000 tons of potatoes, with great quantities of cattle, and meat, and cheese, and butter were imported; that, in fact, 80,000,000*l.* sterling in value were imported, nearly all of which it was the object of the Corn Law and other protective laws to exclude from the country. More than half the working men of England, with their families, are fed on bread which comes from abroad, and it is obvious that the continuance of the protective system as applied to agriculture would have spread famine among the people, and would have plunged the nation into anarchy.

I have not time to write more to you, and I feel certain that to add to what I have said would be of no use to your opponent, as he must be very ignorant, and I fear quite unable to reason on a matter of this nature. If you turn to the newspapers from 1839 to 1846, or to the debates in Hansard, you may obtain all the facts and arguments you require.

I am, respectfully yours,
JOHN BRIGHT.

ON CANVASSING AT ELECTIONS.

Written to Mr. James Eddy, of Stockton, who had asked Mr. Bright's opinion on the subject, and read at a meeting in the Temperance Hall of that town on the 28th of October, 1874.

Rochdale, October 26, 1874.

DEAR SIR,—I can give no opinion of much value on the subject on which you have written me. I suppose that so long as many electors are careless and ignorant it will be impossible to put an end to canvassing. I think the proposal to make it illegal is absurd. To canvass in an honourable manner is an innocent act, and in many cases it is useful, and any attempt to make it unlawful would fail. I speak of canvassing by friends of candidates; for candidates in person to solicit votes is, in my view, humiliating, and the best constituencies have abolished it, though it still prevails in many boroughs.

Yours respectfully,
JOHN BRIGHT.

ON SUNDAY CLOSING IN IRELAND.

Written in reply to a communication from Mr. T. W. Russell, Secretary of the Sunday-closing movement in Ireland, who had complained that although forty-two of the Irish members voted for the Sunday-closing Bill in the preceding session, and only ten against it, the Bill was thrown out by the English vote.

Rochdale, October 27, 1874.

DEAR SIR,—I think you have a grievance to complain of in the mode in which the House of Commons treated your Bill for closing public-houses on Sunday. This seems to be one of the questions on which the opinion of the Irish members should have a special weight.

There is no great principle involved. Drapers and grocers cease from business on Sundays, and public-houses are allowed to be open only because it is supposed to be necessary for the convenience of the public; but if the public, as represented by a great majority of the Irish members, are willing or wishful to have public-houses closed on Sundays, as the shops of other traders are closed, it seems a most unreasonable course for English members to prevent it.

I should recommend you to make a direct and

earnest appeal to the Government, with a view to induce them to discourage the opposition made to the Bill.

I have no doubt that the Treasury Bench, if willing to aid you, could easily enable the Irish members, who are friends of the Bill, to pass the measure through Parliament.

By the help of the Government, and the further discussion which the Bill will receive next session, I hope you may succeed; and I believe your success, whilst it will aid the cause of temperance, will be more beneficial to the publicans themselves than to any other class of your population.

I am, very truly yours,
JOHN BRIGHT.

Mr. T. W. Russell, Dublin.

ON SECRET VOTING IN REPRESENTATIVE BODIES.

At the beginning of 1875 attention was drawn in a local newspaper to the fact that the Birmingham Board of Guardians voted by ballot. As a consequence, some of the ratepayers, feeling that by the divisions of their representatives being kept secret, they could not see in what degree the promises made at the hustings were fulfilled, wrote to Mr. Bright, asking his opinion on the subject. Mr. Bright replied as follows:—

Rochdale, January 12, 1875.

DEAR SIR,—I know nothing as to the law of the case, whether a Board of Guardians can, according to its own pleasure, vote secretly or openly. Probably there is no law on the subject, it not having been supposed possible that a body of representatives would endeavour to escape from under the oversight and criticism of those whose interests and wishes they assumed to represent. I should think the protests of the minority, and the condemnation of the public expressed through the newspapers, would correct this practice, unless there be arguments in its favour which do not occur to me. I am afraid I can be of no use to you in the matter. In Birmingham public opinion is generally strong enough to correct eccentricities which occasionally show themselves, and I shall hope it will not be powerless now.

I am, very truly yours,
JOHN BRIGHT.

ON WORKING-MEN CANDIDATES.

In a speech delivered at Birmingham on the 28th of January, 1875, Mr. Bright deprecated the selection of working men to represent constituencies on the mere ground of their being working men. He contended that a man's fitness to discharge the duties of a Member of Parliament ought to be the consideration which should induce the electors to send him there, and that to choose men because they belonged to the working class was a mistake. "If," he said, "we are to have a Parliament composed of two classes—one working-men representatives, and one that are not representatives of working men, it appears to me it would be one of the greatest calamities that could happen in our representative system. If you can find a man, let him be a first or second-class or third-class passenger, if you can find a man with intelligence, and honesty, and firmness, and the kind of capacity which you understand for Parliamentary duty, then I say lay hold of him at once and make him a Member of Parliament."

In reference to these remarks Mr. Bright received a letter from Stoke-on-Trent, in which the writer expressed his surprise that such observations should have been made. Mr. Bright thereupon replied as follows:—

Rochdale, February 13, 1875.

DEAR SIR,—It seems impossible to say anything in public which will not be misunderstood and misrepresented.

I have no objection to working men as candidates. What I object to is that a candidate should be chosen only or mainly because he is a working man, and that I should be expected to vote for him for the same reason. I do not vote for a candidate because he is a middle-class man, or a man of high family connections; and I refuse to be under any obligation to vote for one who is chosen as a candidate because he belongs to some other class or section of the community.

If the Liberal party in a constituency, speaking and acting through its recognized organization, selected a working man as its candidate, I hope I should give him my hearty support; but I object to have him thrust upon the party merely because he is a working man. The policy now recommended to working men in regard to this matter is, in my judgment, fatal to unity, as it is to an honest representation of all classes and interests.

I hope I need not say that, if I were one of your constituency, I should have no difficulty in giving my vote to Mr. Walton.

I am sorry you should have misunderstood me. Your letter has only just reached me, and I send you this hasty reply.

I thank you for the kind expressions in your letter, and am,

Very truly yours,
JOHN BRIGHT.

Mr. Joseph Hulme, Burslem.

ON HOME RULE.

Written to the Rev. Thaddeus O'Malley, Dublin.

London, Reform Club, February 25, 1875.

DEAR SIR,—I thank you for your letter and the little book on "Home Rule; or, the Basis of the Federation." I have read the book. Shall I tell you what I think of two Irish plans on this Irish question? The Mitchell plan is easy to understand, and if Ireland were unanimous and strong enough, it might be attempted, and might succeed. It is very simple, and under the conditions I have mentioned is not, or would not be impracticable; but the conditions are wanting, and therefore there is this fatal objection to it, that it is impossible, and only men partly mad or wicked will urge Irishmen to attempt it. As to your Federation plan, the Home Rule scheme of which you are evidently proud to be thought the author, is in my opinion quite as impossible as the other, and I must say that it seems to me far more absurd. To look at it only for a moment raises wonder that any man or number of men should imagine or think seriously of such a scheme. How many Home Rulers, how many men of that faith are there in Ireland? Certainly not more than a million. If I give you four millions of the disaffected Home Rulers, Repealers, Irish Republicans, or other antagonists of Great Britain—and this is more than you can fairly claim—they will give you only one million of men, and of these not one half have any knowledge of political and public affairs; and yet you propose, in order to allay the discontent of this part of your population, not only to make a revolution in Ireland, but to do the same in England, Wales, and Scotland. In Great Britain nobody wants two Parliaments of Lords and Commons. Nobody wants a third Imperial Parliament. And yet you propose, with a childish sympathy and enthusiasm, to force upon England, Wales, and Scotland these additional representative and legislative bodies, in order, apparently, to justify or balance the creation and establishment of like arrangements in Ireland. Surely so absurd and monstrous a proposition was never before heard of! You propose that twenty millions in Great Britain shall, in a manner, turn everything to which they are accustomed, and with which, in the main, they are satisfied—upside down, in the hopeless attempt thereby to allay the discontent of a portion of the people of Ireland—the said portion of your people never having been able to make a clear statement of its grievances, and being, as you must feel, totally unable to agree in any remedy for them.

I do not enter into any examination of the details of your little book, or I might point out many inaccuracies into which you have fallen. I confine myself, in this reply to your letter, to the main features of the two plans for the regeneration of Ireland. I believe them both to be impossible, but your plan of Home Rule seems to be eminently childish and absurd. I must ask you to forgive the plain speaking or writing of this letter, but I am unwilling to leave you in any doubt of my views, after I have read the little book you have been kind enough to send me. Since I have taken my part in public life I have thought myself, and have intended to be, one of the best friends of Ireland, and I think now that I have never been more so than I am at this moment.

I am, very faithfully yours,
JOHN BRIGHT.

Rev. Thaddeus O'Malley, 1, Henrietta Street, Dublin.

ON THE TICHBORNE CASE.

Written to a correspondent at Sheffield, who

urged Mr. Bright to support Mr. Whalley in his efforts to obtain protection for a man in New Zealand claiming to be Arthur Orton.

132, Piccadilly, London,
July 15, 1875.

Sir,—You may rely upon it that Arthur Orton will not come from New Zealand. During the trial 1000*l.* was offered for him, and nobody could produce him. It was a large bribe, and I only wonder it did not bring over a score of Ortons. The Arthur Orton is in Dartmoor, and nobody, I suspect knows this better than some of those who are pretending to expect him from New Zealand. I have read all the evidence and all the speeches of both trials, and the summing up of the Lord Chief Justice. This last I have read again during last month. And I have read more than once the evidence taken before the Chili Commission. I know, therefore, as much about the matter as you can know, and much more than is known by nine out of ten of those who are clamouring for the release of the convict at Dartmoor. I have before me now the handwriting of the real Roger Tichborne, of the real Arthur Orton, and of the convict, and this alone is sufficient to convince any man of common sense and observation what is the truth in the case. If you could see this handwriting, and if you could examine the evidence of the Chili Commission, the evidence of the convict's own friends, to whom he referred for proof that he was what he pretended to be, you could hardly fail to be convinced that your belief in the convict is wrong, and your sympathy with him wholly misplaced.

I mention these two points as conclusive against him. There are many other points in the evidence on the two trials which are fatal to his claims. He seemed to know the names of two dogs, but he did not know the name of his own mother. Mr. Turville, in Australia, asks him a last question, whether his mother was stout or thin. He said, "Stout, a tall, large woman." It is not denied that Lady Tichborne was leanness itself. Miss Nangles said she was more like a skeleton than anything else, and this was not contradicted by any one. If you can believe in a man who did not know his own mother's name, and who stated that his mother, who is admitted to have been leanness itself, was "stout, a tall, large woman," when he first came forward in Australia, and when he had no opportunity of picking up information and facts to support his case, I fear you are of that credulous nature that it may be useless to reason with you.

I can take no part in the proceedings of Mr. Whalley and his friends. To me the convict in Dartmoor is the greatest criminal of our time. His crime has extended over many years; it is most base in character, and includes in it almost every crime for which evil men are brought to punishment.

You are much impressed, I dare say, by the declarations of those who traverse the country creating agitation on this question. I must ask to be permitted to value my own judgment at least as highly as that of these persons. One of them is believed to have invested money largely in the case, and pecuniary interest is not favourable to an impartial decision. Another suffers from a complaint which I call "Jesuit on the brain,"[1] and this seems grievously to distort almost everything he looks at. The third is the lawyer who failed, after a trial which lasted 188 days, to convince three judges and twelve jurymen, or any one of the judges or of the jurymen, that his client was anything but an impostor and a man most odious from his character and his crimes.

I shall be glad if you, and such as believe with you, will not ask me to correspond further on a question about which only honest men who are in entire ignorance of the facts can in my view differ in opinion.

I am, respectfully yours,
JOHN BRIGHT.

Mr. Mark Harrison, 1, Elliott Road, Sheffield.

ON THE FOREIGN CATTLE TRADE.

Mr. George Whitehead, of the Calder Vale Ironworks, Wakefield, wrote to Mr. Bright on the 2nd of September, 1875, to ask him whether the restrictions placed upon the impor-

---

[1] The late Mr. Whalley, M.P., to whom Mr. Bright here alludes, had an exaggerated idea of the influence of the Jesuits on the private and public affairs of men, and this led him to the belief that there existed a Jesuit conspiracy to keep Roger Tichborne out of his estates.

tation of foreign cattle into our markets were necessary for the preservation of our English herds, or whether some other unworthy object was brought about to serve the interests of some selfish few. Mr. Bright replied as follows:—

Rochdale, September 3, 1875.

DEAR SIR,—I shall not venture to give you a confident opinion upon the matter on which you have written to me, but my impression when the Bill was passing through Parliament was that the country gentlemen were anxious to make it as restrictive as possible, and that its operation in the direction of protection made restriction popular among them. I have not much confidence in the legislation to prevent cattle disease, and I distrust it entirely when it is fixed at the point which meets the views of county members of Parliament. High prices and high rents, by the help of legislation, were once greedily sought after, and will not be refused now if offered under cover of an Act to prevent the importation of diseased cattle. An impartial inquiry into this question would, I suspect, discover that the restrictions imposed are needlessly severe, and that they tend sensibly to diminish the supply and to raise the price of butchers' meat throughout the country.

I am, respectfully yours,
JOHN BRIGHT.

Mr. George Whitehead,
Calder Vale Ironworks, Wakefield.

ON FUNERAL REFORM.

Written to a Birmingham constituent.

Rochdale, October 26, 1875.

DEAR SIR,—If your friends or any sensible people wish to reform the funeral exhibitions and expenses, let them observe and copy the practice of the sect to which I belong, that of the "Society of Friends." Nothing can be more simple, and nothing can be better. They would be wise also to follow them in rejecting the fashion of wearing mourning, which is always costly, and, as worn by many women, hideous. I am sorry to say, however, that the wearing of mourning has of late been rather increasing with "Friends," among whom are many who apparently do not comprehend, or do not value the principles on which the practice of their forefathers was based.

I am, yours, &c.,
JOHN BRIGHT.

ON SUNDAY CLOSING IN IRELAND.

Read at a public meeting held at the Town Hall, Birmingham, on the 14th of December, 1875, in favour of the Irish Sunday Closing Bill.

Rochdale, November 27, 1875.

DEAR SIR,—You must excuse me if I do not attend your proposed meeting at Birmingham. I do not feel that I have anything to say on your question to my constituents. If you do not succeed in the House of Commons, you may blame the Government, and your pressure should be brought to bear upon them. They refuse what Irish opinion asks for, because they fear to break up the alliance between the party and the "drink interest" in England. The publicans say they placed the present Government in office, and the Government admit their obligation to them, and, fearing to offend them, they influence the House to reject your Bill. It is a humiliating condition of things for Ireland and for the whole kingdom. Perhaps the day may come when the morality of the nation will be too strong for the publicans, but till then we must suffer the degradation which now discredits us.

I wish you great success in your labours, and am,

Very truly yours,
JOHN BRIGHT.

ON THE EASTERN QUESTION.

TURKISH RULE IN EUROPE.

Read at a meeting held in the Rochdale Town Hall on the 4th of September, 1876, to protest against the Turkish atrocities in Bulgaria.

Inverinate House, Lochalsh, Scotland,
September 1, 1876.

DEAR SIR,—Your letter has just reached me late this evening. I have no time to write anything for the meeting. The question is not one to be treated hastily, and I almost fear to say anything about it. More than twenty years ago I explained my views of the Eastern or Turkish difficulty. The Government of the day differed from me, as did the vast majority of the nation, and the war with Russia was entered upon. Some of its results we now know. It is said to have cost England 40,000 lives and 100,000,000*l.* of money. It cost all the parties to the war more than half a million of lives. Since then it has cost us 10,000,000*l.* a year in increased military expenses, or 200,000,000*l.* in all, and in loans to the Turkish Sultan it has probably cost England another 100,000,000*l.* sterling. The money account thus comes to four hundred millions (400,000,000*l.*) sterling; the loss of life was enormous. The policy of that day was popular, and the result is what I have described. I was assailed and insulted in and by almost all the newspapers in the kingdom because I condemned the war and the policy which led to it.

The present Government accepts the policy of the Government of 1854. It is now understood throughout the world to be the main if not the one supporter of the Turkish rule in Europe. If it had acted with Russia and the other Powers, it is almost certain the Servian war would not have taken place; and but for the confidence caused by the support of England, the Turks would not have dared to have committed the horrid crimes of which they have been guilty in Bulgaria. In these crimes there is nothing new. They are familiar to all who know anything of Turkish history. What is new is that the English Government cannot see the crimes till an English newspaper describes and denounces them; and that an English Minister, speaking for himself and his colleagues, treats them as of small account, and as the common incidents of insurrection and war. I am not sure that a Minister truly representing English opinion would not have withdrawn the Queen's Ambassador from Constantinople, and have refused longer to receive a Minister from Turkey at the Queen's Court. The Government of England should clear itself of all partnership in the interest and the policy of the Turkish Government. It is a partnership in no degree necessary to our interests, and degrades us in the estimation of every Christian nation. Every town should have its meeting, and protest against our country being stained and disgraced by a participation in the policy and crimes of the Turkish Government. I do not think this can reach you before your meeting is held, but it is some relief to have written it.

I am, very truly yours,
JOHN BRIGHT.

Mr. R. Hope Brown, Rochdale.

ON THE EASTERN QUESTION.

THE POLICY OF ENGLAND TOWARDS TURKEY.

Read at a town's meeting held in the Birmingham Town Hall on the 2nd of October, 1876, to consider the policy of the Government in the East.

The admission of the Prime Minister alluded to in this letter occurred in a speech delivered by Lord Beaconsfield at Aylesbury on the 20th of September, 1876, in the following passage :—

"The noble lord the Secretary of State who, on the part of the Government, is conducting negotiations at this present moment has to fulfil two most difficult tasks, and to accomplish two most important ends. He has at the same time to secure permanent British interests of the highest importance, and he has to secure the maintenance of European peace. Gentlemen, under ordinary circumstances a minister so placed, whatever might have been his difficulties, would have the consolation of knowing that he was backed by the country. Gentlemen, it would be affectation on my part for a moment to assert that that is the position of her Majesty's Government at this moment."

Rochdale, September 30, 1876.

DEAR SIR,—I regret that I cannot come to your meeting on Monday. An engagement in Manchester which I may not break will keep me away from you. You meet to urge the immediate assembling of Parliament. Lord Hartington and Mr. Gladstone have supported such a course, and though full of inconvenience, it seems to me both constitutional and wise. The Government will refuse it doubtless. Their mechanical majority might break up or break down. The House might adopt a policy which the ministers with their engagements would not accept.

There are two ways out of the existing difficulty, a difficulty which is not denied; for has not the Prime Minister admitted that the Government is not in accord with and is not backed up by the nation? One way is by a complete turnabout of the Foreign Office in regard to the Eastern Question. It has been, and is now, pro-Turk. Henceforth influence must be honestly given in favour of freedom and security to the populations of the European provinces of Turkey. The policy of 1854 to 1856 must be abandoned and revised. To enable the Government to do this it must decapitate itself, for after the Aylesbury speech nothing can be hoped for from its chief.

The other way is for the Government to resign. To remain in office, not backed by the nation, to negotiate in a spirit opposed to that of the nation, to continue a policy which the nation has emphatically condemned, is unconstitutional and dangerous.

I am, yours truly,
JOHN BRIGHT.

Mr. F. Schnadhorst.

ON PEACE AND WAR.

Read at a "Peace Conference of Christians," held at Philadelphia in 1876.

Rochdale, ninth month 22, 1876.

DEAR FRIEND DANIEL HILL,—I cannot come

to your conference, and I do not feel that I can write anything that will be of service.

There seems nothing cheerful to write on the subject of peace or war except this—that the influences in favour of peace are now become so strong that with millions of men in arms in Europe, still peace is the rule; and nations are not so much in the hands of monarchs and ministers as they have been in past times.

When the boundaries of nations and races are well adjusted, and when the hindrance to trade created by hostile tariffs is removed, I think the time will have come when the intelligence and Christian feeling and the true interests of nations will overcome the motives and passions which lead to war.

We may hope that in Europe there will arise a monarch or a statesman of sufficient authority and influence to lead his own country, and to induce other countries, to unite in some resolute effort for a great reduction of armaments.

We may hope, too, that as duelling is gradually being condemned for the adjustment of differences between private persons, so war may be condemned as a practice fitted only for savage nations, and wholly disgraceful and infamous when waged by nations pretending to civilization and professing the religion of the Prince of Peace.

I wish your conference a good result, although I am not able to take any part in it.

I am, sincerely thy friend,
JOHN BRIGHT.

ON WAR.

Written in reply to a communication from a number of Bristol working men, asking Mr. Bright's opinion, whether it would be patriotic on their part to engage in a demonstration on behalf of the Christian populations of Turkey.

Rochdale, November 25, 1876.

Dear Sir,—You need not fear being unpatriotic in objecting to war for Turkey or against Russia on account of Turkey. I advise you to protest against war in connection with the Eastern Question, and in any interference on the part of England, to urge that we support the propositions offered by Russia as the best that can be done for the Christian populations of the Turkish provinces in Europe. You should condemn this foolish and wicked jealousy of Russia, which springs from ignorance among our people, and is fostered by writers in the press. It suits those who live out of the 25,000,000*l.* spent annually, and for the most part wasted on our monstrous armaments, to keep up this feeling, and the influential among them are constantly acting on the proprietors, editors, and writers of the London newspapers. Working men everywhere should resist this feeling and influence. It is their blood which is shed in war; the destruction of capital and the injury to industry and trade fall upon them with crushing weight. But for the wicked wars of past times, which now we all see to have been wicked, the working classes of this country might have been surrounded by the comforts of home and blessed with education, as are the families of what is termed the middle classes in our English society. In every city and town the working men should denounce the idea of this threatened war, and they should condemn the minister whose loose and reckless tongue makes peace more difficult to secure. I hope Bristol will not be behind other towns in expression of opinion on this great question.

I am, very truly yours,
JOHN BRIGHT.

Mr. W. H. Godfrey, Pennywell Road, Bristol.

ON MR. JOSEPH KAY.

Written on the occasion of the bye-election at Salford in April, 1877, caused by the death of Mr. Cawley, M.P. Mr. Kay was the Liberal candidate, and Mr. O. O. Walker represented the Conservatives. The election resulted in the return of Mr. Walker.

House of Commons, April 11, 1877.

DEAR SIR,—I need not tell you that I feel a great interest in your Salford election. The time has been when I might have asked permission to say something on behalf of your candidate at a meeting of electors, but now I must abstain from the excitement of election contests.

I am glad that Mr. Kay is the candidate selected by the Liberal committee. For many years I have wished to see him in Parliament.

His full knowledge of the land question, his sound opinion upon it, his valuable writings in the volume published many years ago, and in his admirable letters from time to time in the *Manchester Examiner*, all point to him as one qualified in an especial manner to be useful in the settlement of one of the great questions, not of the remote, but of the near future.

There is no other political question, in my opinion, in which the working classes of Great Britain and Ireland have so distinct and pressing an interest as the land question. To free the land will be as great a blessing to the nation as we have found it to have been to free the produce of the land. Mr. Kay understands this question thoroughly, and his return to Parliament will be of essential service in the discussion of it. If I could speak to every working man among your electors, I would urge him to support Mr. Kay on this ground. I need not dwell on his other claims on the good opinion of every section of the Liberals of Salford.

Englishmen and Irishmen may cordially unite in support of a man whose policy on the land question is so broad and so wise, and so calculated to advance the interests of all who seek to live by honest industry.

I am sorry to hear that Mr. Kay is for the moment unable from illness to meet his friends in Salford. I believe they will only the more earnestly exert themselves to secure his election.

I wish you every success, and am always,
Sincerely yours,
JOHN BRIGHT.

ON PARLIAMENTARY REPORTING.

On the 20th of April, 1877, a debate took place in the House of Commons with respect to the manner in which speeches delivered in the House were reported, and Mr. Hanbury-Tracy, who opened it, moved the following resolution: "That a Select Committee be appointed to consider the expediency of providing official reports of the debates of this House," which, on being put to the vote, was lost. Mr. Bright spoke in favour of the resolution, and the *Times*, in an article on the debate in its next day's issue, criticized his remarks. The Editor of the *Times* explained in a footnote to the letter, that the sentence imputed to Mr. Bright, which he repudiated, was spoken by Lord Eslington, who followed him in the debate.

TO THE EDITOR OF THE *TIMES*.

SIR,—I am afraid the writer of the leader in the *Times* of this morning on last night's debate has not read the report on which he comments. He quotes one sentence as from my speech, which I did not utter, and which is not even in the *Times*' report of it. He further attributes to me the opinion that "every speech ought to be reported verbatim, for a member ought to be able to prove that he was not responsible for expressions that had been attributed to him, and which he had never uttered" —an opinion which I did not express, and which I do not hold; and towards the close of the article he asks: "Are the members to be reported word for word, as Mr. Bright insists?" I have not even suggested that members should be reported word for word, still less have I insisted upon it.

All I insist upon is, that with the present size of newspapers, a size which at the present price cannot be increased, the pressure of advertisements, the most profitable source of a newspaper's revenue, does make, and will make, it impossible for newspapers to give such reports of the proceedings of Parliament as are required by Parliament and by the country. I advised the House to appoint a committee to consider if any improvement could be made in the mode of reporting its debates.

I am, respectfully yours,
JOHN BRIGHT.

Reform Club, April 21.

ON FREE TRADE.

A PROTECTIVE POLICY IN THE ENGLISH COLONIES.

At a banquet given at Melbourne in June, 1877, in honour of Mr. John Young, the Canadian representative at the Industrial Exhibition held at Sydney in that year, some of the speeches turned on the subject of Free Trade, and Sir Charles Gavan Duffy, Speaker of the Victoria Legislative Assembly, said that, seeing that the tendency of opinion in that colony was in favour of Protection of some sort, he had consulted three eminent gentlemen in England—

John Bright, John Stuart Mill, and Thomas Carlyle. He said to John Bright: "All my life will be spent in Australia. I am a Free Trader, as you know. They are going to have a protective policy there. Am I to retire, therefore, from public life?" John Bright, a practical man, said, "If there are particular industries that can flourish in that country, and if it is the determination of the people to encourage them, I would grant bonuses on certain industries liberally, in order to promote them; or I would come to an agreement with the Protectionists to protect a certain number of articles for a certain number of years, and let them try their experiment."

Mr. A. Langton of Melbourne, a Free Trader, who was present at the banquet, wrote to Mr. T. B. Potter, M.P., and asked him to call Mr. Bright's attention to these remarks, and in reply to the letter which was sent him, Mr. Bright wrote as follows:—

Rochdale, July 31, 1877.

Dear Mr. Potter,—I thank you for sending me Mr. Langton's letter of the 10th of June, from Melbourne. By the same mail I have three other letters on the same subject on which Mr. Langton has written to you: one from the Secretary of the Free Trade League of Victoria; one from Sir Charles Gavan Duffy; and one written at Suez by Mr. John Young, of Montreal, to whom the dinner at Melbourne was given.

I need not tell you that I am surprised and

amused at the stir which so small a matter has caused among our friends on the other side of the globe.

I recollect meeting Sir Charles Gavan Duffy on his visit to this country; but I have not the least recollection that we had any conversation on the subject of Protection, or on the policy of the province of Victoria on that question. If any such conversation occurred, I can say with confidence that my views have been entirely misunderstood and misrepresented by Sir Charles. The words he puts into my mouth are much like in meaning what I think I have seen in some of the writings of Mr. John Stuart Mill, and it may be that Sir Charles may have inadvertently attributed to me what he has heard from Mr. Mill, or read in some of his works.

If a Government voted a sum of money to support a steamboat enterprise which was deemed of great service to the country, but which, from its novelty, or its risk, private capitalists would not undertake, I should say that in doing this no sound principle would be broken, and that the public interest might possibly be wisely served. So, if a Government thought that if a new culture might be introduced into the country, such as the grape or tea, it might appropriate a sum of money to make that experiment, leaving its future progress or fate entirely to the industry and disposition of the people. But to enact a tariff imposing heavy duties on most important articles of import, to establish an oppressive and costly system of custom-houses, to build up special interests before their time, or industries which might never thrive in the free air of competition, at the expense of taxation upon the whole people, levied partly at the custom-houses, and partly by the high prices which are sought to be obtained on the home-made and protected article, is a policy so unsound and so injurious that I am greatly surprised that any one in the least acquainted with me or with my life should have supposed it possible that I should have given it my support.

Englishmen form colonies at a distance from the mother country. They throw off many of the superstitions which are still to a large extent cherished in England. In respect of Protection by means of a prohibitive or restrictive tariff, the colony of Victoria clings to a superstition or error which we in England have abandoned. Our experience is conclusive as to the wisdom of our policy. Victoria is young, and thinks she knows more and better than we know. But when she finds herself, not at the head, but at the tail of the great Australian communities as to her success and the growth of wealth, she may discover that industry has no greater enemy than a protective or restrictive tariff.

If you will kindly send this letter to your correspondent, Mr. Langton, it will not be necessary for me to write to Sir Charles Duffy or to the Secretary of the Free Trade League of Victoria.

Believe me, &c.,
JOHN BRIGHT.

ON KINDNESS TO ANIMALS.

Read at a meeting held in the Birmingham Town Hall on the 28th of November, 1877, when prizes publicly subscribed for were distributed to such of the Board School children as had succeeded either by writing essays or answering questions in connection with the subject of kindness to dumb animals.

Rochdale, November 22, 1877.

Dear Miss Goddard,—I cannot come to your meeting, but I am very glad your good cause excites so much interest as to enable you to hold a public meeting in its favour. If children at school can be made to understand how it is just and noble to be humane even to what we term inferior animals, it will do much to give them a higher character and tone through life. There is nothing meaner than barbarous and cruel treatment of the dumb creatures who cannot answer us or resent the misery which is so often needlessly inflicted upon them.

Wishing you a constant success,

I am, very sincerely yours,

John Bright.

ON "CONSECRATED GROUND."

On the 20th of November, 1877, the Bishop of Peterborough delivered a speech on the occasion of the foundation-stone of a new parish church at Loughborough being laid. In the course of his remarks the bishop said:—" It was his fortune, or his misfortune, to have been in the gallery of the House when Mr. Bright was delivering what appeared to him to be an exquisitely beautiful and touching speech upon a sorely-vexed question—the Burials Bill. He never heard a speech more full of pathetic beauty and power; but when speaking on that subject it occurred to the great orator to stop and to sneer at the observances of the Church of England, and, speaking of his own burial grounds, to say, 'they have not been—what do they call it?—consecrated.' He confessed, when he heard that, it seemed to him to be an entirely unworthy jeer, unworthy of the speaker, unworthy of the subject, and unworthy of the place—a jeer at the cherished religious feelings and observances of many who stood around him."

On reading the bishop's speech, Mr. Bright addressed the following letter to his lordship:—

Rochdale, November 23, 1877.

DEAR BISHOP OF PETERBOROUGH,—I have read your speech, and write to make one correction in it. You refer to my speech on the Burials Bill, to which you give too much praise, but you condemn what you term the "sneer" intended in my mention of the ceremony of "consecration." I assure you there was no sneer intended. The speech was entirely unpremeditated. I had no intention of saying anything on the question when I went down to the House, and what I said arose from feelings excited during the debate. When I came to the word "consecration," it entirely escaped me, and for the moment I could not recall it. In my difficulty I turned to my friends on the bench near me and said, "What is it called?" or, "What do they call it?" One or more of them answered, "Consecration," and one or more laughed, I suppose, at my ignorance or forgetfulness, and this laugh, which was somewhat ill-timed, made that seem a sneer which was never so intended by me.

This charge has been made against me more than once, but always, I think, in party newspapers, to which I did not think it needful to reply; but coming from you, I write now to correct an error and misrepresentation which perhaps I ought to have corrected before.

You will not blame me if I do not believe in the virtue of "consecration." I cannot believe in what is called "holy ground" any more than you can believe in "holy water," and for the same reason, that there is nothing in it; but it is not necessary to ridicule all that one cannot believe, although it is certain that ridicule has had its share in clearing the world of some portions of the superstitions which have misled and afflicted it.

I am, with great respect,
Very sincerely yours,
JOHN BRIGHT.

The Right Rev. the Bishop of Peterborough.

ON INDIA.

THE INDIAN IMPORT AND EXCISE DUTIES.

London, February 7, 1878.

MY DEAR ARMITAGE,—I am surprised at the

line taken by some of our friends of the Chamber of Commerce in the matter of the Indian import duties.

It seems dictated by passion and disappointment, rather than by reason and a sound judgment.

India has an interest in the question as well as England. If the people of India could speak and act as we can in England, they would oppose to the last degree of resistance any attempt to impose an excise duty of five per cent., or of any amount, on the produce of their factories. If they were in theory Free Traders, and wished to be so in practice, they would oppose any such tax, and in my opinion most rightly. They would say, as we ought to say, an excise duty on the produce of the mills is odious on every ground and cannot be permitted. They would look for the power to remove the import duties to greater economy in the public expenditure, or the regular growth of the public revenue, or the imposition of some new tax which might raise the needful 800,000*l.* a year. The grievance complained of in the Chamber can only be remedied in one of these three ways, for I feel very confident the House of Commons will never compel the Indian Government to adopt the odious and intolerable proposition which seems strangely to have found favour with some of the members of your Chamber.

I see in the same discussion in the Chamber objection is made to anything being done there which may be termed political. What is more political than a question of revenue and taxation? This dread of all serious questions is the cause of the feebleness and general uselessness of Chambers of Commerce.

I suppose the excise proposition is merely a weapon to use against the Government, and to compel it to act against the import duties. It must fail, for it is impossible to defend it. It would be much more wise to put pressure on the Indian Government to lessen its expenses, to reduce its English and native forces by the amount required, which surely may be safely done, if our Indian Government is so intelligent and so just as it constantly declares itself to be.

I write this rather hastily, after reading the report of the proceedings of the Chamber. I am not a member of the Chamber, but I shall be very sorry to see it take a course which must lessen its character for wisdom, and therefore lessen its influence.

If you think any one will care about my opinion, you need not conceal it. I am sorry to be compelled to differ from any of our friends on this question.

Believe me, always sincerely yours,
JOHN BRIGHT.

Benjamin Armitage, Esq.,
48, Mosley Street, Manchester.

ON FREE TRADE.

FREE TRADE AND ARMAMENTS.

Written to Mr. J. R. Morrison, of Hampstead, London, in reply to a letter from that gentleman, suggesting that Mr. Bright should assist in the formation of an International Free Trade League.

Rochdale, March 18, 1878.

DEAR SIR,—I thank you for your letter. You greatly over-estimate the force of any influence I may possess. The formation of an International Free Trade League is a grand idea, which some of our Free Trade friends have often suggested; but the difficulty is great, if not insuperable. The difference of language is in itself one great difficulty, and the jealousy between nations is another. For myself I am too far on in life to be able to undertake any great work of this kind. My lamented friend, Mr. Cobden, did something towards it, or attempted something; but wars and national jealousies have barred the way against the growth of his beneficent ideas. Just now Europe is disturbed, the chief disturber being our own Government. The war between Russia and Turkey is over, and England is the Power which threatens to reopen the contest on a wider field. So long as our people are so ignorant as to their true interests, and so long as a war party of any considerable influence exists among us, I fear we shall do little to encourage other nations to enter the Free Trade path. To abolish tariffs is the only way which leads to the abolition of great armies. Free Trade between nations would give the nations peace, but war, anxieties, and menaced conflicts make it impossible for the nations calmly to consider their true interests. If any opportunity offers, I hope I shall be ready to do anything in my power in furtherance of the policy you suggest.

I am, yours,
JOHN BRIGHT.

Mr. J. R. Morrison,
11, Buckland Villas, Hampstead, N.W.

ON IRISH MEMBERS OF PARLIAMENT IN RELATION TO THE LIBERAL PARTY.

Written to the guardians of the Tullamore Union, in reply to a request to present a petition for an amendment of the Bright Clauses of the Land Act.

132, Piccadilly, London, April 4, 1878.

DEAR SIR,—I will present your petition to the House of Commons. Nothing can be done this session; a committee is now taking evidence on the matter. I fear that while the present Government is in office there will be no remedy for the evils you complain of. I do not see any chance for a better Government so long as Irish members refuse to unite with the English and Scotch Liberal members. An Irish party hostile to the Liberal party of Great Britain insures the perpetual reign of the Tories.

I am, yours respectfully,
JOHN BRIGHT.

To the Clerk of the Tullamore Union, King's County.

ON THE FOREIGN POLICY OF LORD BEACONSFIELD'S GOVERNMENT.

Read at a conference of representative working men, held on the 4th of May, 1878, in the Concert Hall, Liverpool, to consider the crisis as affecting labour. The circular convening the meeting stated: "We ask you to attend a conference to discuss the momentous issues referred to, and give such an answer to our rulers as will help to save us from a blunder and a crime, and thus add to the honour and the true interests of our country."

At this time England seemed in imminent danger of being plunged into war with Russia. The vote of credit for 6,000,000*l*. had been given, the fleet had gone to the Dardanelles, the reserves had been called out, the Indian troops were on their way to Malta, and the prospect was anything but promising.

Rochdale, May 2, 1878.

Dear Sir,—I cannot come to your meeting to-morrow, but I am glad to hear that you are to meet.

After my speech on Tuesday evening at Manchester, I have not much to write. I ask your friends to notice three points, to two of which I referred at Manchester. I charge the Government with constant deception practised on the House of Commons and the country, by professions of a wish for peace whilst engaged in acts which are distinctly provocative of war. I charge them, further, with constantly interposing obstacles in the way of any arrangement with Russia or the other European Powers for the settlement of the Eastern Question on any basis favourable to the freedom of the oppressed Christian population of the Turkish provinces in Europe.

There is a third charge which may be brought against them, as seen in the action of their party organization in London and in many of the large towns of England. Through that party organization they attempt to suppress the expression of opinion of thoughtful and peaceful citizens, through the ordinary means of public meetings, by an exhibition of violence and rowdyism from which, for many years past, the country has happily been free; and they are willing to accept this violence and riot as the voice of the English people.

This Government is no friend to freedom at home or to peace abroad; and, to add to its other offences, it now introduces into its contemplated European warfare an armed force of Mahometans from India, whose numbers have not been voted by Parliament, and the cost of whose maintenance and employment has not been given in any Parliamentary estimate.

The people of England will begin to ask themselves if they have gone back to the times of Charles I., and if the prevalent idea of English freedom and of constitutional principles and practice is only a dream. I wish I could speak to every working man in the kingdom, and to all the members of your trade societies. I would urge them to meet and speak at this moment of supreme interest, it may be of supreme peril. The country and its dearest interests are in evil hands, and it is possible for a Cabinet by the same policy to betray both Crown and people.

I am, very respectfully yours,

JOHN BRIGHT.

Mr. J. W. Julian, Liverpool.

ON THE LIBERAL PARTY IN ACCRINGTON.

Written to Mr. John Hartley, of Accrington, in reply to a letter from that gentleman, informing Mr. Bright of the result of a municipal contest, when the Liberals of Accrington elected twenty-four Liberals as members of their first Town Council, carrying every man they nominated in each ward, against a non-political party, which included about twelve Conservatives.

Rochdale, May 4, 1878.

DEAR SIR,—I thank you for sending me the result of your municipal contest. I hope it may be only the beginning of your municipal and political career, and that you may always stand among the foremost of the northern populations in favour of Liberal principles. At this moment your election has a special significance. You are not in favour of war, nor in favour of a party that is clamouring for war, and you take the first opportunity of declaring your adherence to the party which is truly anxious for peace. When the working men of England comprehend their own interests, they will give no support to the war party. They will have discovered that the wounds and sufferings of war are mainly for them, and its profits, if there be profits, are reserved for those far above the men of their social scale.

We owe you thanks for your efforts and services in the late contest. You have spoken with no uncertain voice, and all true Liberals will thank you. You have chosen twenty-four Liberal Town Councillors, and have rejected by a large majority every Tory, or Conservative, or non-political—which last word means Tory in disguise—who offered himself as a candidate for your vote. You have done well.

I am, yours very truly,
JOHN BRIGHT.

ON THE FOREIGN POLICY OF LORD BEACONSFIELD'S GOVERNMENT.

Read at a Conference of Delegates from various working men's associations, held at the St. James's Hall, Leeds, on the 4th of May, 1878, to take into consideration the subject of peace or war, and to express the opinions of working men on that question.

May, 1878.

DEAR SIR,—If the trades' societies would speak out for peace, there would be no war. There are men and classes to whom war is sometimes gain; to the working men it is only loss. Hitherto they have had little voice in determining whether war should be entered into. They have had to bear the sufferings inseparable from it, and their blood has been mainly shed at the bidding of monarchs and statesmen. Now, in a question of this kind the voice of the working classes is powerful, if not omnipotent; and if the sufferings of war are again to be endured, their silence at this supreme moment would throw no light responsibility upon them. I would advise you to take some means whereby the famous and unanswerable speech of Lord Derby shall be widely circulated among the householders and electors in the districts represented by the members of your Conference. Lord Derby's name and character, his late high position and great office in the Government, and his perfect knowledge of the whole question now before the country, will give immense force to his arguments and opinions.

Wishing you all success in your attempt to defeat the war policy of the Government,

I remain, &c.,

JOHN BRIGHT.

THE LIQUOR TRAFFIC AND THE TORY PARTY.

Written to Mr. T. S. Leedle, of York.

Rochdale, September 4, 1878.

DEAR SIR,—I have read your interesting letter, and wish something could be done in the direction to which you point; but I despair of anything being done at present and for a long time to come. The "drink question" has become a political question, and the unscrupulous political party will take care that it shall remain so, and the alliance between drink and the Tories will continue, and the question will still be one which many will talk about, but which none can deal with. I have had some plan of reform on this subject in my mind, but there seems yet no suitable time for saying anything in public about it. Foreign policy has filled men's minds, to the exclusion of all matters of home and social interest, and while the present party is in power there is small hope of any improvement. You will have observed the manner in which the Tory party in Parliament hold together. It is difficult to say what it will not vote for, or what it will not resist, to maintain its supremacy and its power; but certainly it will not break up its alliance with the great publican combination.

The Permissive Bill seems to me a great error. It is not a good Bill, and men anxious for something to be done are forced to vote against it, while almost all who vote for it condemn it in private conversation. It blocks the way, and the most eager foes of the drink curse, by their pertinacity in supporting a bad Bill, are thus a great difficulty in the way of any considerable and effective remedy being applied.

I suppose we must wait; perhaps by-and-by opinion will rise to the point of action; but advance is slow, and we may almost despair.

I think your letter must be useful in its appeal to thoughtful minds, and I wish all men and women could read it.

I am, very respectfully yours,
JOHN BRIGHT.

Mr. T. S. Leedle, 3, Micklegate, York.

THE PREVENTION OF WAR.

Written in answer to an invitation to attend the Peace Congress held in September, 1878, at Savona. The Advocate, Pietro Sbarbaro, to whom the letter was written, was Professor of Law in the University of Macerata, and prime mover in the commemoration of Alberigo Gentili, who from his chair in Oxford first propounded the doctrine of international arbitration.

Rochdale, September 23, 1878.

DEAR SIR,—I cannot write to you at any length on the interesting subject of which you have spoken to me, and I fear my short letter will not reach you in time for your Peace Congress.

The situation of Europe at this moment is deplorable; its nations are groaning under the weight of enormous armies and burdensome taxation. They are at the same time disjoined in interests and sentiments by tariffs, which form an insurmountable barrier between the peoples of the different States, and prevent that reciprocity of interests which would make it impossible for their statesmen to drag them into war.

How can wars be avoided and standing armies dissolved? This is the great question for Europe, and for every nation of Europe. In my own view the directest way—I was going to say the only way—to this great end lies in Free Trade between the peoples of Europe. If tariffs were abolished, or even if they were made very moderate, the nations would trade freely with each other, their commerce would increase enormously, and they would bit by bit become like one grand nation, their commercial interests would multiply on such a scale, and their natural knowledge and intercourse would become so intimate, that the ambition of monarchs and of statesmen would be impotent to drive them to war.

The treaty between France and England, negotiated eighteen years ago by Mr. Cobden, has entirely changed the sentiments of the two nations to each other, and if the tariff of France were as free as that of England, the two States would, through their interests, become as one. If the tariffs of Europe were abolished, Europe would not fear war, and her armies would in a short time be reduced.

Monopoly in commerce, high tariffs, protection of the trading classes at the expense of society and the consumers, such are the allies of great armies and the grand obstacle to a general and lasting peace in Europe. Destroy the tariffs, or reduce them greatly, and standing armies will be dissolved, for then almost every pretext on which they are kept up will have disappeared.

For the disbanding of great armies and the promotion of peace I rely on the abolition of tariffs, and on the brotherhood of the nations resulting from free trade in the products of industry.

Let us try to impress on public opinion the conviction that the protectionist system, the system of high tariffs, and the monopoly which some classes are eager to keep, to the detriment of the people, are the principal cause and the most powerful support of standing armies and of frequent wars. If this idea could prevail in Europe, then indeed should we be able to welcome the dawn of that day in which armies will no longer be considered necessary, and high tariffs a crime against the interests and the happiness of the people.

I am, with great respect, yours, &c.,

JOHN BRIGHT.

To Professor Pietro Sbarbaro, Bologna.

ON THE LIQUOR TRAFFIC.

Written to Mr. Joseph Leicester, President of the Workmen's Political League for the Annihilation of the Liquor Traffic, in reply to a resolution passed at a meeting of working men held on the 28th of September, 1878, at Clerkenwell, calling upon Mr. Bright to frame a Bill for the purpose of controlling the liquor traffic.

Rochdale, October 7, 1878.

DEAR SIR,—I thank you for your letter, and for the copy of the resolution which you forwarded me. I cannot undertake to frame a

Bill on the subject of the drink traffic, or to take the part you and your friends invite me to assume. I watch the discussion which is now in progress, and I hope it may yield some fruit, some plan of procedure which may prove useful to the cause of temperance. The subject is one of great difficulty—the inveterate custom of our people, their belief that stimulants are wholesome and necessary, their habitual and almost universal self-indulgence in them, are obstacles which seem insurmountable. While these opinions and habits prevail, it is difficult to alter the law; a change of law, though not absolutely useless, will do much less for temperance than many sanguine people expect. I hope, however, that what change of law can do may be done, and that a more intelligent public opinion may gradually be created to do more than even the wisest legislation can do. I hope the extension of education may give our people more self-respect, and thus save them from the miserable degradation to which multitudes of them are now subjected by a pernicious indulgence in intoxicating drinks. I am sorry I do not see my way to say or do more in connection with this great and difficult question. If an opportunity offers in which I can be of service I hope I shall not neglect it.

I am, very respectfully yours,
JOHN BRIGHT.

ON THE "VIRTUOUS POOR."

At a meeting of the Haddington Established

Presbytery in November, 1878, Dr. Whitelaw, in calling the attention of his colleagues to the condition of the virtuous poor of Scotland, but more particularly of those who were in communion with the Church of Scotland, read the following letter he had received from Mr. Bright on the subject:—

November, 1878.

DEAR SIR,—I do not see what law can do for what you term "virtuous poor," unless it is to assist them under the action of the poor law. The question which should be asked is, "Why are there so many virtuous poor?" It would take, not a letter, but a volume, to answer this question—but in a letter one or two points may be indicated. If the law or laws make land a virtual monopoly, as it is in the United Kingdom, and especially in Scotland, then we may expect that the population, divorced from the soil, will be in possession only of a precarious income or living, and that they will be subject to fluctuation and reverses which will inflict upon many of them the sufferings of poverty, even when their lives have been fairly prudent and virtuous. I cannot go fully into the question, but I am persuaded that enormous evil to the people comes from this cause. The public exactions and expenditure have much to do with poverty. To raise not less than eighty millions sterling per annum for purposes of government, to expend thirty millions of it in military preparations and means of offence and defence, the bulk of which is only rendered apparently necessary by a mistaken foreign policy, must act as a burden on the people, and must press multitudes of prudent and virtuous families to poverty.

These are two of the great causes and sources of the sufferings of the people. They are both capable of remedy, and the ignorance of the people—not of the working classes, but of the classes above them—is the only difficulty in the way. If you could persuade your General Assembly to look at these matters, and to thoroughly examine them, perhaps its members might make a discovery that would startle them, and benefit the people to whom they minister. I do not touch upon other questions. Some of them will suggest themselves to you. The great whisky question is one which your friends may consider with some advantage. If all the ministers of the Scottish Churches were to banish whisky from their houses, and the consumption of it from their customs or social habits, they would do much to discredit and to withdraw one fertile source of poverty and suffering in Scotland. Many of what you term "virtuous poor" suffer much from the evil of whisky in connection with members of their families. I am burdened with correspondence, and so write hastily and briefly. I do not suppose what I write will be of service: if you think otherwise, you are at liberty to add this letter to the other contributions of your friends.

I am, very respectfully yours,
JOHN BRIGHT.

Rev. Dr. Whitelaw.

ON PROTECTION IN THE UNITED STATES.

One Ash, Rochdale, January 21, 1879.

My dear Mr. Field,—I never write for reviews or any other periodicals. It is so long since I have written, that my hand has lost its cunning, if it ever had it. I do not think anything an Englishman could say would have any effect upon an American protectionist. The man who possesses a monopoly by which he thinks he gains is not open to argument. It was so in this country forty years ago, and it is so with you now. It is strange that a people who put down slavery at an immense sacrifice are not able to suppress monopoly, which is but a milder form of the same evil. Under slavery the man was seized, and his labour was stolen from him, and the profit of it enjoyed by his master and owner. Under protection the man is apparently free, but he is denied the right to exchange the produce of his labour except with his countrymen, who offer him much less for it than the foreigner would give. Some portion of his labour is thus confiscated. In our protection days our weavers and artisans could not exchange with American flour. They exchanged with an English farmer, who gave them sometimes only half the quantity the American would have given them. Now, your farmer is forbidden to trade with the Englishman, and must give to an American double the quantity of grain and flour for many articles he is constantly requiring that he would give if your laws did not forbid his trade with England.

A country may have democratic institutions, its government may be republican, and based on a wide suffrage, and yet there may be no freedom to men for that which is the source of life and comfort. If a man's labour is not free, if its exchange is not free, the man is not free. And whether the law which enacts this restriction be the offspring of republican or autocratic government and power, it is equally evil, and to be condemned and withstood by all who love freedom and understand what it is.

Nations learn slowly—but they do learn; and therefore I do not doubt that the time will come when trade will be as free as the winds, and when freedom and industry will do much to put down great armies and the peril and suffering of war. But I am writing you almost an article instead of a short note—as if I would teach you, which would be an impertinence. If you could teach your farmers, and ask the "solid South" to help them and you, you might soon succeed.

Believe me, always sincerely your friend,
JOHN BRIGHT.

Cyrus W. Field, Esq., New York.

ON JUVENILE SMOKING.

Written in reply to a letter from a Birmingham constituent, who had urged legislative action against juvenile tobacco smoking amongst the working classes.

February, 1879.

DEAR SIR,—I do not think such a law as you recommend would receive support in the House of Commons. We have rather too many laws already, and I prefer to leave such evils as you refer to to parental supervision and the effects of a better education among the working classes.

I am, yours, &c.,
JOHN BRIGHT.

ON PERPETUAL PENSIONS, SEPTENNIAL PARLIAMENTS, AND THE BEACONSFIELD GOVERNMENT.

Written in reply to a letter from the Secretary of the All Saints' Branch of the Workmen's Peace Society in Birmingham in March, 1879, asking him whether he would support the Government in proposing a simultaneous reduction of all standing armies; whether he would support an inquiry into the present system of pensions, with a view to the abolition of such as those of the Duke of Marlborough and the Duke of Schomberg; whether he would support Mr. Macdonald's Bill for liability of employers for injuries, and a Bill for shorter Parliaments.

132, Piccadilly, March 11, 1879.

DEAR SIR,—I cannot say "Yes" or "No" to the questions you put to me. Any answer I could give to them would require explanation and more length of writing than I can put into an ordinary letter. I may say, however, that generally I doubt not that my views are much in harmony with yours on the points you have raised.

With regard to the liabilities of employers, if I remember correctly, I was willing to support the conclusions of the Committee appointed to consider the whole question. The Bill then before the House seemed to me to require amendment.

The pensions to which you refer should have been terminated by purchase long ago. Perpetual pensions should never be granted.

I think no Parliament should sit for more than five years; probably three or four years would be a better time.

With regard to the reduction of armies, it is ludicrous to think of supporting this Government in any attempt of the kind. The policy of this Government for three years past has made the reduction of armies less possible than it was before, and has been the cause of nearly all the war or wars which have afflicted the world during that period. They have made needless wars in Asia and Africa, and were a main cause of the great war in the east of Europe. I hope they have convinced the nation that Parliament does not exert a sufficient control over the disposition to go to war shown by the Ministers of the Crown; but it must be remembered that the Parliament has partaken largely of the guilt of the Administration. A better House of Commons must precede any of the good things which you are hoping for.

I am, respectfully yours,
JOHN BRIGHT.

Mr. Herbert Ball, Birmingham.

ON TORY MISREPRESENTATION.

In March, 1879, a member of the Barrow Conservative Club read a paper before the members of that institution on "Liberal principles and Liberal arguments," in which he made the following statement:—"Is it fair play, then, to try and make it appear that the repeal of the Corn Laws was entirely a Liberal measure, and that it was almost entirely for the benefit of the working man, which bait they know some are always ready to swallow, whereas it was the employers of labour (as these Liberals like to be called) that expected to reap the most benefit? For what did they do? Why, as soon as the working man got cheap bread they lowered his wages, told him he could do with less now that he had bread so cheap, and I do believe the Brights were among the first to do this."

A Liberal in Barrow forwarded a letter and newspaper to Mr. Bright, containing this report, and received the following letter in reply:—

132, Piccadilly, London,
March 28, 1879.

Dear Sir,—I thank you for your note and for your newspaper. I do not know which is more apparent among the Tory speakers—their ignorance or their faculty for lying. The man whose speech you send me is largely guilty of both. He may not know that he is ignorant, but he cannot be ignorant that he lies. And after such a speech the meeting thanked him,—I presume because they enjoyed what he had given them. I think the speaker was named Smith. He is a discredit to the numerous family of that name.

>I am, very truly yours,
>JOHN BRIGHT.

Mr. J. C. Baynes, Barrow-in-Furness.

ON FREE TRADE.

THE CONDITION OF ENGLAND UNDER FREE TRADE.

Written to Mr. Abraham Sharp, who was chairman of a meeting of working men held at Bradford in March, 1879, in favour of Free Trade.

>132, Piccadilly, April 1, 1879.

DEAR SIR,—I thank you for your note and the newspaper. The meeting seems to have been a very good one, but the report of the speeches is not good. The "reciprocity" notion is exactly adapted to catch the considerable class of simpletons who have no memory and no logic. But for this lack of memory and of reasoning power they would know that the "distress" in this country was ten times greater in the period from 1839 to 1842 than it has been from 1877 to the present time, or than it is at this moment, although in the former period we had protection, as much as Parliament and the law could give. They would know, also, that in the United States the most "protected" nation in the world, the distress during the last five years has been more prolonged, more widely spread, and far more intense than in this country. If your "reciprocity" neighbours could reason, surely these facts would help to convince them of the silliness of their views.

You wish to learn something of the distress of the former period. I recommend you to read a volume written lately by my friend, Henry Asworth, of Bolton. Its title is "Cobden and the League." Any bookseller will get it for you. If England could be reduced this year to the condition it was in after the bad harvests from 1839 to 1842, we should have insurrection and anarchy all over the country, and the simpletons who are writing pamphlets and delivering lectures in favour of protection would be flying for their lives. If your working men ask for protection and reciprocity after what they have seen and known during the past thirty years, it is clear that neither facts nor arguments nor experience can be of any service to them. I am not afraid that this heresy and lunacy will make much way amongst them.

I am, very respectfully yours,
JOHN BRIGHT.

Mr. Abraham Sharp.

FREE TRADE AND THE DEPRESSION IN TRADE IN 1879.

Addressed in May, 1879, to the editor of the *North American Review*, who had asked his opinion as to the nature and extent of the so-called movement in favour of Protection in England.

May, 1879.

MY DEAR SIR,—I have no difficulty in replying to your letter of the 31st ultimo. Do not think there is any chance of a return in this country to the doctrines of protection. We export everything but agricultural produce. To protect our manufactures is manifestly impossible. From another cause the protection of our land produce is not more possible. Half our population exists on imported food. To limit this import by customs duties in order to raise the price of home-grown food is a proposition that cannot be entertained for a moment. Such a scheme offered to Parliament and the country would destroy any Government and any party.

We are passing through a time of commercial depression. Its causes are apparent to those who examine and consider the facts of recent and past years; but in times of trouble ignorant men seize upon unlikely and impossible propositions and schemes for relief. There is no special remedy for this malady. Time, patience, the working of natural laws, the avoidance and cessation of the half-madness of the past, and a general economy will bring about a cure, not without some or much suffering, but without failure. We adopted Free Trade in the year 1846, but our landowners and farmers and multitudes of our people did not comprehend the principles we taught, and a new generation is on the stage, ill acquainted even with the facts of forty years ago. There has been no great distress since our corn law was abolished, and now when trouble has come for a time some of the sufferers, and some of the quack doctors, who are always ready to prescribe for the public, cry out for protection as if we had never tried it before, and as if it had been found a specific in other countries. There is no danger of our going back to protection. The present trouble will pass away. It has been aggravated by the evil policy of our Government, and that also will pass away, and the simpletons who are looking for relief to an exploded doctrine and practice will relapse into that silent obscurity which becomes them.

It is a grief to me that your people do not yet see their way to a moderate tariff. They are doing wonders unequalled in the world's history in paying off your national debt. A moderate tariff, I should think, would give you a better revenue, and by degrees you might approach a more civilized system. What can be more strange than for your great, free country to build barriers against that commerce which is everywhere the handmaid of freedom and of civilization?

I should despair of the prospects of mankind if I did not believe that before long the intelligence of your people would revolt against the barbarism of your tariff. It seems now your one great humiliation. The world looks to you for example in all forms of freedom. As to commerce, the great civilizer, shall it look in vain?

Believe me, very sincerely yours,
JOHN BRIGHT.

ON THE DEPRESSION IN TRADE IN 1879 AND ITS CAUSES.

Written in reply to a letter asking Mr. Bright to support a motion in the House of Commons for an inquiry into the causes of the depression in trade.

132, Piccadilly, London,
June 26, 1879.

DEAR SIR,—Mr. Chaplin is about to move for an inquiry by Royal Commission into the existing agricultural distress, and I do not see how or why such an inquiry should be granted without including in it a more general inquiry as to the present depression in other branches of industry. Some people still have faith in Parliamentary Committees and Royal Commissions on matters of this kind; I confess that I have none.

A few years ago we had a panic about the scarcity and price of coal, and a Parliamentary Committee sat upon it and about it. The Committee led to nothing. More recently we had a Committee on the Fall in the Value of Silver, and the inquiry led to nothing. Just now we have a Committee on Co-operative Stores, and it will lead to nothing, except to show generally the uselessness of such inquiries. If Mr. Chaplin gets his Committee or Commission it will lead to nothing, except to prove that, with free imports of corn, bad harvests are bad for farmers, and that the omnipotence of Parliament fails when it seeks to control the seasons; and that, therefore, Parliament cannot step in by legislation materially to mitigate the admitted sufferings of the farmers.

As to the present depression of trade, we owe some of it to the bad harvests, which have impoverished many farmers, who are not an inconsiderable portion of our home-trade customers; we owe much of it to famines in India and China, and to the commercial and manufacturing distress which has prevailed in almost every country, and not least in those countries which have sought to secure themselves by high protective duties. If our harvest this year is unfavourable, I fear the recovery we all hope for will be delayed; if it is abundant, which seems not probable, we shall soon see, not symptoms only, but proofs of a revival.

In the United States, with a great harvest last year, trade is reviving. We followed them in their depression, but not to so deep a depth, and we shall follow them in their recovery. These great changes are not in the power of Congresses or Parliaments; they are in the ordering of nature, and we must accept them, always endeavouring not to aggravate them by our own follies.

There is one great consolation in our present condition; the food of our people is cheap. But for the free imports the price of bread would be more than double, the price of sugar would be three times its present price, the price of cheese and bacon would be double, or nearly so, and of the price of labour it may be said that it would be much lessened by a greater prostration of every industry in the country not immediately connected with the growth of food. The freedom of our imports will enable us to pass through the present time of depression with less suffering than at any former period of disastrous seasons.

As to Parliament and its inquiries, I have seen much of it and of them. If Parliament would keep out of foreign broils; if it would conduct the government of the country at an expenditure of sixty millions instead of eighty millions in the year; if it would devote its time and labours to questions of home interest rather than to those which involve the sacrifice of the blood and treasure of our people in remote lands, we might have hope and faith that Parliament could serve the nation in times of depression, and we should find that such times of suffering would visit us more rarely.

If an inquiry, such as you refer to, is granted, I hope it may do some good, if it only shows once more how useless such inquiries are. I need not tell you that the friends of Free Trade can have no objection to Commission or Committee if the Government wishes to appoint one.

I am, respectfully yours,
JOHN BRIGHT.

Mr. Frederick Blood,
32, Charlotte Street, Birmingham.

FREE TRADE—ITS PROGRESS AND RESULTS.

Mr. Russell, a working man, residing in Glasgow, who described himself as having been an enthusiastic member of the Anti-Corn-Law League, wrote to Mr. Bright in July, 1879, asking his opinion as to the existing widespread depression in trade. Mr. Russell said there could be no doubt about the excellence of the principle of Free Trade abstractedly considered, but, he added, the good effects of the principle in a commercial point of view could only be felt when other nations met us in the same spirit.

Mr. Bright, in reply, wrote :—

One Ash, Rochdale, August 1, 1879.

DEAR SIR,—There are two passages in your letter that I must dispute. You speak of depressed trade from 1839 to 1843 as being nothing like that which now exists. If you will read Mr. Ashworth's book, "Cobden and the League," you will learn that the distress now is not to be compared with that of the former period. This I can confidently assert from my own knowledge, but Mr. Ashworth gives abundant proofs of it.

You say that in our agitation, now nearly forty years ago, we urged that a necessary consequence of Corn Law repeal would be that "war would cease, and that there would be no more commercial and agricultural depression."

We never said this. We said that Free Trade greatly tends to promote peace between nations, and that commercial depression caused by the Corn Law on the occasion of every bad harvest would be prevented. Before 1846, and during the thirty years of Corn Law, there were five or six parliamentary committees on agricultural distress; during more than thirty years of free imports of corn, until this session, there has been no such committee appointed or asked for; and now all sensible men know that the commission to be appointed is a mere delusion held out to cajole the farmers.

War has not ceased. *We* made the Russian war in 1854, and since then the armaments of Europe have much more than doubled. Free Trade—imports of corn—cannot make Englishmen or Scotchmen sensible or moral. But with regard to France, every man must know that our relations with France have been much more friendly since Mr. Cobden's treaty came into force; and that now we are on most friendly terms with the nation with whom in past times we have most frequently contended on the battle-field.

As to Germany and its tariff, its military expenditure demands more taxes; and by offering higher duties to her manufacturers, higher taxes are made less unwelcome to many of her people. I am not aware of any movement towards Protection in Italy, or Belgium, or France. In France the cause of Free Trade is far more powerful now than at any former period. America has had her tremendous civil war; but for that and her enormous debt Protection would have been dead and buried long ago; and nobody surely expected or said that the repeal of our Corn Law could make or prevent a civil war on the great question of slavery in the United States.

Why don't you and your friends ask why American commercial distress has been much deeper and more prolonged than our own? Yet America has all the good which Protection can give her.

We are suffering from many bad harvests at home, from famines and poverty in India and China, from depression in North and South America, from like suffering in Germany, from war in the east of Europe, and from the extravagance and inflation of the years preceding the present bad times. And, after all, our people as a whole suffer infinitely less than in the three years from 1839 to 1842; and our farm labourers, who were to be specially ruined, are receiving nearly double the wages, and of that which wages can buy, that they received in the three years to which I have referred.

If you use your faculties as well now as you did in the days of the Free Trade contest, you will not doubt the wisdom of our present policy.

I am, respectfully yours,
JOHN BRIGHT.

Mr. Wm. Russell, Glasgow.

ON CANADIAN POLICY.

Written to a gentleman in New York. Sir John Macdonald, who was appointed Premier of Canada in the beginning of 1879, signalized his accession to office by adopting a policy of protection to native industries. Some months later he visited this country and endeavoured to raise a loan for the construction of a railway through Canada to the Pacific.

Rochdale, August 16, 1879.

DEAR SIR,—The policy of the Canadian Government seems to me injurious to the inhabitants of the Dominion, and, if persisted in, will be fatal to its connection with the mother country. To shut out the manufacturer of England is bad enough, but at the same time to seek to borrow money from her on a guarantee for a loan is a scheme and a policy so impudent that it cannot succeed. The great railway project of Canada can only add to the debt of Canada, and this can only cause heavier taxes, and will be made the excuse for still higher protective duties on imports, so that England's generous but foolish help to the colony, if further given, will tend directly to cripple the trade between them. I believe the present policy of the Canadian Government is inflicting a wound on the union between the colony and England from which, if it be not speedily reversed, great changes must come. I watch the progress of the protection malady in the States and in Canada with great interest. I cannot think it will continue very long. Your letters will do something to weaken its hold upon those affected by it.

I am, very respectfully yours,
JOHN BRIGHT.

ON WAR.

In the autumn of 1879, Mr. Alexander H. Urquhart, of Manchester, wrote to Mr. Bright, asking his opinion on war, and particularly whether he would do away with war and armies altogether. Mr. Bright wrote in reply as follows:—

One Ash, Rochdale, August 18, 1879.

DEAR SIR,—I have not time to write fully upon the question. It is one on which men should make up their minds as to their own personal duty. So far men have defended war as if it were a natural condition of things which must always continue. It might be true that war could not always be avoided, and that in some cases it might be justifiable, and yet, granting this, it might be shown that nineteen out of every twenty wars which might have been waged ought to have been avoided, and were criminal in the highest degree. I believe that all our wars since the time and accession of William III. might have been avoided on principles which do not require the absolute condemnation of war in every possible case that may be suggested or imagined. We need not discuss the question as you put it. We shall change the policy and the aspect of our country and of the world, if we leave the demon of war to the cases in which there seems to Christian and rational men no escape from the miseries he inflicts upon mankind. I would advise you not to trouble yourself with the abstract question. The practical question is the one which presses, and when we have settled that, there will remain very little of the mischief to contend about or to get rid of. If you wish to know the best argument against war, I would recommend you to read Jonathan Dymond's "Essays on the Principles of Morality," or his "Essay on War." You may obtain them from Mr. Harris, 5, Bishopsgate Street Without, London.

I am, yours, &c.,
JOHN BRIGHT.

ON THE GAME LAWS.

Written in reply to a letter from Mr. W. A. Sothern of Lowestoft, who had called Mr. Bright's attention to some remarks made upon his conduct as to the Game Laws and Malt Tax by Mr. J. S. Gardiner at a late meeting of the Farmers' Alliance at Ipswich.

One Ash, Rochdale, November 16, 1879.

DEAR SIR,—Mr. Gardiner, who spoke at the Farmers' Alliance meeting, is very ignorant or very unjust in what he said about my conduct on the Game Law question. I never promised the repeal of the Malt Tax or the Game Laws. I undertook to bring the subject of the Game Laws before Parliament, and in the session of 1845 I moved for and obtained a committee to inquire into it. The evidence was laid before Parliament and the public, and I went to the expense of 300*l.* in publishing an abstract of the evidence, in the hope that farmers especially might be made acquainted with it. I am sorry

to say that I discovered that farmers did not
buy books, and my digest of the evidence did
not, I fear, circulate largely among them. It
was prepared by my late friend, Mr. Welford,
who was a good farmer and a good lawyer, and
the case made out in it against the Game Laws
was unanswerable. After this I submitted a
Bill for the removal of the same nuisance to the
House of Commons, but it received no support
from the large party in the House who call
themselves farmers' friends. On other occasions I have spoken against the Game Laws,
and ten years ago, when I was a member of the
late Government, I spoke strongly against them,
and declared my opinion that farmers would
never have their rights in this question until
they were in absolute possession of all the
animals which fed on their farms.

I may tell Mr. Gardiner that I unfortunately
found that farmers dared not or would not
make any combined effort to do themselves
justice; that they still voted for "farmers'
friends," who in Parliament do nothing for
farmers but watch keenly after the interests of
landlords; and I was, therefore, compelled to
abandon a question and a cause in which I
found that I could do no good. I turned my
attention to other questions, leaving Game Law
reform, which means Game Law abolition, to
some time of calamity, when farmers' rights
and the public interest would force themselves
on the notice of Parliament. If that time has
now come, I shall be as willing as I was thirty-
four years ago to offer to Mr. Gardiner and his

friends any help it may be in my power to render them.

I would now advise speakers at meetings of the Farmers' Alliance not to attack their friends, and Mr. Gardiner will do well to inform himself more accurately before he again speaks to a meeting of farmers on the subject of the Game Laws.

I am, very truly yours,
JOHN BRIGHT.

Mr. William Alexander Sothern, Lowestoft.

ON THE STUDY OF POLITICAL QUESTIONS.

Read at the annual meeting of the Hollinwood Liberal Association on the 6th of December, 1879.

One Ash, Rochdale, November 17, 1879.

DEAR SIR,—I thank you for your invitation, although I shall not be able to be present with you on the 6th of December. It is pleasant to hear of your success in the district you represent, and I hope it may increase, and that your strength may grow. If men knew how much the good of their country and their own interests are affected by wise or unwise governments, they would study political questions more, and many evils from which we now suffer might, and would be, removed. I hope your efforts may do something to promote the change of Government and change of policy which the conduct of the present administration has made so needful. I trust you will have a successful meeting, and that the Liberal unity and opinion among you may be largely interested.

Believe me, very truly yours,

JOHN BRIGHT.

ON THE CRIMEAN WAR.

On the 11th of December, 1879, Mr. Sidebottom, M.P., addressed his constituents of the Dukinfield portion of the borough of Stalybridge, and in the course of his remarks, alluding to the Crimean war, with which he charged the Liberal Government of that time, said :—" Mr. Bright went to St. Petersburg as the apostle of peace. The Government hesitated and vacillated, played fast and loose, blew hot and cold, until Russia was encouraged to believe that our ancient spirit was decayed and degenerated, that we should talk for ever, but never fight, till at last we drifted into one of the most dreadful wars of modern times." Mr. Sidebottom also said that Mr. Cobden once uttered these words in the House of Commons :—" I declare before God and this House that in my conscience I believe if the Tory Government had been in power we should have had no Crimean war."

Mr. Bright's attention having been called to these remarks by Mr. W. Summers of Sunnyside, Ashton-under-Lyne, elected member for Stalybridge in 1880, the right hon. gentleman wrote the following reply :—

One Ash, Rochdale, December 13, 1879.

DEAR SIR,—We do not expect the Tory speakers to be accurate.

I was never in St. Petersburg, and had nothing to do with the deputation to which Mr. Sidebottom, I presume, refers.

As to his quotation from Mr. Cobden, I know nothing of it. If the Tory party had been in office and the Liberals in opposition, nobody can say positively what would have happened, but what we know is that the Whig leaders blundered into the war, and the Tory Opposition did their utmost to urge them into it. They incessantly attacked Lord Aberdeen on the ground that he was disposed to submit to Russia.

I am, very truly yours,
JOHN BRIGHT.

ON FAGOT VOTING.

A correspondent of the *Birmingham Daily Post* having called Mr. Bright's attention to a speech delivered by him in 1845 in which, speaking of the Anti-Corn-Law League, he said "they had asked their Free Trade friends in the northern counties to invest some of their property so as to be able to defend their rights and liberties at the hustings," and that accordingly "their friends in Lancashire, Cheshire, and Yorkshire had invested a sum of not less than 250,000*l.* in the purchase of county qualifications," and having asked whether this did not savour of fagot voting, received the following reply:—

One Ash, Rochdale, December 20, 1879.

Sir,—The votes obtained by friends of Free Trade in 1845 were obtained by the real possession of a real property. The fagot votes to which objection is made are created by a deed giving a rent-charge upon a property for which it is understood nothing is paid, and on which nothing is received; the whole thing being on paper or parchment, and no real ownership being created or intended.

I am, respectfully,
JOHN BRIGHT.

ON READING THE BIBLE IN BOARD SCHOOLS.

One of the candidates for election on the West Bromwich School Board in 1880 having asserted that Mr. Bright, among other leading Liberals, was in favour of giving religious instruction in Board Schools, another candidate wrote to Mr. Bright on the subject, and received the following reply:—

House of Commons, February 20, 1880.

Dear Sir,—I must not take any part in your discussions or contests, but my opinion is that if you go beyond the old practice of the British School system of reading a portion of scripture without note or comment, you will find yourselves in great difficulties, without doing anything to promote religion or peace.

I am, yours respectfully,
JOHN BRIGHT.

ON THE TRADE BETWEEN ENGLAND AND THE UNITED STATES.

Written to Mr. Alfred Gray, Secretary of the Agricultural Board of the State of Kansas, acknowledging receipt of a copy of one of Mr. Gray's agricultural reports.

One Ash, Rochdale, January 3, 1880.

DEAR SIR,—I have received the volume you have kindly forwarded to me. It contains much apparently exact and interesting information on agricultural affairs and on land in your State. There is a growing desire here to know more of your progress, and there are signs that emigration is on the increase. There is, too, among both farmers and landowners, a great fear that you will beat them in their own markets. I am inclined to think that the panic will subside, and that if we have good seasons our agriculture will return at least to a moderate prosperity. I hope your world and ours may help each other. We take everything you have to sell freely, without customs duties, except tobacco and spirits, and on these our duties are only for revenue, for we have equal duties on spirits, and we prohibit the growth of tobacco, while you charge with extravagant duties nearly everything you take from us and that we can or could send you. If in commercial matters and in agriculture you could annex the United Kingdom, it would be a great and good thing for both.

Believe me, truly yours,
JOHN BRIGHT.

ON THE BEACONSFIELD GOVERNMENT AND ON COUNTY MEMBERS.

Written to a Nonconformist minister at Torquay, and read at a meeting held in that town in March, 1880, in support of the candidature of Lieutenant-Colonel Sterling, the Liberal candidate for East Devon.

March, 1880.

Dear Sir,—I have received your friendly letter this morning. Sir Stafford, I suspect, will not feel very lively. Your meeting will be in good spirits. The conspiracy at headquarters is exposed and broken up, and every additional Liberal vote will speak more distinctly the general condemnation of the worst Government we have had for more than fifty years. The counties are opening their eyes to the imposture they so long believed in and supported; their "friends," the "farmers' friends," are being found out. The county gentlemen, the county members, are the great obstructive party in the House, and they are the supporters of every form of extravagance the Government may indulge in. I hope in your county the farmers may see something of their true interests. The Liberal party have given freedom and much legislation to the towns. Freedom for the counties can only come from the same source. I hope on Friday next you will have to rejoice over another great victory gained by the Liberal electors of the division of your county.

Yours, very sincerely,
JOHN BRIGHT.

ON THREE-CORNERED CONSTITUENCIES.

Read at the opening of a new Liberal club at Platt Bridge, near Wigan, on the 20th of July, 1880.

Wigan is in the south-west division of Lancashire.

London, July, 1880.

DEAR SIR,—I cannot hope to be present at your meeting; but I may congratulate you on your activity, and upon your resolve to do something to change and improve the representation of your division of our county. Much may be done by labour bestowed on registration and organization, and you have a good field before you. In our division of the county a great change has been made. There is now, I believe, only one Tory member returned from the constituencies of the south-east division, and he is in the humiliating condition of being the minority member. He sits by virtue, not of the goodwill or vote of a majority of the electors of Manchester, but by a contrivance invented to cripple the Parliamentary influence of the great populations and constituencies. His sitting in Parliament is by a direct violation of the ancient principle of the Constitution, which in all past time gave to majorities the right to select and to elect members of the House of Commons. hope you will be able, by the time another general election occurs, to place your division in a position as advantageous and as creditable as that now occupied by the south-east division and by the boroughs within its limits.

I am, yours very truly,
JOHN BRIGHT.

ON BEING ELECTED LORD RECTOR OF GLASGOW UNIVERSITY.

Written to the President of the Glasgow University Liberal Club :—

Stratford-on-Avon, November 22, 1880.

DEAR SIR,—I beg to thank you for your letter informing me of my election to the office of Lord Rector of Glasgow University. I am much indebted to you and your friends for the high favour that has been shown to me, but I cannot, I fear, reciprocate the enthusiasm of which you speak. If I am sensible of the kindness and good opinion of the students, and desire to rejoice in the success of your efforts, I am not less conscious that I have very little claim to the distinguished position in which I am placed. It is fortunate for me that the duties of the office to which you have called me, but to which I did not aspire, are light, and not immediately pressing. During its term I shall hope to have an opportunity of presenting myself before your constituency, and of delivering the address which is expected from me.

I can now only ask you and those by whose support I have been elected to accept my grateful thanks for the confidence they have placed in me.

I am, &c.,
JOHN BRIGHT.

ON MONARCHS, ARISTOCRACY, AND LANDOWNERS.

On the 16th of November, 1880, Mr. Bright delivered a speech at Birmingham, in which, alluding to Lord Beaconsfield's remark that the affairs of the world were conducted by monarchs and statesmen, he said: "I for my share do not learn from history that everything has been wisely done that has been done by monarchs and by statesmen. On the contrary, almost all the greatest crimes of history have been committed, and all the greatest calamities have been brought upon mankind, through the instrumentality of monarchs and of statesmen. I would rather have the judgment of an intelligent and moral people informed as to their interest and their duties."

Mr. Bright then proceeded to comment upon the misgovernment which had characterized the treatment of the Irish people by England, and he condemned the system of land tenure in Ireland, by which the land was kept in the hands of a few proprietors, and the tenants were denied any security for their holdings. Finally he blamed the House of Lords for throwing out Mr. Forster's Compensation for Disturbance

Bill. It was in this speech that occurred the famous sentence, "Force is not a remedy."

The Earl of Carnarvon, who was staying at Madeira, on reading the speech, addressed a long letter to Mr. Bright, in which he defended the institutions of monarchy and the House of Lords, protested against censure being applied to the aristocracy and landowners, and remonstrated with Mr. Bright for having used language which he considered unbecoming in a Minister of the Crown. Lord Carnarvon concluded his letter as follows:—" In conclusion, I will only add that in what I have now said I am not assailing the principle of democracy, or desiring to limit its fair and full scope. Rightly understood, it has its part in our form of government, and the greatest thinkers and statesmen have endeavoured to combine in harmonious proportions the everlasting principles of monarchy, aristocracy, and democracy. My object in this remonstrance is to protest against the public repudiation of two of these principles by one who, by the office which he has undertaken, is bound to be a faithful guardian of the Constitution in its integrity."

Mr. Bright replied to Lord Carnarvon as follows:—

Rochdale, December 25, 1880.

Your letter of the 8th of December, which appeared in the London papers of yesterday morning, reached me last night. You condemn me for attacks on the sovereign, the aristocracy, and the landowners.

I have defended the monarchy; the defence is little needed in this country and in this reign. I have warned the aristocracy of danger I wished them to shun. As to landowners, I have been one of the most prominent supporters of a policy so necessary for the country and so wise for them, that, had it been obstinately resisted, the great landowners of England and Scotland would long ago have been running for their lives, as some Irish landowners are reported to be doing now.

I will not reply at length to your letter; it is enough to acknowledge the receipt of it. I am content to leave my speech and your letter to the judgment of the public.

I am, yours faithfully,
JOHN BRIGHT.

The Right Hon. the Earl of Carnarvon, Madeira.

ON TORY CLERGY.

Written to Mr. G. Pratt, of Southend, Essex.

132, Piccadilly, January 11, 1881.

DEAR SIR,—I thank you for sending me the report of the speeches at the dinner of the Conservative Association. It is sad to witness the recklessness of Tory clergy when they speak at Tory dinners. The ignorance and untruthfulness displayed are amazing and shocking. In their clerical reading they seem never to have met with the passage, "Thou shalt not bear false witness." I do not know what Mr.

Thackeray is in the pulpit, but surely on a platform, as a public speaker, he is an example to be carefully avoided.

I am, very respectfully yours,
JOHN BRIGHT.

ON THE POLICY OF THE GLADSTONE GOVERNMENT IN THE TRANSVAAL, AND ON THE HON. JAMES LOWTHER.

Addressed to Mr. George Howard while a candidate for the representation of East Cumberland, in February, 1881.

February, 1881.

DEAR SIR,—I am sorry to hear that an attempt is being made to injure your cause by a condemnation of the course taken by the Government in the deplorable conflict which has arisen in the Transvaal. This difficulty, as you know, has not come from the conduct of the Government; it is one of the legacies left us by the policy and blunders of our predecessors. I may tell you that the Government is most anxious to restore peace in South Africa, and that efforts are now directed to be made to bring about a cessation of hostilities, and to promote a negotiation for the restoration of peace on terms which there is reason to hope the Transvaal people will be willing to accept.

I see that your opponent is not careful as to what he says on the state of Ireland. He has been Chief Secretary to the Lord-Lieutenant of

Ireland, and a secretary less qualified to show sympathy for the people of the country, or to aid in its pacification, I have not known during my public life, extending over forty years. He considers the great Acts of 1870, the Church Act and the Land Act, one as a measure of spoliation and the other as one of confiscation. If he were now in office I know not to what sad end the present confusion in Ireland might be brought. I hope your electors may consider the policy of the Government, and may compare it with that of the Government they have succeeded, and that your farmers may remember that during last session the attempt to do justice to them in the matter of ground game was bitterly opposed by the party to which your opponent belongs.

I am, yours, &c.,

JOHN BRIGHT.

George Howard, Esq.

ON THE TRANSVAAL PEACE.

An International Address, which was proposed during the presence in this country of Mr. Stuyt, Mr. Zylstra, and Mr. Schmüll, the delegates of the Dutch Transvaal Committee, and which had received numerous signatures in Holland, Germany, Hungary, France, and Italy, was forwarded to Mr. Bright in March, 1881, by Mr. Karl Blind, to whom the right hon. gentleman returned the following reply:—

132, Piccadilly, March 14, 1881.

DEAR SIR,—I thank you for the memorial

you have forwarded to me, and for the friendly letter from yourself on the sad question of the Transvaal difficulty. I hope the prospect is one of peace, and not of further war, and that an arrangement may be made satisfactory to the Transvaal people, and honourable to this country. I scarcely need to assure you that whatever influence I possess is being and will be exerted in favour of peace. The conflict is one in which England can gain nothing, not even military glory, which is the poorest kind of glory, in my view, which men and nations strive for. I hope the time may come when nations will seek and obtain honourable renown by deeds of mercy and justice.

This reply to your letter and the memorial is brief, but, under the circumstances, I feel sure you and your friends will excuse its brevity.

Believe me to be, very sincerely yours,

JOHN BRIGHT.

Karl Blind, Esq.,
3, Winchester Road, South Hampstead, N.W.

ON THE TRANSVAAL PEACE.

Another address with reference to the Transvaal difficulty was presented to Mr. Bright by Mr. Buisson, a French journalist resident in London. The address emanated from a number of leading French Liberals, and was signed by about thirty members of the French Senate, certain deputies and members of the Paris Municipal Council, the French Academy, &c. To this memorial Mr. Bright wrote the following reply:—

London, March 23, 1881.

DEAR SIR,—I was glad to have the opportunity of speaking to you yesterday during your short visit, when you presented to me an address on the subject of the Transvaal war from the eminent French Liberals whose names I find appended to it. They have done me great honour in selecting me as in any manner worthy to be considered a representative of the friends of international justice, peace, and good-will between nations. I accept the address with much pleasure, and I can ask now to be permitted to rejoice with them in the happy settlement of a difficulty and of a conflict which has excited in their minds, as in mine, so deep a grief. I believe the English people will gladly sustain a Government which has restored peace by a course at once magnanimous and just, and I feel entire confidence that its policy will be approved in all foreign countries by "friends of international justice, peace, and good-will between nations." I ask you to convey to the eminent Frenchmen who have signed the address my warm thanks for the great compliment they have paid me.

I am, &c., &c.,
JOHN BRIGHT.

M. Buisson, Saville Club.

ON FREE TRADE.

MR. HERMON'S PROTECTIVE PROPOSALS.

On Tuesday, the 15th of March, 1881, Mr. Hermon, member for Preston, delivered a speech in the Area of the Corn Exchange of that town, in which he advocated a return to Protection. A Preston gentleman sent a copy of the speech to Mr. Bright, and received the following reply:—

132, Piccadilly, March 18, 1881.

DEAR SIR,—I have read Mr. Hermon's speech to which you refer me. I am not amazed at the ignorance it displays, or its misrepresentation of facts. He does not tell how he proposes to protect by new tariff duties the factory-workers or the mill-workers of Preston. His constituents are exporters of cotton goods to all quarters of the globe; they compete with all foreign manufacturers in all foreign markets. How can he protect them by re-imposing duties on the import of cotton goods, which they so largely export?

Does he intend to give a bounty out of the general taxes on all goods they export, as he says "he would give a bonus on every acre of land that a farmer of this country chooses to till and crop with corn"?

He proposes to give out of the taxes a bonus, how much he does not say, but so much per acre on all land growing corn, doubtless to enable the farmers to pay a higher rent than the land is worth, and to limit our supplies of corn from the United States, Canada, and other countries!

Mr. Hermon did not tell his audience that between the harvests of 1879 and 1880, that is in the year after the bad harvest of 1879, *out of every four loaves of bread eaten by the people of the*

United Kingdom three loaves came from abroad, and that in no other year in his lifetime or in mine have our people been fed so cheaply or on bread of such excellent quality.

What must Mr. Hermon think of the mental condition of his constituents when he ventured to utter to them the confused nonsense of his speech, and what must every intelligent elector of your town think of a representative in Parliament who has not advanced a step beyond the benighted ignorance of forty years ago?

If you wish to see this question of Free Trade and our trade well discussed, I advise you to pay sixpence for the little book published by Messrs. Cassell, Petter, and Galpin, of London, entitled "Free Trade and English Commerce," written by Mr. Mongredin. I wish every elector in Preston could have it and read it, and I may recommend it to Mr. Hermon as a book out of which he may begin to learn something of correct facts and sound arguments on the question of Free Trade, and on the results of our policy as adopted by Sir Robert Peel and Mr. Gladstone since the year 1841. I have not time to write you at greater length. The little book I have mentioned will tell you the truth on the facts and results of our Free-Trade policy.

I am, very truly yours,
JOHN BRIGHT.

ON FREE TRADE.

THE FRENCH AND AMERICAN TARIFFS.

In March, 1881, Mr. Ephraim Rigg, of Drigh-

lington, near Leeds, addressed to Mr. Bright a
few questions on the subject of Free Trade
versus Foreign Tariffs, and received the following reply :—

London, March 29, 1881.

DEAR SIR,—I have not time to answer your
letters at length. If you will read the little
book to which I referred in my letter on the
speech of the Member for Preston, you may
learn much from it—more than I can tell you
in any letter I can write.

We all regret that France, the United States
of America, and other countries continue to
maintain their high tariffs; it is, we believe, a
misfortune to them and injurious to us; but
we can only legislate for our own country and
not for them. If you think that, *not being able
to sell freely*, we should mend ourselves by
giving up the power to buy freely, I must leave
you to that opinion, only expressing my wonder
at it. But you will perhaps say that we can
force other nations to reduce their tariffs if we
impose a tariff against them. You forget probably that we have tried this in past times, and
that it has wholly failed. Sir Robert Peel
taught this nearly forty years ago, and he
believed, as I believe, that the best defence we
can have against the evils of foreign tariffs is
to have no tariff of our own.

You speak of France. The French Senate is
in favour of more protection. The Chamber of
Deputies is disposed to Free Trade and a more
liberal policy. The Free Trade party in France
is more powerful than in past times, and it is

not certain that the proposed treaty will be less favourable to trade between the two countries. As to America, how will you compel its Government to reduce their tariff? By placing duties on American exports to England? If so, on what exports? On cotton for the mills of Lancashire, or on corn for the food of all our people? The American Protective Tariff makes it difficult or impossible for Americans to become great exporters of manufactures. If you fight them at the Custom Houses, you can only assail them by duties on cotton or on corn, and this surely will not benefit Lancashire or the West Riding. When the debt of the United States is much reduced, when their revenue is in excess of their wants, then their tariff will be reformed and their import duties will be reduced.

If you doubt what Free Trade has done for England, go back to your histories, and read what was the condition of our working men and their families for the first forty years of this century, when everything was supposed to be protected, and compare it with what it is now.

For some years past manufacturers and farmers have suffered greatly, and workmen have suffered much, but they have not seen one-tenth of the part of the distress which afflicted them during the forty years of the high duties from 1800 to 1840. The country suffers now, not from our purified tariff, and not wholly, or in chief part, from foreign tariffs. It suffers from want of sunshine—from the short harvests of several years; and till we have again good harvests we must suffer and endure. Parliament cannot give sun and heat for our fields, and it will be no compensation to re-impose import duties and to deny us the right to purchase freely what we need from foreign nations.

I am, very respectfully yours,

JOHN BRIGHT.

Mr. E. Rigg Drighlington, near Leeds.

ON RECIPROCITY.

A gentleman from Bradford, having written to Mr. Bright on the question of Reciprocity as it affected that town, received the following reply:—

One Ash, Rochdale, April 15, 1881.

SIR,—I cannot reply at length to letters like yours. Only last week, I think, a letter from me on the subject on which you have written was published in your newspapers. I can only refer to it.

The home trade is bad mainly or entirely because our harvests have been bad for several years. I believe the agricultural classes—owners and occupiers of land in the three kingdoms—have lost more than 150,000,000l. sterling through the great deficiency of our harvests. This great loss must inevitably and seriously depress all our other industries. It is not Bradford alone that has suffered, the whole cotton trade of Lancashire has suffered greatly, and much of all this is to be attributed to the condition of our great farming interest, and this again to the unfavourable seasons of several recent years.

The remedy will come with more sunshine and better yield from the land; without this it cannot come. To imagine that your suffering springs now from hostile tariffs is absurd, because you have had great prosperity with the same tariffs; but to suppose your case will be improved by refusing to buy what you want from foreigners, to punish them for not buying freely from you, seems to me an idea and a scheme only worthy of the inmates of a lunatic asylum.

To return to protection, under the name of reciprocity, is to confess to the protectionists abroad that we have been wrong and that they are right, and protection will henceforth be the justified policy of all nations. If protection is needful and good, surely at this moment it is needful for our farming class, and yet who dares to propose another sliding-scale or a fixed duty on the import of foreign corn? Bradford must be watchful and patient, to look out for new markets or new products for her looms, and to endure a temporary reverse, to be followed, I trust, at no remote period, with a revival of prosperity. Bradford has had a good innings since 1860; she gained more than other towns from Mr. Cobden's treaty with France. Great success and great expansion of business are followed by depression, to be followed, I hope and believe, by a return to a fair measure of prosperity. But our recovery depends more on the produce of our harvests than on foreign tariffs, or on the changes in the fashion of dress to which you refer.

I am, respectfully yours,
JOHN BRIGHT.

Mr. W. G. Lord, 1, Norfolk Street, Bradford.

ON LIBERAL RULE.

Read at a Liberal meeting, held at Newtown, Montgomeryshire, on the 22nd of April, 1881.

April, 1881.

DEAR MR. HANBURY TRACY,—If I were in your neighbourhood, I should be glad to go with you to meet the members of your workingmen's club at Newtown. I hope you may find the club well sustained and prosperous. Wales has done much for the Liberal cause, and England and Scotland and I hope Ireland too have reason to be grateful to the intelligent constituencies of the principality.

When I speak of the Liberal cause, I mean the cause which is represented by increasing freedom at home, and by justice, honourable dealing, and peace abroad. In the triumph of this cause no portion of the people have a greater interest than that which is most directly connected with your club. I hope your members will make themselves acquainted with the history of our country during the last two centuries, and especially since the accession of George the Third.

In this last period of twenty years they may trace the fruits of the two systems of Government, the Tory and the Liberal. The Liberal Government has made some blunders, but their policy and career have been marked by great and wise concessions, and by many services to the people. The possession of power by the Liberal party since the passing of the Reform Bill of 1832 has made a beneficent revolution in the nation, and there is yet great work for the party to do.

I hope your Welsh constituencies will attend carefully to their registration of voters, and that they will find themselves at the next general election as powerful as they showed themselves last year.

With every good wish for the friends you are about to meet,

I am, very sincerely yours,
JOHN BRIGHT.

To Hon. H. S. A. Hanbury Tracy, M.P.

ON THE FRENCH TREATY.

Written to the Secretary of the National Trades' Defence League in reference to a resolution passed at a meeting in Birmingham on the 3rd of August, 1881, protesting against the conclusion of any treaty of commerce with France which did not materially reduce the high duties hitherto levied by France upon British manufactures, and which did not also provide for England's withdrawal from such treaty upon giving twelve months' notice to do so.

House of Commons, August 10, 1881.

DEAR SIR,—The French treaty, as a matter

of course, if negotiated at all, will be liable to termination by either of the parties to it on giving due notice to the other party. As to our having a treaty at all or not, I hope you will allow the Government to do what is best in the matter. We cannot expect to deal with the French tariff as if it was our own. Each Government has its own people and interest to care for, and all that can be done is what the two Governments can agree upon. We may fail in doing anything good, but we shall do our best, and may possibly succeed. I hope if this negotiation fails, they who ask to have no treaty except such a one as is impossible will not turn round upon the Governments and blame them for not accepting an arrangement which might have been of great value to some branches of our varied industry. I think you may trust the Government to do what, under the circumstances of the case, is best for the country.

I am, respectfully yours,
JOHN BRIGHT.

THE IRISH LAND BILL OF 1881.

Written to the Secretary of the Kilrea Tenant-Farmers' Association.

One Ash, Rochdale, August 19, 1881.

DEAR SIR,—I have just received a copy of the resolutions passed by the tenant farmers of the Kilrea district on the subject of the Land Bill. I write to thank you and them for your friendly expressions towards myself. I believe the Bill to be a great and just measure, and that it ought to give great satisfaction to the Irish people. During Mr. Gladstone's administration the great questions of the Irish Church and Irish land have been, I hope, finally disposed of. The education question is no longer one of difficulty or of heated conflict. The Imperial Parliament has endeavoured to be liberal and just, it remains now with your people, by increased industry and by a regard to public order, to make Ireland not less prosperous and not less tranquil than England and Scotland now are.

With every good wish for you and your country,

I am, very truly yours,
JOHN BRIGHT.

ON RECIPROCITY.

Mr. Thomas Barrow, of Kegworth, near Derby, who was the first traveller under a well-known carpet firm, under the Cobden treaty in France, wrote to Mr. Bright, in September, 1881, stating his experience in French trade—namely, that as soon as the French adopted steam-power for their manufactures we should not be able to compete with them, their labour being obtainable at such a low rate. He therefore asked Mr. Bright whether he did not consider in the case of France that we should adopt a system of reciprocity.

Mr. Bright replied as follows:—

One Ash, Rochdale, September 2, 1881.

SIR,—I do not know what you mean by a system of reciprocity; if you mean that we are only to trade freely without duties at our ports with nations who will do the same with us, then I am against reciprocity as a stupid and impossible proposition.

If you mean that we are to put on duties at our ports with the notion that we shall compel other nations to take off their duties, then I am against it, from the conviction that such a plan must fail, as it has done in all past time. For thirty years before our Free-Trade times this plan was made use of and offered to foreign ports, and it entirely failed, as it would fail if again offered.

If you begin to put on duties at our ports, the protectionists of all other nations would say we were adopting their policy and admitting that our Free-Trade policy was unsound, as we had repented and begun to adopt theirs.

The true course for England is to open her ports as widely and completely as possible, whatsoever may be the tariffs of other countries.

I am, respectfully yours,
JOHN BRIGHT.

Mr. T. Barrow, Kegworth, Derby.

ON FREE TRADE.

Written to a gentleman at Newport, Isle of

Wight, in reply to questions on the subject of protective duties.

One Ash, Rochdale, November 20, 1881.

DEAR SIR,—If you keep a particular trade employed at the cost of taxing persons engaged in other trades, what is it but a system of relief, or like feeding a dog with its own tail? Our people are not turned out of work by foreign imports. How do we employ and feed ten millions increased population since the Free Trade era—or since 1840? They are far better employed and paid and fed now than they were forty years ago, when they were ten millions less in number. The present state of things is one of steady and general improvement. Poor-rates are decreasing everywhere. All these ideas are delusions and falsehoods.

Yours truly,
JOHN BRIGHT.

[Read Mr. Medley's "Reciprocity Craze," published by Cassell, Petter, and Galpin, for facts.]

ON COMPLETING HIS SEVENTIETH YEAR.

Written to the Chairman of the Manchester Liberal Association, in reply to an address presented by the Association on the occasion of Mr. Bright's 70th birthday.

Rochdale, December 13, 1881.

DEAR MR. BEITH,—I thank you for your kind letter, with which you send me the address of the Manchester Liberal Association, presented to me on the occasion of my birthday. I will ask you to convey to your Committee and to your members my warm thanks for the kindness with which they have greeted me, and for the good wishes they express for me. It is a great consolation to me to know that I have had, in my public career, the approval of so many of my countrymen who are qualified to form a just opinion on the great questions which affect the interests of the State. I hope, by our combined efforts, we have been able to do some good and to increase the sum of comfort and happiness among our people. To have been permitted to partake with you in these efforts, and in the labours of many years, is a large compensation for the burden which public life has laid upon me.

Believe me, yours very sincerely,
JOHN BRIGHT.

John Alexander Beith, Esq., Manchester.

ON NATIONAL EXPENDITURE.

Written in reply to Mr. Colborne, a member of the Monmouthshire Chamber of Agriculture, on the subject of national expenditure.

February, 1882.

DEAR SIR,—I must refer you to reports of my speeches for what I have said on the subject of expenditure. Some are in newspapers, perhaps, and some are in the published volumes of my speeches. As to the complaints of

Chambers of Agriculture about public expenditure, I can only say that they are just enough; but I would remind you and them that every increase of expenditure during the nearly forty years I have been in Parliament has been supported by the representatives of the farmers. County members are the most eager supporters of whatever extravagance our administration has been guilty of. I shall be very glad if now they take a turn, but I observe them more willing to throw the burden on to some other shoulders than to insist that the burden shall be lessened.

Yours truly,
JOHN BRIGHT.

ON SLAVERY IN THE UNITED STATES.

Written to Mr. John Lobb, the editor of the "Life and Times of Frederick Douglass," a history of an American slave's experience, and prefixed to the work.

132, Piccadilly, London,
March 8, 1882.

DEAR SIR,—I am glad to hear that you are about to publish an English edition of the "Life and Times of Frederick Douglass," in his youth a slave in the State of Maryland, now holding an honourable office in the district of Columbia, in the United States of America. I have read the book with great interest. It shows what may be done and has been done by a man born under the most adverse circumstances—done not for himself alone, but for his race and for his country. It shows also how a great nation persisting in a great crime cannot escape the penalty inseparable from crime. History has probably no more striking example of the manner in which an offence of the highest guilt may be followed by the most terrible punishment than is to be found in the events which make the history of the United States from the year 1860 to the year 1865. The book which you are about to offer to English readers is one which will stimulate the individual to noble effort and to virtue, whilst it will act as a lesson and a warning to every nation whose policy is based upon injustice and wrong.

I hope it may find its way into many thousands of English homes.

I am, with great respect, yours sincerely,
JOHN BRIGHT.
To Mr. John Lobb.

ON THE SALVATION ARMY.

Written to Mrs. Booth in reference to the opposition to which the Salvation Army was then exposed. In the case alluded to in the letter a sentence of one month's imprisonment with hard labour had been passed at the petty sessions at Whitchurch, on four members of the Salvation Army for an assault on the police, who attempted to prevent their forming a procession. The chairman admitted that the assault was only a technical one, and on the case being submitted to Lord Chief Justice Coleridge, he stated that "hard labour was ignominious, and that the defendants might be religious enthusiasts, but such sentences were not to be tolerated for one moment." Sir W. Harcourt said he agreed very much with both of these opinions, and that he was happy to think that the sentence was under review by the Lord Chief Justice.

House of Commons, May 3, 1882.

DEAR MADAM,—I gave your letter to Sir W. Harcourt. He had already given his opinion in the House of Commons, which will be, to some extent, satisfactory to you. I hope the language of Lord Coleridge and the Home Secretary will have some effect on the foolish and unjust magistrates, to whom, in some districts, the administration of the law is unfortunately committed. I suspect your good work will not suffer materially from the ill-treatment you are meeting with. The people who mob you would, doubtless, have mobbed the Apostles. Your faith and patience will prevail.

I am, with great respect and sympathy, yours sincerely,

JOHN BRIGHT.

To Mrs. Booth, 101, Queen Victoria Street, London.

ON THE WAR IN EGYPT.

In September, 1882, the Rev. Thomas Rippon, of Warrington, in a letter to Mr. Bright, discussed the question of war in the abstract, holding that "peace at any price" was an untenable position, and that the Egyptian war seemed a righteous one from that stand-point. He reminded Mr. Bright of the prevailing opinion of many of his countrymen that his was a policy of "peace at any price," without reserve, and that it was that alone which led him to give up office. He also called his attention to a letter which appeared in the previous week's *Spectator*, in which the writer said "Mr. Bright gave up office and association with an admired leader, solely because he believed the war to be a departure from national morality, and therefore from the principles of the Liberal party;" together with the editor's note thereon, that "Mr. Bright did not oppose the Egyptian war in particular, but all wars."

Mr. Bright replied to the letter as follows:—

Cassencary, Creetown, N.B.,
September 25, 1882.

DEAR SIR,—The *Spectator* and other supporters of this war answer me by saying that I oppose the war because I condemn all war. The same thing was said during the Crimean war.

I have not opposed any war on the ground that all war is unlawful and immoral. I have never expressed such an opinion. I have discussed these questions of war, Chinese, Crimean, Afghan, Zulu, Egyptian, on grounds common to and admitted by all thoughtful men, and have condemned them with arguments which I believe have never been answered.

I will not discuss the abstract question. I

shall be content when we reach the point at which all Christian men will condemn war when it is unnecessary, unjust, and leading to no useful or good result. We are far from that point now, but we make some way towards it.

But of this war I may say this, that it has no better justification than other wars which have gone before it, and that doubtless when the blood is shed, and the cost paid, and the results seen and weighed, we shall be generally of that opinion.

Perhaps the bondholders, and those who have made money by it, and those who have got promotion and titles and pensions, will defend it, but thoughtful and Christian men will condemn it.

I am, &c.,
JOHN BRIGHT.

Rev. Thomas Rippon, Warrington.

ON THE RULES OF PROCEDURE.

Written in reply to a resolution passed by the Birmingham Trades Council in favour of the resolutions for the reform of the Procedure of the House of Commons. These resolutions were passed in the autumn session which was held in 1882.

One Ash, Rochdale, October 19, 1882.

DEAR SIR,—I thank you for sending me a copy of the resolution of your Trades Council on the subject of the improvement of Parliamentary Procedure. I hope the propositions about to be submitted by the Government will be adopted by the House of Commons. In my opinion the only fault to be found in them is that they are not sufficiently stringent to be an effectual remedy for the evil they are intended to meet. They merit, however, the hearty support of all who wish the House to be able to do the work for which it is elected and for which it exists.

I am, very truly yours,
JOHN BRIGHT.

ON COMPLETING HIS SEVENTY-FIRST YEAR.

On the 16th of November, 1882, Mr. Bright completed his seventy-first year, and on the occasion the overlookers of the large manufacturing works at Rochdale, owned by Messrs. John Bright and Brothers, sent the right hon. gentleman an address of congratulation. The following is a copy of Mr. Bright's reply :—

132, Piccadilly, London,
November 21, 1882.

DEAR SIR,—Your letter, so unexpected, but so welcome, I have received with much pleasure. I am grateful to you for your good wishes, and for the friendly feelings you express towards me. May I ask you to tell my friends on whose behalf you have written that it is very pleasant for me to know that you and they observe the course I take in connection with public affairs, and that my conduct has secured your approval.

I thank you and them for the kind remembrance in which you hold me.

I am, very sincerely yours,
JOHN BRIGHT.

Mr. Thomas Waller, Field House Mill, Rochdale.

ON AN INVITATION BEING SENT MR. BRIGHT TO VISIT AMERICA.

At the beginning of 1883 Mr. Bright received from Mr. Evarts a resolution unanimously adopted by the Union League Club of New York, inviting the right hon. gentleman to visit the United States as the guest of the club, which was to celebrate its twentieth anniversary on the 6th of February in that year. Mr. Evarts in his letter, after referring to Mr. Bright's support of the Northern cause during the civil war, said :—" The Union League Club has always counted among the important political aids to the support of the authority of our Government, under the stress through which it passed, the firm, unflinching, and impregnable attitude which you and your and our great friend, Mr. Cobden, opposed to the great current of commercial, social, and political interest and opinion which, both in England and on the Continent, set so strongly against the success of the loyal power of the country in dealing with so powerful a revolt. We have never attempted to measure the extent of our obligations to you, nor to calculate the misfortune to our cause had it missed the support of so great a defender.

"These sentiments of the Union League Club are shared by the great body of the sober and thinking people of this country, and the hospitality which we proffer you will be but one form of the general acclaim which your presence in the United States will call forth .... In asking you to be our guest from the time you take the sea to make this desired visit through the whole of your travel in our country, and until you again reach your home, we can promise you that every eye and every heart of all our countrymen will greet you with its blessing, and that, beyond this, our people will encroach as little upon the quiet and freedom which you may think suitable to your health and enjoyment, during your stay with us, as you may desire."

Mr. Bright replied as follows:—

Rochdale, January 16, 1883.

MY DEAR MR. EVARTS,—I have received your kind letter of the 16th of December, along with a letter signed by yourself as President of the Union League Club of New York, and on behalf of the members of the club, inviting me to visit the United States, and to be present on the 6th of February next at the celebration of the anniversary of the foundation of the club in the year 1863.

The receipt of these letters and this invitation has caused me a very mixed feeling. I am pleased to think, and indeed to know, that I have many friends in your country who remember with kind feelings towards me the part I took in the discussions in England at the great crisis in your history, when the unity of your great Republic and your free Government seemed for a time to be in peril.

But if I am glad to have so many friends amongst you, I am grieved that the time has never come when I could visit a country and a people in whose greatness and welfare I have always felt the strongest interest. And now, when you send me the most friendly invitation the obstacles in my way are not to be overcome.

Your celebration is fixed for the 6th of February. Besides the ordinary duties of a member of Parliament, I have special engagements for the spring—for March and May—which I cannot escape from or postpone. It is quite impossible, therefore, for me to accept your invitation for the coming month, and I cannot hope to take part in the interesting proceedings to which you have invited me.

But I must say something more. I never liked the sea, and my once strong appetite for travel has subsided, and I cannot but feel that the friendly welcome promised me on your side of the Atlantic would force me into a publicity from which I shrink.

What can I say, then, in reply to letters so complimentary, and yet, I cannot doubt, so friendly and sincere? That I am deeply grateful to you and to your and my friends on whose behalf you have written, and that I regret with a feeling not less strong that I am not able to accept the kind invitation you have sent me, and the most kind welcome you have offered and promised me. I write with difficulty; but you will understand how hard it is to make a fitting, when an unfavourable, reply to such letters as you and your friends have addressed to me. You will forgive me if I cannot come. I can never forget your great kindness and the honour you have conferred upon me.

Believe me always, very sincerely yours,
JOHN BRIGHT.

ON THE OATHS QUESTION.

Read at a meeting of the Hebden Bridge Parliamentary Debating Society in February, 1883, in a debate on the question of permitting members of Parliament to make an affirmation instead of taking the oath.

One Ash, Rochdale, February 14, 1883.

DEAR SIR,—On the question of oaths, probably there is nothing in the New Testament more especially condemned and forbidden than oaths. To those who do not care about the New Testament this fact will be of no weight.

The practice of swearing to the truth of anything makes two kinds of truth or truthfulness. If oaths are of any avail, by so much as they make truth more certain, by so much they lessen the value of an ordinary statement, and diminish the probability of its truth.

If ignorant persons are not sworn, they think they may tell lies with impunity, and their lying is made to a large extent blameless in their eyes.

I think oaths and oath-taking have done more than any other thing to impair and destroy a regard for truth. If you wish to see the question treated more at large, you will find it in an admirable book, "Dymond's Essays on Morality," which you may obtain from any bookseller, or from Mr. Harris, 5, Bishopsgate Street, London.

I am, respectfully yours,
JOHN BRIGHT.

Mr. W. Pickles, Royd Terrace, Hebden Bridge.

ON THE INCOME TAX.

Mr. Peter Lee, a Rochdale tradesman, wrote a long letter to Mr. Bright in April, 1883, complaining of the harsh operation of the income tax on the middle classes, including tradesmen and others engaged in commercial pursuits, "who are expected to maintain a respectable appearance out of incomes ranging from 100*l.* to 200*l.* a year." Mr. Lee submitted that there should be always a disposition to reward merit, whereas the income tax operated in the opposite direction, "grinding energy at every turn, and claiming nothing from indolence."

Mr. Bright replied as follows:—

132, Piccadilly, April 6, 1883.

DEAR SIR,—There are many cases like yours. The income tax is very unjust; but our foreign policy, so stupid and so often wicked, and so costly, makes it necessary. I preach against the policy, and am much condemned by public writers. What can I do more? I agree with much that you say, but I have no means of helping you. I am, respectfully yours,

JOHN BRIGHT.

Mr. Peter Lee, Church Stiles, Rochdale.

ON THE MARRIAGE LAWS.

Written in reply to the Rev. Alfred R. Tucker, of Bristol, who wrote to ask an explanation of Mr. Bright concerning a passage in his speech at a meeting of the Liberation Society at the Metropolitan Tabernacle, on Wednesday, May 2nd, 1883. The following is the passage in question:—" A handful of ecclesiastics . . . condemn thousands of families to unhappiness during their lifetime, and condemn thousands of children who are wholly guiltless, *as I believe their parents are guiltless.*"

Mr. Tucker asked that " for morality's sake " Mr. Bright would give an explanation of the words italicized.

Mr. Bright replied as follows:—

132, Piccadilly, London,
May 7, 1883.

SIR,—I spoke of those who are married, but whose marriage is by the existing law not legal in this country. These marriages are legal in Canada and in the Australian Colonies, and hence a man may have a legal wife in the Colonies and another legal wife in England. He may bring his Canadian legal wife to England, where, when she touches our shores, she is not a legal wife, and where her children born here are not legitimate. If you can justify this, I will not argue with you. Excuse me if I do not discuss the main question with you. It is asserted, I believe truly, that the Queen is in favour of the change of law. It is known that the Prince of Wales is so.

In the Lords I learn there is a majority in favour of the change; last year the Bishops prevented it. In the Commons a majority of 150 or more support the change. When it becomes law your Church, Bishops and Clergy, will have to support it, which I doubt not they will do without much difficulty.

I only regret they do not see the light before it is forced upon them. When I speak of a handful of ecclesiastics I refer to the members of Convocation who have been discussing this question.

Pray excuse this hurried note.

I am, very truly yours,

JOHN BRIGHT.

To Rev. Alfred R. Tucker, The Paragon, Clifton, Bristol.

ON THE GOVERNMENT OF INDIA.

Written to Major Evans Bell, who was about to proceed to the United States on a lecturing tour.

One Ash, Rochdale, August 25, 1883.

DEAR MAJOR BELL,—I am always glad to hear that Englishmen are going to the States, and that Americans are coming here. The more we know of each other the better for both. I doubt if India is a subject which Americans will find or think very interesting; but if you can make it so, they will learn something on a great question, which, as it concerns 250,000,000 of the world's population, must now and in future, for an intelligent people like our American brethren, have a great and growing interest. You are supposed to judge somewhat harshly of our Indian Government. In describing its course I do not doubt you will give it credit where credit is due, and that you will point out how much the people of England are disposed, so far as they are concerned, to govern wisely the vast population conquered by their fathers. The task of the wise government of so vast an empire may be an impossible one—I often fear it is so—we may fail in our efforts, but, whether we fail or succeed, let us do our best to compensate for the wrong of the past and the present by conferring on the Indian people whatever good it is in our power to give them. Perhaps when the United States are wise enough to abolish what they call protection—that is, protection of a class or classes at the expense of the nation—they may find a market in India, from which now their costly system shuts them out. I hope you may have a pleasant voyage out and home, and that your excursion to the States may be in every way satisfactory to you.

I am, very truly yours,
JOHN BRIGHT,

ON THE WORK OF LUTHER.

Mr. S. Lloyd, of The Farm, Sparkbrook, having compiled a small volume on the work of

Luther in the Reformation, as a remembrance of Luther on the fourth centenary of his birth, forwarded a copy to Mr. Bright, and received the following letter in reply :—

One Ash, Rochdale, September 3, 1883.

DEAR SIR,—I have read your little book on "Luther" with interest and with pleasure. I hope it may have a wide circulation. Every conflict does not need a Luther: our battles are not so fierce, and the strength and passion of the great reformer are scarcely called for in our time. Our triumphs are not after battles with "confused noise and garments rolled in blood;" they come of discussion and gradual change of opinion, and not of great catastrophes—which is a thing to be thankful for. I hope, though we may not have Luthers, we may have teachers whose voice or pen may reach all corners of the land, and guide our people to a higher moral standard. There is a growth—we may wish it were more rapid—but must learn to have and to exercise more patience in this as in other things.

I thank you for sending me your little book, and am, very sincerely yours,

JOHN BRIGHT.

THE FUTURE OF IRELAND.

Written to Mr. Barry O'Brien in reference to his work, "Fifty Years of Concession to Ireland," published in 1883.

One Ash, Rochdale, October 4, 1883.

Dear Sir,—The handsome volume you have sent me reached me last evening. I occupied a portion of the evening in reading it. I am sure I shall find much valuable matter in it, and I wish it could be extensively read in England and in Ireland. Ireland needs to be informed as well and as much as England; but while England is willing to learn, and is now well disposed, a large portion of Ireland is not willing to learn, and has put itself into the hands of men whose purpose is that it shall only learn what is hostile to England, and, as I think, must be injurious to itself.

As to the future, I do not take so gloomy a view as many writers do. I believe in just measures, and in their effect, and in time and patience, and I am ready to hope, and even to believe, that within a reasonable period we shall see a change for the better in Irish affairs. If men will read your book of the "Fifty Years" they will know more about Ireland and may make more allowance for the present unhappy state of the relations between her and the more powerful island. I thank you for your kindness in sending me your book. I hope it will be extensively read and extensively useful.

I am, very truly yours,
John Bright.

ON ELECTION "FADS."

A member of Parliament, in an address to his constituents, said that he desired to see in connection with the County Franchise Bill, a plan whereby a moderate proportion of members of the House—say, 60 out of 600—should be chosen, not by the constituents, but by the members already elected in the usual way. Thus, every ten members of any party could, as it were, appoint a member, the object of this plan being to secure the admission to the House of able men, who, through weakness of voice or any other personal reason, cannot make the customary appeal to a constituency. This project was brought under the notice of Mr. Bright, who wrote as follows:—

One Ash, Rochdale, October 8, 1883.

SIR,—I can give you no favourable opinion of the plan you refer to. It is wholly opposed to the spirit and principles of our Constitution, and offers no advantage to compensate for this. As to admitting men into Parliament, whom electors will not elect, or whose condition of health or voice will not allow them to undertake an appeal to a constituency—the proposition seems to me not a little ludicrous. Men feeble in health and men not able or willing to go through the ordeal of an appeal to a constituency, may take other means of serving the public—the Parliamentary path is not their path—and to open a new gate for those incapable of making use of the ancient and constitutional road, is a proposition not seriously to be regarded. Parliament has already an abundant supply of clever men—men who can both think and talk. We need no new plan of admitting feeble folk—feeble in body and in voice—and in the powers and qualities which recommend men to the notice and confidence of electors. I advise you to keep to the old ways—for the "fads," minority clauses, and new modes of making a Parliament, all tend to mischief; they show mistrust of the people, and they are mainly intended to weaken the popular voice. I am for none of these things.

I am, respectfully yours,
JOHN BRIGHT.

ON ELECTION "FADS."

MR. HARE'S SCHEME.

The remarks made by Mr. Bright in the previous letter induced an inquiry as to whether he included Mr. Hare's scheme in his general condemnation of "'fads,' minority clauses, and new modes of making a Parliament." To this inquiry Mr. Bright replied as follows:—

One Ash, Rochdale, October 16, 1883.

DEAR SIR,—I think Mr. Hare's plan more of a "fad" than any other yet submitted to the public, and it has this disadvantage—that scarcely any one can understand it. It aims at making Parliament an exact photograph of every phase of public opinion, and under it there is no fancy or folly which might not, and probably would not, have its representative in the House. Parliament would be broken up into busy cliques, led by the political lunatics who would have entrance within its walls. My advice is, keep to the old ways—they are the safest, and the "wayfaring man, though a fool" (in some sense) "shall not err therein." I have known several or a few of Mr. Hare's supporters; but not one of them has seemed to me to possess the common sense which is as useful and necessary for legislation and government as in the ordinary pursuits of life. I am in favour of the Constitution which has come down from our forefathers, with such amendments as circumstances and our experience seem to warrant. I think they would have looked on Mr. Hare's scheme with mingled amazement and ridicule. You have asked my opinion, and I have given it. I do not seek the protection which its friends claim for the patent constitution of Mr. Hare.

I am, very respectfully,
JOHN BRIGHT.

ON PROTECTION IN YOUNG COUNTRIES.

Written in reply to a correspondent who had asked Mr. Bright's opinion as to a policy of protection in young countries.

Llandudno, N. Wales, November 30, 1883.

DEAR SIR,—I have but a short answer to your letter of the 17th of October.

If you impose duties on foreign manufactures, you tax all who consume them. With this tax you hope to induce your own neighbours to begin to manufacture what they had hitherto received from abroad. You succeed in this object to some, and perhaps to a considerable, extent. During this process you create and build up a new industry, which, the larger it becomes, becomes more exacting, and insists on a continuance of, even on an increase of the protecting duties under which it has been created. The system soon becomes one which taxes a multitude for the profit of a few, and the few by combination soon become so powerful that the multitude is more and more burdened, and the evil and unjust system is confirmed. Two results follow: If you have produce to export, the demand for it is lessened, for if you put obstacles in the way of your purchasing, you put them also in the way of your selling, and in the course of time your protected industries are in trouble, for they, forced into an unnatural activity, produce more than you can consume, your home market becomes glutted, and you have no foreign market to relieve it.

A protected industry is confined to its own market—its productions are necessarily so costly that it cannot relieve itself by exportation, for in foreign markets it cannot compete with other non-protecting nations. If your Government offered some definite sum of money to establish a certain manufacture as an example or encouragement to others, the evil would be small, and could be measured, and no claim or demand would be created for a general system of protection, and the public might gain or suffer only a certain and moderate loss in the experiment. This might be done in a given case, without harm, and without the departure from any sound principle.

If I were one of your community, I should steadfastly resist the introduction of any system of tariff protection—it is evil in principle, and an evil which tends to grow, and which in time, by combination, defies the efforts of honest men to abolish it.

I would trust to time and to individual effort to open up new industries, and I should feel that in doing so I was only doing what, in the end, was most likely to do good to the community in which I was living. Your colony, from all I can learn of it, is more prosperous than Victoria. You are on a safe basis. Free Trade, or a low tariff, only for revenue, is the true policy, and will last longest. Any departure from it is evil, and tends at once to breed an interest hostile to the interest of the whole community. The experience of this country ought to convince all our colonies of the wisdom of low tariff or no tariff; but it does not, for men are selfish and men are ignorant, and the selfish act upon the ignorant and bewilder them.

There is nothing in public affairs that tends more to make men dishonest than the system of protection. It was so in this country before our Free Trade era; it is so now in the United States.

There is no meanness to which those who gain by tariff obstructions to trade will not stoop to continue a system by which they profit at the expense of the consuming public.

The efforts of all honest men should be directed to prevent the beginning of such a mischief, and to destroy it where unhappily it has been permitted to take root.

Your colonies should learn from us to shun our many errors, and to follow us where, after long and bitter experience, we have discovered true principles and the right path.

Yours, &c.,
JOHN BRIGHT.

Mr. Frederick Jones,
235, Pitt Street, Sydney, New South Wales.

ON VACCINATION.

A Leicester gentleman wrote to Mr. Bright, asking his opinion as to the enforcing of the Compulsory Vaccination Acts, the seizure of goods and the imprisonment of persons for refusing to have their children vaccinated, and as to whether it was consistent with personal freedom that respectable men should be put in prison on any such matter of conscience. A case was also stated in which a workman in a condition of distress was apprehended by the police while his four children were at his knee saying their prayers, and the correspondent asked whether this was the sort of man for whom the State ought to provide prisons. Mr. Bright replied as follows :—

December, 1883.

Dear Sir,—I fear I cannot help you in your complaint against the Vaccination Laws. I think compulsory vaccination doubtful, and the repetition of penalties as now practised monstrous. The repetition of penalties creates or intensifies the agitation against the law, and so long as they are inflicted I suspect we shall see only a greater hatred of the law.

As to compulsory vaccination, I am of opinion that if it had never been insisted on or enforced, vaccination might have been as general as it now is without the fierce opposition to it which now prevails in many quarters. The facts appear to me to be in favour of vaccination, but that it often fails of any good effect, and sometimes causes much evil and even death, is admitted even by its warmest supporters. To me it is doubtful if persuasion and example would not have been more effective than compulsion, but to inflict incessant penalties upon parents, and to imprison them for refusing to subject their children to an operation which is not unfrequently injurious and is sometimes fatal, seems to me a needless and monstrous violation of the freedom of our homes and of the rights of parents.

The instances of harshness and cruelty you mention shock me greatly. After so much contest for mildness in our laws, are such things still possible in our country?

I am, very truly yours,
JOHN BRIGHT.

ON THE FACTORY ACTS.

Written to a gentleman in the Fylde district, who had called Mr. Bright's attention to the criticisms of a Tory newspaper with respect to his opposition to factory legislation.

One Ash, Rochdale, January 1, 1884.

DEAR SIR,—I was opposed to all legislation restricting the working of adults, men or women. I was in favour of legislation restricting the labour and guarding the health of children. I could not therefore support Bills which directly interfered with and restricted the working hours of women, and which thus were intended to limit the working hours of men. I still hold the opinion that to limit by law the time during which adults may work is unwise, and in many cases oppressive. As to your Tory newspaper, you may remind the writer that I sought to give the workman two loaves of bread, when his party wished to give him only one.

I am, truly yours,
JOHN BRIGHT.

ON WAR.

Read at the annual meeting of the Workmen's Peace Association, held in London on the 13th of February, 1884.

London, February 13, 1884.

DEAR SIR,—I thank you for sending me your map of our national expenditure for the last fifty years. It affords a lamentable exhibition of our folly as a nation, and it should be put up in some prominent place in the dwelling of every working man in the three kingdoms. In war the working men find the main portion of blood which is shed, and on them fall the poverty and misery which are occasioned by the increase of taxes and damage to industry. Household suffrage in boroughs and counties will provide means by which our people may defend themselves against these enormous evils. It will now rest not with a few, but with multitudes, to say whether the future shall be as the past, whether the blood and treasure of our people shall continue to be shed and squandered on distant shores in causes in which we have no real interest. I hope your Workmen's Peace Association may send your chart of expenditure through the country. It can only do good in every family in which its figures are examined and understood.

Yours, &c.,
JOHN BRIGHT.

ON THE LAND LAWS.

Written to Mr. Hope Hume, of Torquay.

132, Piccadilly, February 27, 1884.

DEAR SIR,—The time is near when our land laws will be revised, some of them abolished. The law of primogeniture will vanish, and entails and settlements will be got rid of, or will be so far limited as to be deprived of their pernicious influence on the public welfare. I believe that opinion has so far advanced on these questions that Parliament will consent to changes which a few years ago men thought almost impossible. The ease with which the Settled Estates Bill, brought in by Lord Cairns, passed both Houses is a proof that opinion has changed, and that landowners have been instructed by the adverse times through which they have recently passed. I need not tell you that I have no sympathy with some wild propositions which have been brought before the public. The path of justice and honesty in regard to land and the owners of land is one from which I would not depart, and I believe all our people of every class have no real or permanent interest in schemes of confiscation which have recently been offered for public acceptance. When the measures of parliamentary reform now contemplated have become law, I think the changes which are required in our land system will not be difficult to accomplish, if undertaken in an honest spirit and on honest principles. I am satisfied that in the main the owners of the soil will profit by the change not less than other classes of our population. Our reforms hitherto have been good for the whole nation. Acting on the same lines we shall meet with a like result. Some may be timid, some may doubt, but future years will prove the wisdom of the changes we have suggested, and which cannot now be long delayed.

I am, &c.,
JOHN BRIGHT.

ON AMERICA, PEACE, AND WAR.

Written to Augustin Jones, of the Friends' Boarding School, Providence, in reply to a letter announcing that a marble bust of Mr. Bright was to be erected there.

London, March 10, 1884.

DEAR FRIEND,—I regret that I have so long delayed an answer to your most kind letter, which reached me some weeks ago. It informed me of the singular and great compliment you were about to pay me by placing a marble bust of me in the lecture-hall of your noble school. I was surprised to hear of the project; but I cannot but be much gratified at the friendly feeling manifested to me by yourself and the authorities connected with your institution. You say that I was a friend to your country in the day of need. I did what I could to prevent discord between the two English nations, and to teach our people the nature of the great issue which depended on the conflict in which twenty years ago your people were engaged. I lamented the conflict; but I wished that England should offer her sympathy on the side of freedom to the slave, and in favour of the perpetual union of your great Republic. I look back on the part I took with unalloyed satisfaction, and would withdraw no word I uttered in connection with a contest on which England and the civilized world looked with a profound interest.

The question of peace, to which you refer, claims the sympathy of all Christian nations. On your continent we may hope your growing millions may henceforth know nothing of war. None can assail you; and you are anxious to abstain from mingling in the quarrels of other nations. Europe, unhappily, is a great camp. All its nations are armed, as if each expected an invasion from its neighbour, unconscious, apparently, that great armies tempt to war the moment any cause of dispute arises. The potentates and Governments of Europe, I doubt not, dread war. They seek to guard themselves against it by enormous armaments.

We, in England, are not free from blame; but with us the love of peace is increasing, and no Government can engage in war without risking, and even losing, the support of our people. We are so involved with territory and populations over half the globe that difficulties are almost constantly arising, and our danger of war is greater than that of any other nations. I am, however, confident that our feeling against war is sensibly increasing, and I trust and believe the moral sense of our people will more and more condemn it.

I have read with much interest the report of your great school which you sent me. I hope your efforts in behalf of a sound, liberal education may prosper, and that your students, as they enter and pass through the world, may strengthen the moral sentiment which pervades so large a portion of your population. I can only wish you success in your great work, and thank you and all connected with your institution for the kindness you have shown me.

England and your United States are two nations, but I always like to regard them as one people. On them the growth of all that is good in the world greatly depends.

Believe me, your sincere and grateful friend,
JOHN BRIGHT.

ON FAIR TRADE.

Mr. J. Gething, of Birmingham, having sent Mr. Bright a copy of a resolution passed at a Fair Trade conference held in Birmingham in March, 1884, in favour of the appointment of a Royal Commission or a Parliamentary Committee to consider the state of trade, received the following reply:—

April 1, 1884.

DEAR SIR,—I have received the copy of the Fair Trade resolution, and thank you for it. I cannot undertake to urge upon the Government or Parliament the inquiry you suggest, although I am certain it would result in a complete overthrow of your case. Your friends greatly exaggerate what you call "the unsatisfactory and unprofitable state of trade." I have known trade on many occasions in a far more "unsatisfactory and unprofitable" state than it is now, and I have seen a gradual restoration of activity and prosperity, which I do not doubt we shall again see.

As to the condition of agriculture, if a commission or committee could give us plenty of sunshine and hot or warm summers, I should gladly vote for it. For the produce of our farms a high or a fair price is given except for wheat. If wool is cheap, mutton is dear; and in this respect the farmer is more than compensated. The inquiry you suggest could not lessen injury caused by diseases which occasionally and in some localities afflict our cattle. What we want in agriculture is more capital on the land, and more skill and enterprise among those who rent and cultivate it. Parliament has made the land and its owners its special favourites for fifty years past, and can do no more in that direction. The farmer cannot now be helped by higher prices caused by the restrictions on the import of foreign corn. If produce and prices will not yield the accustomed rents, then rents must be reduced. Parliament can do nothing, and will not attempt to do anything, to sustain rents.

As to industry generally, I believe the artisan and working classes throughout the country are at this moment better fed, and clothed, and sheltered, than at any former period within our knowledge or recollection. There is still poverty and suffering, but it lessens in amount, and the spread of education and the growth of habits of temperance will, we may hope and believe, diminish the suffering and add to the comfort of our people. Your "Fair Trade" notion is a delusion which comes from an ignorance of the facts bearing on the industrial condition, or from a want of power to reason from them. To establish what you call "Fair Trade" you propose to restrict our trade, to enact that our people shall not buy in the markets where to buy would be most profitable for them. In some branches of business you would restrict, in others you would not restrict, and this you call "Fair Trade." I am surprised at the want of sound reasoning in your dealings with the question, and in your daring to give the name of "Fair Trade" to the policy which you are offering for the acceptance of your countrymen. Rest assured that "freedom of industry" is a far greater blessing than any you can confer by parliamentary tinkering with individual trades which you would subject to your "Fair Trade" theories.

As to the future, I do not doubt that if our harvests are more favourable, we shall witness a general improvement in the agricultural department of industry, and this will aid the restoration to greater activity of the various manufactures on which so large a portion of our people depend for their employment and their means of living.

I have written you a long letter in return for yours. I have not done so because I am likely to convince you, but because of the earnestness with which you have addressed me. You are, as you say, my political opponent. In the course I take on the question we have been discussing I am not an opponent of your true interests, but your friend.

I am, respectfully yours,
John Bright.

ON A LLANDUDNO PENSIONER.

Written to Mr. Thomas Williams, Llandudno, in reply to a letter announcing the death of a poor widow who was one of Mr. Bright's pensioners, and was always visited by him and his family when staying at Llandudno.

132, Piccadilly, London,
April, 1884.

DEAR SIR,—I send you cheque and stamps for coals. And so the poor old woman is gone—I doubt not, to a happier world. To visit her was a lesson. Her cheerfulness and patience were wonderful, and her faith seemed always to sustain her. She was in bed for nineteen years, and yet life appeared to have a pleasant side even to her, with all her prolonged affliction. I am much better, and wait only for change of wind and weather.

Yours very truly,
JOHN BRIGHT.

FREE TRADE AND DEPRESSED INDUSTRIES.

In June, 1884, a gentleman interested in the Nottingham lace trade wrote to Mr. Bright, pointing out the injury likely to be done to that important industry by the measure then before the German Parliament—increasing the duties on lace goods to such an extent as practically to close the German market to British producers, whilst, at the same time, Nottingham manufacturers were exporting some of their machinery to Germany, where it could be worked cheaper, and whence the goods came back to injure the home market for Nottingham produce. The writer expressed doubts as to the value of the Free Trade system, under which such results were possible, and hinted that the right hon. gentleman should suggest a remedy, or use his influence with the Government for the benefit of the lace trade. Mr. Bright replied as follows:—

One Ash, Rochdale, June 19, 1884.

DEAR SIR,—I cannot give you any decided answer to your letter, for I have no definite statement of facts before me.

Free Trade intends that you should buy where you like to buy, and sell where you can sell, and that this should be and is the right of every workman and trader.

If I understand your letter, your idea is that your present customers in this country should not be allowed to exercise this right; they must buy such goods as are made in Nottingham from the manufacturers and workmen of Nottingham, and not from German manufacturers or workmen, although, and indeed because, these offer their goods at somewhat lower prices. I cannot see the justice or reasonableness of this. The right to buy freely is as sacred a right as the right to sell freely, and the customer may justly complain if he is shut out from a cheap market and forced only to purchase in a dear one.

We export more manufactured goods than any other country in the world. We have a greater interest in freedom to buy and sell than any other country, and I should strongly object to any measure intended to tax all our people with a view of sustaining any special industry among them. If this were done for one, why not for others, and for all? And if for some, or all, we should give the greatest encouragement to foreign nations to combine and make more strict and injurious their exclusive policy.

I know little of the conditions of your trade. It may suffer under a depression which has visited many trades of late, and must wait for the revival which will doubtless come.

The most depressed trades in England for several years past are those connected with coal and iron, and yet coal and iron are not imported into this country in any quantities to affect prices. The depression comes from causes which Governments and Parliaments cannot reach.

As to your own case, surely with as good machinery and as much skill and as much industry as the Germans you can meet them in your own or in any foreign market.

If you wish to compel me and others to give you a higher price than the article is worth in the world's market, what is it but something like a "rate in aid" that you are asking, and that all your countrymen should subscribe to support the special industry of your town? We do not ask it for the cotton industry of Lancashire, although we have our depression and difficulties.

I hope we shall see better days for all our industries. All countries have suffered, and the protected countries, I believe, have suffered more than England, whose trade is free.

I am, respectfully yours,
JOHN BRIGHT.

THE HOUSE OF LORDS.

Read at a great reform demonstration at Accrington on the 19th of July, 1884. The meeting was held shortly after the rejection by the House of Lords of the Bill for extending household suffrage to the counties.

132, Piccadilly, July 18, 1884.

DEAR SIR,—I am glad to hear of the arrangements for your great meeting to-morrow. Accrington and the surrounding district will not fail in its duty at this crisis. The question is not one of the Franchise Bill only—that Bill will *not* be defeated, or long delayed. There has arisen another and a greater question. Shall the House of Lords subject to its will the Ministry, which represents the Crown, and the House of Commons, which represents the nation? Shall the policy of a great and free country be thwarted by men sitting in their hereditary chamber, who are there by no right of votes given them, and through whom the voice of the millions of the United Kingdom is not heard? Their veto is a constant insult to the House of Commons, and if the freedom of our people is not a pretence and a sham, some limit must be placed upon a power which is chiefly manifested in, or by, its hostility to the true interests of the nation. A parliament controlled by hereditary peers is no better, perhaps it is worse, than a parliament influenced by and controlled by a despostic monarch. Ask your friends to consider this question seriously. Let them join with their countrymen in demanding a change which shall free the House of Commons from fetters as humiliating to it as they are injurious to the country.

Believe me, sincerely yours,
JOHN BRIGHT.

Mr. John P. Hartley, Accrington.

ON LORD SALISBURY'S MISREPRESENTATION OF MR. BRIGHT'S VIEWS.

During the recess following the first session of 1884, in which the House of Lords rejected the Franchise Bill, the Marquis of Salisbury accused Mr. Bright, by means of a mutilated quotation from a speech delivered by the right hon. gentleman in 1859, of having, in that year, insisted on the union of Franchise with Redistribution. Shortly afterwards, Mr. W. Lord, of Manchester, published, through the National Reform Union, a pamphlet entitled "Mr. Bright on Redistribution, being a Refutation by Lord Salisbury himself of his misrepresentation of Mr. Bright," in which he completely disposed of the charges of the Tory leader. Mr. Bright, in acknowledging a copy of the pamphlet, wrote as follows:—

Kelso, N.B., October 9, 1884.

Dear Sir,—I thank you for the trouble you have taken with the pamphlet, and for the interest you have shown in defending me against the monstrous charge made by Lord Salisbury and his followers. I do not fear that any Liberal in the country will accept Lord Salisbury's word as more worthy of confidence than mine. I suppose some one has sent him the paragraph, and he has used it without ascertaining whether the argument founded upon it was just or not. There is no other man in England who has so repeatedly and consistently urged the dealing with Franchise first and with the seats afterwards as I have. But the Tory managers do not object to a good, and as they think, a thoroughly useful lie, and so they have placarded this in all the towns of England and Scotland. It will not do much for them, but your quotations from Lord Salisbury's and from my speeches will make the matter clear to all who read them. The Tory papers will avoid the subject or will misrepresent the statement you have made.

I thank you for your kindness in this matter, and am, very sincerely yours,

John Bright.

THE SUNDAY POSTAL DELIVERY.

Mr. Bright, having received an invitation to a conference proposed to be held with a view to the closing of all post offices and to the non-delivery of letters on Sundays, forwarded the following reply to Mr. Aston, of the Sunday Rest Association:—

One Ash, Rochdale, October 23, 1884.

DEAR SIR,—I cannot attend your proposed conference, or support the object for which it is to be held. To close all our post offices on Sundays would, in my view, be not only an intolerable inconvenience, but a great evil. To continue at least one delivery of letters in the day seems to me needful for the public service, and not unduly interfering with the labour and service of the letter-carriers.

The post office is our great means, not only of commercial but of family communication, and it is with reference to the "family" that I am most strongly opposed to your views. There are scores of thousands of young men and women in this country who are away from their homes and parents, engaged in cities and towns in the various occupations by which they live. To these Sunday is, to a large extent, a day of rest. It is a day on which their thoughts naturally turn to the homes they have left. It is the day on which the letter from the loving but absent father or mother is most frequently received; and it is the day on which the absent son or daughter has the greatest leisure to write to the home circle.

If your plan were adopted, how many thousands of letters of wise and loving counsel from parents to absent children would be unwritten, or received under circumstances less favourable for good than if received, and read, and re-read during the quiet and leisure of the Sunday? In cases of sickness or of death the closing of the post would often be a grievous inconvenience and a cause of great and prolonged distress. I have known two instances of it in my own family; and what has happened in my case must have taken place in many others. I think the closing of the post in London on Sundays is a great inconvenience, and on the grounds to which I have referred, as to its effects on family correspondence, a great evil. But if the London system were extended to the whole kingdom it would cause an amount of confusion that would be intolerable. If I am not mistaken, the House of Commons did once pass a resolution in favour of your object, but was compelled to rescind it. I have no fear that you can succeed. If you obtain a momentary success, it must be followed by failure.

The one round of the postman in the day is not a heavy burden—not heavier than that borne by great numbers in almost every class in life. It is a great public service, an honourable labour, and it must be compensated for as other services are. There is not a word in the New Testament leaning to your views, so far as they are influenced by religious considerations. The Sabbath was made for man, and not man for the Sabbath.

I am, very respectfully yours,

JOHN BRIGHT.

Mr. T. H. Aston, 197, High Street, Birmingham.

ON INTEGRITY IN BUSINESS.

In answer to a question as to how a man can succeed in business and yet be thoroughly a Christian, addressed to him by the Secretary of the Hackney branch of the Young Men's Christian Association, at the instigation of the members, Mr. Bright replied as follows:—

November, 1884.

DEAR SIR,—I do not think I am specially qualified or in any way entitled to give an opinion upon the question with regard to which you have written. My own experience does not carry me further than other men. There are men who profit by practices of meanness and dishonesty in business, and I have heard of trades in which an honest man is said to be at a serious disadvantage in the competition to which he is subjected. But, on the other hand, I know many men who seem to me to prosper, in part on account of their high character for honour and justice, in their dealings as shopkeepers, manufacturers, or merchants. If a man is able to be strictly honest in all his dealings, in the quality of his goods, as well as in every business transaction, his character undoubtedly serves him in some sort as capital, because he gains the respect of those from whom he buys and those to whom he sells; and I believe this will in many, perhaps in most cases, balance or even exceed whatever gains may be secured by mean or dishonest practices to which some tradesmen have recourse. That honesty is the best policy I firmly believe, as it is also the most righteous, and it will leave no stain upon the conscience. There are trades offering more temptations to dishonest practices than others, and parents may wisely consider this when seeking employment for their sons; and sons may likewise consider it when looking out for the business of their lives, and seek that trade which offers the least possible temptation. In my judgment the value of a high character for strict honour and honesty in business can hardly be estimated too highly, and it will often stand for more in the conscience, and even in the ledger, than all that can be gained by shabby and dishonest transactions.

Yours truly,
JOHN BRIGHT.

ON INDIAN GOVERNMENT.

Written on the receipt of a work which had been sent to Mr. Bright by its Bengali author:—

London, November, 1884.

DEAR SIR,—You speak of my services to your country. I wish I could have done more for your vast population now connected and subject to the rule of my country. It is to me a great mystery that England should be in the position she now is in relation to India. I hope it may be within the ordering of Providence that ultimately good may arise from it. I am convinced that this can only come from the most just government which we are able to confer upon your countless millions, and it will always be a duty and a pleasure to me to help forward any measure that may tend to the well-being of your people. I think I perceive an increased interest here in your welfare, and a growing intelligence and influence among the natives of India in anything that is calculated to promote their wise and just government. The principles which have distinguished the administration of Lord Ripon seem to me to be those which promise to be beneficial to you and creditable to us. I hope every future Governor-General may merit the confidence of our Government at home and of the vast population whose interests may be committed to his charge. I thank you for the gift of your volumes. I shall value them as you desire, and as a proof that in the little I have been able to do my small services have been appreciated by those for whom my sympathy and good intentions have been so strongly excited. So far as I know how to do so, I would be as much a friend of India as of England.

I am, yours, &c.,

JOHN BRIGHT.

ON THE RESULTS OF FREE TRADE IN ENGLAND.

Addressed to Mr. Adam Wilde, of the Hackney Liberal Association, during the election in that borough consequent on the death of Mr. Fawcett. Professor Stuart, who was the Liberal candidate on the occasion, was subsequently returned by a large majority over his opponent.

132, Piccadilly, W., November 17, 1884.

DEAR SIR,—I observe that your Tory candidate and his friends are seeking support as Fair Traders in opposition to Free Traders. They complain that we are allowed by our Government and our tariff, to buy freely all the products of foreign countries, and that, owing to some foreign tariffs, we cannot sell our own products as freely as we wish to do. We can fix the duties in our own tariff and on our imports, but we cannot fix the duties in the tariffs of foreign countries and on their imports. All this is true enough and plain enough, but what is not plain and not true is the strange belief held by Fair Traders that being injured by not being able to sell so freely as we wish to do, owing to duties in foreign tariffs, we should remedy the evil by giving up the power to buy freely by putting duties on our own tariff.

To sell freely would be a great advantage, as to buy freely is a great advantage; but neither to buy freely nor to sell freely, as the Fair Traders recommend, would, in my view, enormously increase the injury to our trade arising from the foreign tariffs which now obstruct our foreign trade.

Let your workmen reflect on the change in their condition which Free Trade has wrought within the last forty years since the reform of our tariff. The corn law was intended to keep wheat at the price of 80*s.* the quarter; it is now under 40*s.* the quarter. The price of tea is now less than the duty which was paid upon it in former days. Sugar is not more than one-third of its cost when a monopoly of East and West India sugar existed. As to wages in Lancashire and Yorkshire, the weekly income of thousands of workers in factories is nearly if not quite double that paid before the time when Free Trade was established. The wages of domestic servants in the county from which I come are, in most cases, doubled since that time. A working brick-setter told me lately that his wages are now 7*s.* 6*d.* per day; formerly he worked at the rate of 4*s.* per day. Some weeks ago I asked an eminent upholsterer in a great town in Scotland what had been the change in wages in his trade. He said that thirty to forty years ago he paid a cabinet-maker 12*s.* per week; he now pays him 28*s.* per week. If you inquire as to the wages of farm-labourers, you will find them doubled, or nearly doubled, in some counties, and generally over the whole country advanced more than 50 per cent., or one-half, whilst the price of food and the hours of labour have diminished. It may be said that milk and butter and meat are dear, which is true; but these are dear because our people, by thousands of families, eat meat who formerly rarely tasted it, and because our imports of these articles are not sufficient to keep prices at a more moderate rate. The Fair Traders tell you that trade in some branches is depressed, which is true, though their statements are greatly exaggerated. We have had a great depression in agriculture, caused mainly by several seasons of bad harvests, and some of our traders have suffered much from a too rapid extension in prosperous years. I have known the depression in trade to be much greater than it is now, and the sufferings of traders and workmen during our time of Protection, previous to 1842, when the reform of our tariff began, were beyond all comparison greater than they are now. In foreign countries where high tariffs exist, say in Russia, in France, and in the United States, the disturbance and depression of manufacturing industries are far greater at this moment than with us. Their tariffs make it impossible for them to have a larger foreign trade; we have a wide field for our exports, which they cannot enter. We have an open market for the most part in South America, in China, in Japan, and with a population of more than 200,000,000 in our Indian Empire, and in our colonies, with the exception of Canada, and the province of Victoria in Australia. The field for our manufacturing industry is far wider than that for any other manufacturing nation in the world, and I cannot doubt that we shall gradually rise from the existing depression, and shall reap even greater gain from our policy of Free Trade in the future than we have reaped in the past. In 1846, when the cruel Corn Law was repealed, we did not convert our landowners and farmers, we only vanquished them. Even now there remains among them a longing for Protection; they cling still to the ancient heresy, and, believing in the ignorance or forgetfulness of our working men, they raise their old cry at every election of members of Parliament. If I have any influence with your own or any electors, let me assure them that for centuries past there has been no change of our national policy which has conferred and will confer so great good on our industrious people as that policy of Free Trade which the two greatest Ministers of our time, Sir Robert Peel and Mr. Gladstone, have fixed, I cannot doubt for ever, on the statute book of our country.

The recent contest in the United States has overthrown the party of Protection and monopoly. It may prove a great blessing to the English nation on the American continent. When England and America shall have embraced the policy of free industry the whole fabric of monopoly the world over will totter to its fall.

I am, very respectfully yours,
JOHN BRIGHT.

Mr. Adam Wilde, The Morley Hall, Hackney, E.

ON LAND AND ITS RENT.

Some extracts of a paper on agricultural depression, which was read by Mr. Lywood at the Warminster meeting of the South Wilts Chamber of Agriculture in December, 1884, having been sent to Mr. Bright, he wrote the following reply:—

Rochdale, December 19, 1884.

Dear Sir,—I know nothing of Mr. Lywood, but, judging from the extract of his speech, his mind, I fear, cannot be of a very clear or logical order. I do not know if he quotes me accurately, but I assume that he does so. Surely if the losses of the land in 1879-80 were as great as my authority estimated them to be, and if the harvests have been unfavourable for so many years, as farmers tell me is the case, we can hardly expect all this mischief to be repaired by the occurrence of one good harvest, such as that of the present year.

The present year is remarkable in this—the yield of wheat in almost every country has been good. In America the price of wheat must be lower than with us. Everywhere there is a surplus seeking a market, and a portion of that surplus comes to us, hence the unusually low price of wheat. Why wheat is cheap everybody knows; even Mr. Lywood knows, and yet he would "ask the Government to take immediate steps to find out." The Government knows, the Parliament knows, why wheat is cheap, and we all know that wholly or partially to shut out foreign wheat would immediately stir the markets and raise the prices; how much, would depend on the amount of the duty, and the height of the barrier raised against the import of foreign wheat.

What Mr. Lywood wants is that Parliament should create this barrier, and thus raise the price of wheat in the markets and the price of bread in the home of every English family, and this to give prosperity to the farmer, and, through him, to the general trade of the country. To do this, or to attempt to do it, would be as reasonable as to expect to improve trade by greatly raising the poor-rate to enable paupers to become better customers of our manufacturers and tradesmen. On this system farmers are to be restored to prosperity by the levying of a "rate in aid" on all the consumers of bread throughout the country.

May I suggest to Mr. Lywood that his remedy would at once tend to give steadiness to rents, and would raise the letting value of farms, and that all this would come from the tax levied on the tables and the bread of the millions of our population; whether it would be of permanent service to tenants may be more than doubtful. May I suggest, further, to Mr. Lywood, that if the present or future price of wheat will not yield the present rents of wheat-growing land, would it not be better to adjust the rent to the quality and produce of the soil rather than to attempt to tax all the bread-consumers of the kingdom to sustain rents which the land will not yield? If land is not worth rent, it should be, and will be, rent-free. If land is paying rent which it will not yield, then the question is one between the tenant and the owner, and the taxpayer cannot be called upon to make up the difference between them. So long as rent is charged for a farm the tenant can only look to the owner for redress if rent is excessive.

Mr. Lywood says the depression in agriculture is greater now than when I referred to its great losses. Bad harvests in successive years cause increasing distress, as capital is wasted and tenants are less able to meet the difficulties which assail them. But this is found only with the occupants of wheat-growing soils; in other departments of farming there is no special distress or complaint. There are districts where rents are not only not reduced, but within two years from this time have been raised, and where farms are eagerly sought after by tenants. The present price of wheat is not the permanent price. When wheat was 80s. the quarter, or more, farmers accepted the situation, even though people were starving. Now the price is very low; but fluctuations are inevitable, and probably a change for the better, from a farmer's point of view, is not far off. Mr. Lywood asks for an inquiry. Has he never heard of inquiries in former years? During the Protection period there were frequent inquiries. We had dismal stories from tenant-farmers, as dismal as we have now, but Parliament could discover no remedy. We had a great Commission which reported only three years ago, but it offered no remedy to the farmer in whose behalf it was appointed.

What the land wants is sunshine such as it has had during this year; it wants, further, tenants of energy and intelligence and capital, and it should be held on rational conditions, and at rents which are fair and just, depending on the quality of the soil and the nature and value of its produce. It does not want, and cannot have, a "rate in aid" raised on the tables and the bread of the laborious millions of our people. I have written you a long letter, but the question you put to me is one of much interest.

I am, very respectfully,
JOHN BRIGHT.

Mr. George Heap, the hon. treasurer of the National Industrial Association having written to Mr. Bright to ask for an explanation of the sentence, "If land is not worth rent, it should be, and will be, rent free," contained in the foregoing letter, Mr. Bright replied as follows:—

Rochdale, December 23, 1884.

DEAR SIR,—Surely what I have written is clear enough. If land will not produce anything that will afford a rent, no one will take it on the condition of paying rent for it. There are millions of acres in the United Kingdom that pay no agricultural rent. I do not say this is the condition of wheat-growing land in England, but surely rent must be determined by the nature of the soil and its capacity to produce what the markets require. If it be a question whether rent shall fall, or shall in some cases cease to be paid, or whether the food of our people shall be limited and raised in price by the action of law and by the imposition of a tax, there can be only one answer to the question. In this county there are many mills—probably some scores of mills—which are closed owing to the competition of modern mills of better construction. It is certain that many of them will not work again; but the owners of them do not ask for a contribution from the purchasers of our cotton manufactures, or for a tax collected by the Government, to enable them to reopen their mills and to work them to a profit. How does the profit or rent of a mill differ from the rent or profit of a farm? If the friends of the farmers would tell them that capital and intelligence and industry are necessary for their trade, and that if these fail there is no other resource than a sufficient fall of rent, they would give them the only counsel that can be of use to them. If, as I doubt not is the case in many instances, the farmers' capital is much wasted in your county, it shows that they have paid more rent than the land was worth; but it does not show that a higher price of food should be brought about by law to enable them to recover the excess which they have paid to the owners of their farms. If men suffer, if farmers now suffer, we may all feel much sympathy with and for them; but we cannot depart from sound principles of legislation, and levy a general contribution to restore them to a condition of prosperity. They must be dealt with as mill-owners or renters of mills are dealt with. They must adjust their relations with their landlords, and not ask Parliament to tax the whole people for their benefit.

I am, respectfully yours,
JOHN BRIGHT.

Mr. George Heap.

ON A CONSERVATIVE CANDIDATE'S SPEECH.

In December, 1884, Mr. William Robertson, President of the Ayr Liberal Club, drew Mr. Bright's attention to a charge preferred against him by Mr. Somervell, Conservative candidate for Glasgow, who, in addressing the Bothwell Conservative Association, alluded to the connection of Mr. Bright with the Corn Law agitation, and said Mr. Bright was enabled to put a considerable quantity of size into his goods, but he did not reduce their price for all that. Those goods were sent to India and Africa among the coloured races there, who were unjustly talked about as belonging to the "great unwashed." They, however, objected to size, and washed their clothing until it almost disappeared altogether. So much, added Mr. Somervell, for Mr. Bright's philanthropy. He had done his best to ruin the British farmer, and he had also done his best to wheedle the very niggers who practised habits of cleanliness. In reply to Mr. Robertson's communication, Mr. Bright wrote as follows:—

Rochdale, December 27, 1884.

Dear Sir,—The speech of Mr. Somervell is not worth notice, except to say that it is remarkable that a man capable of such a speech can be accepted as a candidate by any class or portion of the Scotch people. The observations to which you refer me are an example of the exhibition of ignorance and falsehood which are only met with in the lowest ranks of the Tory party. I do not think any audience of Liberals in any part of England or Scotland could be found to applaud language such as Mr. Somervell seems to delight in. To indulge in it is a proof of the low opinion he must have had of those who listened to him, but perhaps he gave them the best which he had. More than that it would be unreasonable to expect from him. What must a Scotch constituency be to which Mr. Somervell can appeal with any hope of success?

I thank you for your note, and am,
                 Truly yours,
                      John Bright.

Mr. Robertson, Ayr.

This letter produced the following rejoinder from Mr. Somervell :—

Sorn Castle, Mauchline, Ayrshire,
December 30, 1884.

Sir,—My attention has been drawn to a letter that has been published, dated the 27th of December, and bearing your signature, in which, referring to a speech of mine, you state it is an "exhibition of ignorance and falsehood." I have to request that you will inform me to what speech you refer, and also state on what observations you base your assertion, and your grounds for so doing.

In the meantime I maintain the accuracy of every public statement I have made.

I pass by the remainder of your letter with the contempt it deserves, but with this single observation, that I challenge you to point to any public utterance of mine that at all resembles your letter, either in its low tone, or the coarseness of its personal abuse.

I remain, yours faithfully,
JAMES SOMERVELL.

The Right Hon. John Bright, M.P.

To this Mr. Bright wrote in reply as follows :—

Rochdale, December 31, 1884.

SIR,—I enclose the paragraph which is published as a portion of your speech, and which caused me to write the letter of which you complain. You assume that the part I took in the Anti-Corn-Law movement was prompted by the fact that the size which is necessary in the weaving of cotton goods would be made more cheap, and that self-interest was my ruling motive. In this you wished to convey to your audience an impression which is entirely false. You then say that I did not reduce the price of my goods for all that. Are you not ignorant if you do not know that the competition among manufacturers will give to the consumer whatever advantage is gained by cheapening the mode or course of manufacture? You speak of those goods sent to India and Africa, countries to which I have not been in the habit of shipping cotton goods. Manufacturers, as you ought to know, make the goods which their customers order, and are not responsible for the countries to which they are sent. You say I have done my best to ruin the British farmer—that is, with the purpose to ruin him—which you cannot know to be true, and which I think you know to be false. What you say about " unclothing the very nigger" is so very silly that I will not comment upon it. If you say that the extract which I enclose is no part of your speech, I shall express my regret at having said anything upon it; but if the extract is a fair representation of what you said, I must adhere to the terms of my letter, although it may not be pleasant reading for you. I shall be glad if you will publish your letter of yesterday and this reply.

I am, respectfully,

JOHN BRIGHT.

ON THE LIBERAL PARTY IN RELATION TO AGRICULTURAL LABOURERS.

In December, 1884, Mr. T. S. Townsend asked Mr. Bright if he would write a short paper or letter which, being distributed, might be useful in giving some political education to the newly-enfranchised electors in South Warwickshire. Mr. Bright in reply wrote as follows :—

Rochdale, December 29, 1884.

DEAR MR. TOWNSEND,—You suggest that I should write something that may be of use to the new voters under the Franchise Bill which has just become law. If I were speaking to your new voters, and especially if to those who are farm labourers, I should say something like that I am about to write.

I should tell them that there is a great difference between the two parties which will ask for their votes in the spring of 1886—a difference which they may see in all things during the last fifty years. The Reform Bill of 1832 was carried by the Liberal party against the violent opposition of the Tories. It was the first step, in our time, towards a better representation of the people in Parliament. In the year 1867, now seventeen years since, the suffrage was first given to working-men, when household suffrage was granted in our cities and towns. This was gained by the agitation promoted by the Liberal party in the country, and was pressed upon the Tory Government during the discussions in the House of Commons in the session of 1867.

The Liberal party in the country and in Parliament has advocated household suffrage for the counties for several years, during which the Tories have constantly opposed it. This year the Bill giving household suffrage in the counties has become law, notwithstanding all the efforts of the Tories to obstruct it.

The Liberal party gave to all voters the protection of the ballot, which the Tory party strongly opposed. Every voter is now able to vote as he wishes. No landlord, or farmer, or employer of any kind can know how any vote is given—and now the poorest man is as safe in giving his vote as the richest. This is a great safeguard for the voter. The arrangement of seats under the Bill now before Parliament is the work of the Liberal party. The Tory party when in office did not propose it, and it is only under a Government of Liberals that so great and wise a measure could have been passed into law.

Political freedom therefore, and a real representation of the people, rich and poor, the country owes to the Liberal party. But we owe much more to the Liberal party.

We owe to it the repeal of the cruel Corn Law, and the removal of the hindrances to trade, caused by monstrous taxes on almost everything brought from foreign countries. The Corn Law, by shutting out foreign corn, was intended to keep the price of wheat at, or near, eighty shillings the quarter; its natural price without Corn Law is probably about forty shillings the quarter.

Bread is, and will be, about half the price at which the Corn Law intended it to be in all years when English harvests were not good.

A great minister, Sir Robert Peel, repealed the Corn Law. The agitation of the Anti-Corn-Law League, the Irish famine in 1846, and the help and votes of the Liberals in Parliament, with the support of a portion of the Tories, gave him power to repeal this wicked and cruel law. Some of the Tories are now proposing to restore it, and again to make the labourers' bread dearer, so that farmers may be able to pay rents which they say are too high unless the law is put in force to raise the market price of wheat, and the baker's price of bread! The Tory party and country gentlemen were very angry with Sir Robert Peel because he would not maintain the Corn Law. His party deserted him, and drove him from office and from power because he preferred the interests of the nation, and the comforts of the labouring classes to dear bread and high rents for the landowners.

When the Corn Law was gone, other bad things went with it. The Liberal Government which came in after Sir Robert Peel destroyed the monopoly in sugar. Other great changes have been made, chiefly by Mr. Gladstone, supported always by the Liberals. The new voters who are not young will remember the price of bread in former days; they will know that sugar is about one-third of the price it once was, and that they now can buy three pounds for the price they formerly paid for one pound; and they know that tea costs less now than the tax alone which was imposed upon it before the Free Traders began the reform in our tariff and the repeal of duties on imports from foreign countries. And during these years there has been a general and large rise in the wages of working-men and labourers in all parts of the country. Farm labourers' wages have risen one-half or more, and in some counties they have nearly doubled since the days of Protection and the Corn Law.

But the Liberal party has done more than give the mass of our people a real representation and a real power in Parliament. It has done more than give them freedom for their industry. It has given them the means to understand what Parliament is doing, and what it ought to do, for it has given them the vast advantage of a free Press, and to their children the not less vast advantage of cheap and good schools. Now almost every labourer can have an admirable newspaper weekly for a penny, or every day one somewhat smaller in size, but not less admirable in quality, for a halfpenny! Newspapers, not so large and not so good as these, cost sevenpence when the Liberal party began to deal with this question. The taxes on paper and on the printed newspaper strangled the Press, and the tax on advertisements was as great when a gardener sought a situation and employment as when a rich man advertised a mansion or an estate.

All this is gone,—these scandals and cruelties of the past are gone. The Liberals spoke and worked; the Tory Opposition, step by step, was overcome, and one after another these great evils vanished, and no longer disgrace English legislation.

And what of the cheap and good schools? The child of the labourer may gain an education that will give him as good a prospect, as regards labour and trade, as the child of a richer man has. He will grow up with a sense of self-respect; he will see before him a path along which he may find independence and comfort. The present gain of this is great; the future gain is beyond all we can estimate.

And what of the future? What will household suffrage in counties and the new arrangement of seats do for the new voters, and especially for the farm labourers? If the new voters know their interests, and if the Liberals are returned in great power to the new Parliament, two things will have a chance of being done. The land laws will be reformed, and much of them reformed out of existence. In past times and now our land laws have been framed to protect the great estates of great families. Great estates lead to great farms, and great farms lead to the result that it is almost impossible for farm labourers to become farmers, and thus the path of the intelligent and hard-working labourer to an improved position and condition for himself and his family is barred and blocked. The holding of great estates under entails and settlements, and often heavily mortgaged and burdened, makes it impossible for them to be well cultivated, and thus the demand for labour is lessened, and a better rate of wages is prevented. This whole system of land laws must be broken down, and the new and great reform will do little if it does not get rid, as far as possible, of the mischiefs of the past.

The Game Laws, too, will come under revision. Parliament may accept the principle that the creatures which live on and from the land are the property, if there be any property in them, of the farmer, at whose cost, and by whose labour, the farm is cultivated. When this principle is admitted in our law, then what is called "preservation of game" may cease; murderous conflicts on game preserves may be no longer known, and labourers may not have before them an almost constant and irresistible temptation to become poachers and breakers of the law. If the new voters will help the Liberal party, the Liberal landowners, the Liberal farmers, the Liberal shopkeepers and tradesmen, in the towns and villages of the counties and county divisions, we may see much good done by a new Parliament.

If what I have written shall give information or useful counsel, I shall be glad. I have for more than forty years endeavoured to press forward in the country and in Parliament the changes to which I have referred. They have all, so far as they have been effected, in my view, been of great service to the country. The period of reform is not yet ended; it will rest, in no small degree, on the good sense of the new constituency, combined with what is intelligent and just in the old body of electors, whether, as on two past occasions, in 1832 and in 1867, a large measure of electoral reform shall be followed by great measures of improvement in the legislation of our country. Perhaps I have written at too great length in reply to your letter—if so you will forgive me. The subject is too grave and too great to be treated in a paragraph.

I am, very truly yours,
JOHN BRIGHT.

T. S. Townsend, Esq., 68, Queen's Gate, London, S.W.

ADDENDUM.

ADDRESS TO THE WORKING MEN OF ROCHDALE.

The following address was issued by Mr. Bright in August, 1842. The country was suffering at that time from a keen and widespread distress consequent upon the action of the duty upon foreign corn, which not only raised the price of food, but hampered and restricted trade, so that shopkeepers were impoverished, and thousands of workmen were thrown out of employment, and they and their families driven into the ranks of pauperism, while even those who were still employed were obliged to work as a rule for the merest pittance. The description of the state of the country given in a letter addressed by a Committee of the Anti-Corn-Law League to every Member of Parliament in June of that year recalls in its startling revelations the famous speech of Sheridan concerning the condition of France immediately before the revolution, when he said that "the manufacturer was without employ; trade was languishing; famine clung upon the poor; despair upon all."

"The great bulk of the people," it was asserted in the letter, "the customers of each other, and of all the other classes, are becoming too poor to purchase, and thus they cease to consume, and profits are destroyed. Confidence no longer exists; trade is everywhere paralyzed; wages are rapidly declining; workmen are being discharged; poor's-rates are fast increasing in the agricultural as well as manufacturing districts; private charity has subscribed nobly, but yields to the overwhelming pressure; peaceable men are made savage and desperate; the loyal and obedient are becoming discontented, disaffected, and revengeful; and society in many parts of the country seems to be on the very verge of dissolution."

In this condition of things a feeling akin to despair spread throughout the country when it was seen that Parliament, despite the forcible and eloquent and repeated appeals of the advocates of the League, refused to give its consent to the free admission of foreign corn into English ports, and the starving workmen now turned away from the peaceful and constitutional movement inaugurated by the League, to follow leaders of a different stamp. "It was represented," says Mr. Archibald Prentice in his History of the League, "that a great commercial convulsion, which should compel employers to join the ranks of the employed, would render the demand for the Charter irresistible; and that the means of obtaining that, through reform of the representative system, would also be the means of gaining a great advance of wages. The plan was, that every worker should cease to work; one absurd enough at any time, but especially absurd at a period when employers had so little work to give."

Having adopted this plan the workmen acted

upon it with remarkable promptitude and decision. On the morning of the 8th of August 23,000 hands turned out of the mills of Ashton-under-Lyne, Dukinfield, and Stalybridge; 9150 from the mills of Hyde followed their example the same morning, and in the afternoon the greater part of the operatives in Oldham took a similar course. The next day several thousand operatives proceeded from Ashton to Manchester, and demanded at various mills that the hands should turn out, which was instantly done, the masters making no objections. The movement spread, and rioting occurred in different parts of the country, but it did not last long, for, becoming sensible of the futility of the course they were pursuing, the operatives gradually returned to their work, and by the beginning of September the disorder had subsided. An address issued by Sir Benjamin Heywood to the working men of Manchester was instrumental in persuading them to resume work, and Mr. Bright's address to the men of Rochdale "was," says Mr. Prentice, "greatly influential in inducing them to think deliberately upon the course they were pursuing." Its influence was not limited to Rochdale, for it was copied into the newspapers, and must have been extensively read throughout Lancashire.

Mr. Bright was only thirty years old when he wrote this address, yet its style differs little, if at all, from that of his latest letters. It contains an array of telling facts and truths driven home with sledge-hammer blows, and its statements are characterized by a fearless candour, and by a plainness of speech which allows no doubt whatever as to the meaning intended to be conveyed by them. The matter of the address is such as might have been produced by a mature and experienced thinker; its predictions have been verified, and the views it enunciates will bear the strictest criticism that can be applied to them, although more than forty years have elapsed since they were written. Masterly in its style, and accurate in its conclusions, this piece of composition demonstrates upon what a rock of sound economic theory the young politician was established, and with what a fund of practical wisdom he was equipped, when he began the career which has been distinguished by so splendid a success.

The following is the address :—

TO THE WORKING MEN OF ROCHDALE.

A deep sympathy with you in your present circumstances induces me to address you. Listen and reflect, even though you may not approve. You are suffering—you have long suffered. Your wages have for many years declined, and your position has gradually and steadily become worse. Your sufferings have naturally produced discontent, and you have turned eagerly to almost any scheme which gave hope of relief.

Your fellow-workmen in Ashton and Oldham turned out for an advance of wages; they invaded your town, and compelled you to turn out. Some of you, doubtless, were willing, but many of you were reluctant to join them. They urged you to treat the men of Bacup and Todmorden as they had treated you. They told you that you had no courage, and that you would be unworthy the good opinion of your fellow-workmen if you refused to act towards others as they had acted towards you. You became an invading force. You visited the peaceful villages of Bacup and Todmorden, and compelled your fellow-workmen to cease their labour. You were regardless of the sufferings you were bringing on their wives and children; you relentlessly, and contrary to every principle of justice and freedom, deprived them of bread! You have had many meetings to deliberate on your position and prospects. An advance of wages to the rate paid in 1840 and ten hours per day were the demands you were urged to make. But when the turning-out in this district was completed, and you had become evicted, these demands were abandoned, and you were urged to refuse to work until the charter became law.

Many of you know full well that neither Act of Parliament nor act of a multitude can keep up wages. You know that trade has long been bad, and with a bad trade wages cannot rise. If you are resolved to compel an advance of wages, you cannot compel manufacturers to give you employment. Trade must yield a profit, or it will not long be carried on; and an advance of wages now would destroy profit. You have a strong case now in the condition of the colliers and calico-printers. The wages of the colliers are not so low as those in many other trades, but they suffer because they are only employed two or three days per week. The wages of calico-printers have only been reduced *once* during twenty or thirty years, and yet they are now earning as little as any class of workmen, having not more than two or three days' work per week. If they combined to double the rate of wages, they would gain nothing, unless they could secure increased regular employment. Your attempt to raise wages cannot succeed. Such attempts have always failed in the end; and yours must fail.

To diminish the hours of labour at this time is equally impossible; it is, in effect, a rise of wages, and must also fail. You can have no rise of wages without a greater demand for labour; and you cannot dictate what hours you will work until workmen are scarce.

Your speakers and self-constituted leaders urge you to give up the question of wages, and stand upon the Charter. Against the obtaining the charter the laws of nature offer no impediment, as they do against a forcible advance of wages; but to obtain the charter *now* is just as impossible as to raise wages by force.

The aristocracy are powerful and determined; and, unhappily, the middle classes are not yet intelligent enough to see the safety of extending political power to the whole people. The working classes can never gain it of themselves.

Physical force you wisely repudiate. It is immoral, and you have no arms, and little organization. Moral force can only succeed through the electors, and these are not yet convinced. The principles of the charter will one day be established; but years *may* pass over, months *must* pass over before that day arrives. You cannot stand idle till it comes. Your only means of living are from the produce of your own labour. Unhappily, you have wives and children, and all of you have the cravings of hunger, and you must live, and, in order to live, you must work.

Your speakers talk loudly. They tell you of your numbers and your power, and they promise marvellous results *if you will but be firm.* They deceive you; perhaps they are themselves deceived. Some of them contrive to live on this deception, and some are content with the glory of their leadership. They flatter you grossly, and they as grossly calumniate your employers. They pretend to be working out your political freedom; they know that *that* freedom can only be obtained through the electoral body and the middle classes, and yet they incessantly abuse the parties whom it is your interest to conciliate and convince. For four years past they have held before your eyes an object *at present* unattainable, and they have urged you to pursue it; they have laboured incessantly to prevent you from following any practical object. They have vilified the substance and extolled the shadow. They have striven continually to exasperate you against those who alone will or can aid you to overturn the usurpations of the aristocracy. They have succeeded in creating suspicion and dissension, and upon that dissension many of them have lived. They have done their utmost to perpetuate *your* seven or eight shillings per week, and by their labours in that cause *they* have enjoyed an income of three or four times that amount.

My fellow-townsmen, you have been in a fever during this week. Your conduct, unopposed as you have been, has been peaceable and such as my intimate knowledge of you led me to expect from you. We are all liable to err; you have committed an error, but it is not a fatal one—it may be retrieved. I believe you to be intelligent men, or I would not address you. As intelligent men you cannot remain out; you cannot permanently raise wages by force; you cannot get the charter *now*. What are you to do then? RETURN TO YOUR EMPLOYMENT. It is more noble to confess your error than to persist in it, and the giving up of an error brings you nearer the truth. When you resume your labour, do not give up the hope of political improvement—that would be even more to be deplored than your present movement. Cherish it still—a brighter day will come—and you and your children will yet enjoy it. Your first step to entire freedom must be *commercial* freedom—freedom of industry. We must put an end to the partial famine which is destroying trade, the demand for your labour, your wages, your comforts, and your independence. The aristocracy regard the Anti-Corn-Law League as their greatest enemy. That which is the greatest enemy of the remorseless aristocracy of Britain must almost of necessity be your firmest friend. Every man who tells you to support the Corn Law is your enemy—every man who hastens, by a single hour, the abolition of the Corn Law, shortens by so much the duration of your sufferings. Whilst that inhuman law exists your wages must decline. When it is abolished, and not till then, they will rise.

If every employer and workman in the kingdom were to swear on his bended knees that wages should not fall, they would assuredly fall if the Corn Law continues. No power on earth can maintain your wages at their present rate if the Corn Law be not repealed. You may doubt this now, but consider the past, I beseech you—what the past tells you the future will confirm. You may not thank me for thus addressing you, but, nevertheless, I am your friend. Your own class does not include a man more sincerely anxious than I am to obtain for you both industrial and political freedom. You have found me on all occasions, if a feeble, yet an honest and zealous defender; and I trust in *this*, time will work no change in me. My heart sympathizes deeply in your sufferings. I believe I know whence they mainly spring, and would gladly relieve them. I would willingly become poor if that would make you comfortable and happy.

I now conclude. I ask only the exercise of

your reason. If possible lay aside prejudices, and you will decide wisely.

To such of you as have been employed at the mills with which I am connected, I may add that, as soon as you are disposed to resume work, the doors shall be open to you. I invite you to come, and you shall be treated as, I trust, you have ever been—as I would ever wish you to treat me.

I am, with all sincerity, your friend,

JOHN BRIGHT.

INDEX.

A.

ABERDEEN, Lord, incessantly attacked by Tory Opposition, 243.
Accrington, Liberal party in, 212.
Address, to electors of Manchester, 39; to electors of Birmingham, 45; to working men of Rochdale, 331.
Agriculture, what is wanted in, 298; future of, will be brighter with more favourable harvests, 299; Parliamentary inquiries into the condition of, 317.
America, war of independence in, 27; Mr. Bright invited to, 98, 275; desirability for a moderate tariff in, 230; Protection would be dead in, but for the civil war, 235; how compel its Government to reduce their tariffs, 259; Mr. Bright's conduct with reference to civil war in, 295.
American Jubilee Singers, 165.
Animals, kindness to, 203.
Aristocracy, monarchs, and landowners, 249.
Armaments, reduction of, desirable, 194.
Army, Salvation, 270.
Atrocities, Bulgarian, 190.

B.

BALLOT, 54, 135, 137; given by Liberal party, 325.
Bazaar, Mr. Bright asked to subscribe to, 46.
Beaconsfield Government, and the Eastern Question, 190; suggestion that it should decapitate itself, 193; the foreign policy of, 210; charged with constant deception, 210; charged with attempting to suppress expression of opinion 211; no friend to freedom, 211; the foreign policy of, 213, 225; its defeat, 246; worst Government we have had for more than fifty years, 246.
Beaconsfield, Lord, admits that his Government is not supported by the nation, 192.

Bible, the, in Board Schools, 244.
Birmingham, Mr. Bright elected member for, 44; address to electors of, 45; the unemployed in, 61; the representation of, 62, 150; Conservative Working Men's Mutual Improvement Association, 156.
Board Schools, reading the Bible in, 244.
Bradford, bad trade in, 261.
Bright, Mr., his representation of Manchester, 36; health of, 37; loss of seat for Manchester, 39; address to electors of Manchester, 39; conduct of, with respect to Russian war, 40; his opponents at Manchester, 41; elected member for Birmingham, 44; asked to subscribe to a bazaar, 46; seconds Mr. Milner Gibson's amendment to proposed second reading of Conspiracy Bill, 60; his representation of Birmingham, 63; his Reform Bill, 69; his proposed extension of the franchise, 71; his proposal as to length of residence for voters, 72; proposes lodger franchise, 73; proposes ballot, 73; prevented from introducing his Bill, 74; receives resolution from Chamber of Commerce of the State of New York, 88; invited to go to America, 98; receives vote of thanks from Committee of National Association of Ireland, 105; receives invitation to a banquet in Dublin, 115; writes to Mr. Garth respecting libels, 117; Mr. Garth's reply, 121; replies to Mr. Garth, 125; proposes Parliamentary Commission empowered to buy large estates in Ireland, 139; becomes President of Board of Trade, 147; letter-writing a burden, 158; treatment by the press in reference to the Crimean war, 190; Sir Charles Gavan Duffy ascribes Protectionist sentiments to, 200; writes to Bishop of Peterborough, 204; declines to frame a Bill on the subject of the drink traffic, 218; his work on behalf of farmers in connection with the Game Laws, 239; elected Lord Rector of Glasgow University, 248; his reply to Lord Beaconsfield respecting monarchs and statesmen, 249; correspondence with Earl of Carnarvon, 250; on completing his seventieth year, 267; his reasons for opposing war, 272; on completing his seventy-first year, 274; again invited to America, 275; dislike to the sea, 277; his conduct with reference to the civil war in America, 295; his advocacy for separation of franchise and redistribution, 305; instances in his family of inconvenience of Sunday closing of post-offices, 307; correspondence with Mr. Somervell, 321.
Bulgarian atrocities, 190.
Burials Bill, Mr. Bright's speech on, 203.
Business, integrity in, 308.

INDEX. 343

C.

Cabinet, English, feebleness of, 32.
Canada, United States and, 97.
Canadian policy, 236.
Candidates, working-men, 179.
Canvassing at elections, 176.
Carnarvon, Earl of, and Mr. Bright, 250.
Catholic population of Ireland, 6.
Cattle trade, foreign, 186.
Chambers of Commerce and political questions, 206.
Church, Irish, 5; funds of, 10, 13.
Circular, the London, 49.
Civil Service, 170.
Civil war in America, Protection in America would be dead but for, 235; Mr. Bright's conduct with reference to, 295.
Clarendon, Lord, his description of his policy with respect to Crimean war, 31.
Clergy, Tory, 251.
Cobden. Mr., 4.
Colonies, the, waste lands in, 64; and a Protective policy, 199.
Commercial Treaty between France and England, effect of, 217.
Consecrated ground, 203.
Conservative candidate's speech, 320.
Conspiracy Bill, the, 57, 59.
Conspiracy of Liberal members, 108.
Constituencies, three-cornered, 134, 145, 247.
Corn, tariff on, would tend to give steadiness to rents, 316.
Corn Law, repeal of, did not convert landowners and farmers, 314; repeal of, due to Liberal party, 325.
Country, condition of, in 1858, 61; in 1842, 332.
County members, the obstructive party, 246; support extravagant expenditure, 269.
Coventry and Free Trade, 155.
Crimean war, application of Vattel's principles to, 26; who has gained by it, 66; its results, 190; letter on, 242.
Currency, the, 68.

D.

Depression in trade, in 1879, and its causes, 231; and cheap food, 232.
Derby Government, and Reform, 130.
Derby, Lord (the late), his Reform Bill, 69.

INDEX.

Derby, Lord (the present), his unanswerable speech on foreign policy, 214.
Disraeli Government, and the publicans, 189.
Disraeli, Mr., and Reform, 108; his opposition to the three-cornered constituencies, 134.
Distress, in England, under Free Trade and under Protection, 227, 259; in the United States, 227; in England in 1842, 332.
Distribution of Seats Bill of 1866, 110.
Duffy, Sir Charles Gavan, and Free Trade, 199.

E.

EASTERN Question, the, 189, 191.
Egypt, war in, 271; no better justification than other wars, 273.
Election fads, 284, 286.
Elections, multiplicity of, an evil, 163; canvassing at, 176.
Emigration, its necessity and causes, 63; Government aid to, 64, 67.
Employers, their right to combine, 80; liabilities of, 225.
Endowments, religious, objection to, 17.
England, committed to war with Russia, 31; policy of, towards Turkey, 191; and Russia, 195; the condition of, under Free Trade, 227; and United States, trade between, 245; dependence of, on foreign food supply, 256; distress in, under Free Trade and under Protection, 259; love of peace increasing in, 296; and United States, one people, 297; distress in, in 1842, 332.
English middle class, 85.
English people and Irish wrongs, 143.
Equality for religious sects in Ireland, 7, 9, 10.
Estates, great, evils of, 328.
Europe, Turkish rule in, 189; a great camp, 296.
Expenditure, national, in 1858, 62; excessive national, a cause of poverty, 220.
Extempore speaking and preaching, 166.

F.

FACTORY Acts, 292.
Fagot voting, 243.
Fair Trade, 297; a delusion, 298.
Fallacies of Protection, 256.
Farmers, their representation, 101-2; easy for, to combine, 102; the Game Laws and, 103, 240.
Food, importations into England, 175; Free Trade in relation to price of, 175.

INDEX.

Foreign policy, 1; of Lord Beaconsfield's Government, 210, 213, 225.
France, demands of, upon Turkish Government, 33; prospects of Free Trade in, 258.
Free land, 160.
Free Trade, and Tory pamphleteers, 148; and French Commercial Treaty, 153; in relation to the price of food, 175; and the English colonies, 199; and armaments, 207; between nations, would give peace, 208; a means of avoiding war, 217; in the future, 223; the condition of England under, 227; and the depression in trade in 1879, 228; its progress and results, 233; predictions with respect to, 234; and foreign tariffs, 257; prospects in France, 258; benefits of, 267; the true policy, 289; and depressed industries, 300; the intention of, 301; results of, in England, 311; effect of, on wages, 312.
Free Traders and fagot voting, 243.
French Commercial Treaty, 153, 263.
French war, just, according to "law of nations," 27.
Funeral reform, 188.

G.

Game Laws, 100, 239; and farmers, 240; will come under revision by future electorate, 328.
Garth's libels, Mr., 117.
Genoa, representation of, 53.
Germany and its tariff, 235.
Gibson, Mr. T. Milner, vote on foreign policy, 4; letter on, 56; moves amendment to Conspiracy Bill, 59.
Gladstone Government, policy of, in the Transvaal, 252.
Gladstone, Mr., speaks against Mr. Roebuck's resolution, 2; supports Mr. Milner Gibson's amendment to Conspiracy Bill, 60; his position with respect to Irish questions, 143; attitude of Whigs and Radicals towards, 144.
Glasgow University, Mr. Bright elected Lord Rector of, 248.
Government and new enterprises, 201.
Government, the Beaconsfield, and the Eastern Question, 190; charged with constant deception, 210; and freedom, 211; the foreign policy of, 210, 213, 225; its defeat, 246.
Government, the Gladstone, policy of, in the Transvaal, 252.
Gray, Sir John, M.P., letter to, 5.
Greece, sympathy of the English for, 24.
Grey, Lord, on the claims of Catholics in Ireland, 8.

H.

Hare, Mr., his election scheme, 286; his supporters, 287.

Home Rule, 149, 181.
Honesty the best policy, 309.
Household suffrage, will enable people to prevent war, 293.
Hume, Mr., his vote on the foreign policy of Lord John Russell's Government, 4.
Hyde Park demonstration, 112.

I.

INCOME tax, 82, 87, 151, 279.
India, Government of, 47, 75; the English people and, 75; import and excise duties, 205; government of, 281; disposition of people of England towards, 282; wise government of, may be impossible, 282; government of, 309; growing interest in England in welfare of, 310; Lord Ripon's administration of, 310.
Indian corn, use of, in England, 159.
Indian troops, employment of, 211.
Industry protected, confined to its own market, 288.
Inquisition of blood, 35.
Integrity in business, 308.
Intervention between Russia and Turkey, the cost of, 34.
Ireland, ecclesiastical arrangements in, 11; Protestant Episcopalian Church, endowments of, 12; Presbyterian Church, endowments of, 12; Roman Catholic Church, endowments of, 12; Catholics in, hardships of, 12; Church Property Commission, 13; parishes in, 14; College of Maynooth, grant to, 14; Presbyterians in, 14; Protestant Episcopalians in, 15, 18; Church endowments, distribution of, 13—16; history of, 18; tranquillity of, means of securing, 20; reforms in, 94; Land Law, reform in, 95; State Church in, 95; anticipated visit to, 116; land question, 138; Church and land, 140; only way to remedy evils of, 142; and the Tories, 142; and the Whigs, 143; Home Rule for, 149, 181; Sunday closing in, 177, 188; future of, 283.
Irish affairs, 105.
Irish Land Bill of 1881, 264.
Irish members and the Liberal party, 209.
Irish questions, 94; 140.

J.

JUVENILE smoking, 223.

K.

KAY, Mr. Joseph, 196.
Kindness to animals, 203.

L.

LAND, monopoly in, a cause of poverty, 220; and its rent, 315; what it wants, 318; if not worth rent, will be rent free, 316, 318.
Land laws, 293; schemes of confiscation with regard to, deprecated, 294; owners of the soil will profit by change in, 294; will be reformed, 328.
Landowners, monarchs, aristocracy and, 249.
Land question, 160; Mr. Joseph Kay and, 197.
Legislation to prevent cattle disease, 187.
Liberal party, its degeneracy under unworthy leaders, 86; letter on, 168; in Accrington, 212; in relation to agricultural labourers, 323; its future work, 328.
Licensing system, 93, 161.
Liquor traffic, and the Tory party, 214; letter on, 218.
Llandudno pensioner, 300.
Lords, House of, 145, 303; veto of, an insult to House of Commons, 304.
Lowther, Hon. James, his qualities as Chief Secretary for Ireland, 252.
Luther, work of, 282.

M.

MALT tax, 92, 158.
Marriage laws, 280.
Marriage with deceased wife's sister, legality of, in colonies, 280.
Menschikoff, Prince, note of, 28.
Middle class, English representation of, 85.
Military expenses, increase of, 62.
Military services, rapacity of, 85.
Mill, John Stuart, and Free Trade, 201.
Minority members, 247.
Minority representation, 284, 286.
Misrepresentation, Tory, 226.
Monarchs, aristocracy, and landowners, 249.
Monopoly, a milder form of slavery, 222.
Morley, Mr. Samuel, letter from, 70; letter to, 71.
Mourning, the wearing of, 188.

N.

NATIONAL crime, followed by punishment, 270.
Nesselrode, Count, 30.
Newspapers and Parliamentary reporting, 199.
New York Chamber of Commerce, 88.
Non-intervention between Russia and Turkey, the true policy, 33.

O.

OATHS, forbidden in New Testament, 278; lessen the value of ordinary statements, 278; effect of, on ignorant persons, 278; have impaired regard for truth, 279.
Orton, Arthur, 184.

P.

PALMERSTON, Lord, his defence of his policy, 2; conduct in 1850, 28; introduces Conspiracy Bill, 58; resigns office, 60; his conception of a country's grandeur, 85; his attitude towards Reform, 97, 100.
Palmerston Government, character of, 60.
Parliament, want of zeal of, for Reform, 107; duties of 233 abundant supply of clever men in, 285; effect of making it a photograph of every phase of public opinion, 286.
Parliamentary reporting, 198.
Parliaments, septennial, 225.
Peace, and war, 193; influences in favour of, 194; love of, increasing in England, 296.
Peel, Sir Robert, character of, 4; imposed income tax, 83; taught futility of war of tariffs, 258; repealed Corn Law, 325; Tory party angry with, because he would not maintain Corn Law, 326.
Peers, and the nation, 147; 303.
Pensions, perpetual, 225.
People, causes of sufferings of, 221.
Permissive Bill, 162, 215.
Peterborough, Bishop of, his description of Mr. Bright's speech on the Burials Bill, 203.
Political economy, neglect of the study of, 77.
Political freedom, due to Liberal party, 325.
Political questions, the study of, 241.
Poor, the virtuous, 219.
Postal delivery, Sunday, 307.
Post offices, effect of closing on Sundays on young people absent from home, 306; public inconvenience of Sunday closing of, 307.
Preachers, majority of, not good speakers, 167.
Preaching, extempore speaking and, 166.
Primogeniture and entail, 293.
Procedure, rules of, 273.
Protected industry, confined to its own market, 288.
Protection, in the United States, 220; the chance of a return to, in England, 230; fallacies of, 256; to return to, would be confession of having been wrong, 261; if needful is

INDEX.

needful for farming class, 261; in young countries, 287; tendency of, to make men dishonest in public affairs, 289; when demanded for an industry is simply a "rate ·in aid," 302; injurious to foreign trade, 313.
Pruth, passage of the, 29.

R.

RECIPROCITY, 260; futility of, 266.
Redistribution, necessity of, 43, 51, 137.
Reform, letters on, 42, 49, 69, 96, 99, 106, 112, 128, 137.
Reform Bill, Lord John Russell's, 44; Mr. Bright's, 69; Lord Derby's, 69, 112; Earl Russell's, 106, 110; Lord Palmerston's, 112; Mr. Disraeli's, 133.
Reform, period of, not yet ended, 329.
Reform resolutions of 1867, 128, 132.
Rent, land and its, 315; of a mill, how does it differ from rent of a farm, 319.
Rents, cannot be sustained by Parliament, 298.
Reporting, Parliamentary, 198.
Republicanism, 152.
Residuum, the, 163.
Retrenchment, the word become almost obsolete, 42.
Ripon, Lord, his administration of India, 310.
Roebuck's resolution, Mr., 1.
Rubery's case, Mr., 90.
Rules of procedure, 273.
Russell, Lord John, his opinion on the religious question in Ireland, 8; conduct in 1850, 28; his Reform Bill, 44; his conception of a country's grandeur, 85.
Russell, Earl, and Ireland, 143.
Russia, and Turkey, cost of intervention between, 34; jealousy of, on the part of England, 195.
Russia, the war with, letters on, 22, 26; professed objects of, 23; the English public and, 24; result of, 24; the record of history concerning, 25; Vattel and, 26, 27, 28.
Russian note, rejected by the Turks, 28.

S.

SALFORD, bye-election in 1877, 196.
Salisbury, Lord, his misrepresentation of Mr. Bright, 304.
Salvation Army, 270.
Scotland, preservation of game in, 66.
Sea, dislike of Mr. Bright for, 277.
Secret voting in representative bodies, 178.
Septennial Parliaments, 225.

Sermons, the reading of, 167.
Service, the Civil, 170.
Settled Estates Bill, 294.
Slavery in the United States, 269.
Slavery, monopoly a milder form of, 222.
Smoking, juvenile, 223.
Somervell, Mr., letter to Mr. Bright, 321; Mr. Bright's reply, 322.
Speaking and preaching, extempore, 166.
Standing armies, principal cause of, 218.
Statesmanship, what it consists in, 20.
Stratford de Redcliffe, Lord, 28.
Strikes, 76.
Sugar, monopoly in, destroyed by Liberal party, 326.
Sumner, Mr. Charles, letter on, 169.
Sunday closing in Ireland, 177.
Sunday postal delivery, 306.

T.

TARIFF, moderate, in America, desirability of, 230; Germany and its, 235; how compel America to reduce, 259; change wrought by reform of, 312.
Tariff protection, nature of, 289.
Tariffs, abolition of, will promote peace, 218; reduction of, futility of attempting to force other countries to, 258; in foreign countries make it impossible for them to have a larger foreign trade, 313.
Taxation and representation, 82.
Temperance, Christian churches and, 172, 174; legislation, 172; friends of, should form opinion, 172.
Tichborne case, the, 183.
Three-cornered constituencies, 134, 145, 247.
Times, the, on the rejection of the Vienna note by Turkey, 29.
Tories and Ireland, 143.
Tory clergy, 251.
Tory misrepresentation, 226.
Tory party, hostility of, to enfranchisement of working men, 111.
Trade, depression in, in 1879, and its causes, 231; depression in, and cheap food, 232; between England and the United States, 245; depression in, cause of, 260; depression in, greater under Protection than under Free Trade, 313.
Transvaal, policy of Gladstone Government in, 252; peace, 253, 254.

INDEX. 351

Turkey, determination of, to declare war, 30; declares war, 31; nature of its Government, 33; cost of intervention between Russia and, 34; the policy of England towards, 191.
Turkish rule in Europe, 189.
Tyranny, force no longer used as instrument of, 85.

U.

UNITED States, 88; no other country in which men have been so free, 89; Mr. Bright invited to, 98; and trade with Canada, 99; and Protection, 222; distress in, 227; and a moderate tariff, 230; and England, trade between, 245; their protective tariff, 259; slavery in, 269; Mr. Bright again invited to, 275; when Protection abolished in, may find market in India, 282; prospect of, being preserved from war in future, 296.

V.

VACCINATION, 174, 290; might have been as general if it had not been compulsory, 291.
Vattel, the justness of the Crimean war according to, 26.
Victoria, the colony of, and Free Trade, 202.
Vienna note, agreed upon by four powers, 28; accepted by Russia, 29; refused by Turkey, 29; origin of, 29; construction put upon, by Russia, 29; French Government's advice to Russia with respect to, 30; agreed to by England, 30; declared inadmissible by Turkey, 31.

W.

WAGES, effect of Free Trade on, 312; cannot be kept up by Act of Parliament or act of multitude, 335.
War, description of, 35; letters on, 195, 292; the prevention of, 216; grounds of Mr. Bright's opposition to, 272; its effects on working men, 293; feeling against, increasing, 296.
War, Crimean, its results, 66; letter on, 242.
War in Egypt, 271; no better justification for than other wars, 273.
Wars, past, and the working classes, 195, 213; which might have been avoided, 238.
Watkin, Mr. Absalom, letter to, 26.
Whalley, Mr., M.P., and the Tichborne case, 186.

Wheat, yield of, in 1884, 315; present price not permanent, 317.
Whigs and Ireland, 143.
Whig peers and three-cornered constituencies, 134.
Whisky in Scotland, and poverty, 221.
Work of Luther, 282.
Working classes, condition of, in 1858, 65; and the Crimean war, 65; their exclusion from the suffrage, 78; and past wars, 195, 213; how affected by war, 293; their present condition, 298.
Working-men candidates, 179.
Workmen, their right to combine, 80.

Y.

Young countries, Protection in, 287; introduction of any system of tariff protection in, should be resisted, 289.

THE END.

A Catalogue of American and Foreign Books Published or Imported by MESSRS. SAMPSON LOW & CO. *can be had on application.*

Crown Buildings, 188, Fleet Street, London,
May, 1885.

A Selection from the List of Books

PUBLISHED BY

SAMPSON LOW, MARSTON, SEARLE, & RIVINGTON.

ALPHABETICAL LIST.

ABOUT Some Fellows. By an ETON BOY, Author of "A Day of my Life." Cloth limp, square 16mo, 2s. 6d.
Adams (C. K.) Manual of Historical Literature. Cr. 8vo, 12s. 6d.
Alcott (Louisa M.) Jack and Jill. 16mo, 5s.
—— *Old-Fashioned Thanksgiving Day.* 3s. 6d.
—— *Proverb Stories.* 16mo, 3s. 6d.
—— *Spinning-Wheel Stories.* 16mo, 5s.
—— See also "Rose Library."
Aldrich (T. B.) Friar Jerome's Beautiful Book, &c. Very choicely printed on hand-made paper, parchment cover, 3s. 6d.
—— *Poetical Works.* Édition de Luxe. 8vo, 21s.
Alford (Lady Marian) Needlework as Art. With over 100 Woodcuts, Photogravures, &c. Royal 8vo.
Allen (E. A.) Rock me to Sleep, Mother. Illust. Fcap. 4to, 5s.
Amateur Angler's Days in Dove Dale: Three Weeks' Holiday in July and August, 1884. By E. M. Printed by Whittingham, at the Chiswick Press. Fancy boards, 1s.; also on large hand-made paper (100 only printed), 5s.
American Men of Letters. Thoreau, Irving, Webster. 2s. 6d. each.
Andersen (Hans Christian) Fairy Tales. With 10 full-page Illustrations in Colours by E. V. B. Cheap Edition, 5s.
Anderson (W.) Pictorial Arts of Japan. With 150 Plates, 16 of them in Colours and Gold. Large imp. 4to, gilt binding, gilt edges.
Angler's Strange Experiences (An). By COTSWOLD ISYS. With numerous Illustrations, 4to, 5s. New Edition, 3s. 6d.
Angling. See Amateur, "British Fisheries Directory," "Cutcliffe," "Lambert," "Martin," and "Theakston."
Archer (W.) English Dramatists of To-day. Crown 8vo, 8s. 6d.

A

Art Education. See "Biographies of Great Artists," "Illustrated Text Books," "Mollett's Dictionary."

Artists at Home. Photographed by J. P. MAYALL, and reproduced in Facsimile. Letterpress by F. G. STEPHENS. Imp. folio, 42s.

Audsley (G. A.) Ornamental Arts of Japan. 90 Plates, 74 in Colours and Gold, with General and Descriptive Text. 2 vols., folio, £15 15s. On the issue of Part III. the price will be further advanced.

—— *The Art of Chromo-Lithography.* Coloured Plates and Text. Folio, 63s.

Audsley (W. and G. A.) Outlines of Ornament. Small folio, very numerous Illustrations, 31s. 6d.

Auerbach (B.) Brigitta. Illustrated. 2s.

—— *On the Heights.* 3 vols., 6s.

—— *Spinoza.* Translated. 2 vols., 18mo, 4s.

BALDWIN (J.) Story of Siegfried. 6s.

—— *Story of Roland.* Crown 8vo, 6s.

Barlow (Alfred) Weaving by Hand and by Power. With several hundred Illustrations. Third Edition, royal 8vo, 1l. 5s.

Bathgate (Alexander) Waitaruna: A Story. Crown 8vo, 5s.

Batley (A. W.) Etched Studies for Interior Decoration. Imperial folio, 52s. 6d.

Baxter (C. E.) Talofa: Letters from Foreign Parts. Crown 8vo, 4s.

THE BAYARD SERIES.
Edited by the late J. HAIN FRISWELL.

Comprising Pleasure Books of Literature produced in the Choicest Style as Companionable Volumes at Home and Abroad.

"We can hardly imagine better books for boys to read or for men to ponder over."—*Times.*

Price 2s. 6d. each Volume, complete in itself, flexible cloth extra, gilt edges, with silk Headbands and Registers.

The Story of the Chevalier Bayard. By M. De Berville.
De Joinville's St. Louis, King of France.
The Essays of Abraham Cowley, including all his Prose Works.
Abdallah; or, The Four Leaves. By Edouard Laboullaye.
Table-Talk and Opinions of Napoleon Buonaparte.
Vathek: An Oriental Romance. By William Beckford.
Words of Wellington: Maxims and Opinions of the Great Duke.
Dr. Johnson's Rasselas, Prince of Abyssinia. With Notes.
Hazlitt's Round Table. With Biographical Introduction.
The Religio Medici, Hydriotaphia, and the Letter to a Friend. By Sir Thomas Browne, Knt.
Ballad Poetry of the Affections. By Robert Buchanan.

Bayard Series (continued) :—

Coleridge's Christabel, and other Imaginative Poems. With Preface by Algernon C. Swinburne.

Lord Chesterfield's Letters, Sentences, and Maxims. With Introduction by the Editor, and Essay on Chesterfield by M. de Ste.-Beuve, of the French Academy.

The King and the Commons. A Selection of Cavalier and Puritan Songs. Edited by Professor Morley.

Essays in Mosaic. By Thos. Ballantyne.

My Uncle Toby; his Story and his Friends. Edited by P. Fitzgerald.

Reflections; or, Moral Sentences and Maxims of the Duke de la Rochefoucauld.

Socrates: Memoirs for English Readers from Xenophon's Memorabilia. By Edw. Levien.

Prince Albert's Golden Precepts.

A Case containing 12 Volumes, price 31s. 6d.; or the Case separately, price 3s. 6d.

Behnke and Browne. Child's Voice. Small 8vo, 3s. 6d.
Bell (Major): Rambla—Spain. Irun to Cerbere. Cr. 8vo, 8s. 6d.
Beynen. Life and Aspirations. Crown 8vo, 5s.
Bickersteth's Hymnal Companion to Book of Common Prayer may be had in various styles and bindings from 1d. to 31s. 6d. Price List and Prospectus will be forwarded on application.
Bickersteth (Bishop E. H.) The Clergyman in his Home. Small post 8vo, 1s.
—— *Evangelical Churchmanship and Evangelical Eclecticism.* 8vo, 1s.
—— *From Year to Year: Original Poetical Pieces.* Small post 8vo, 3s. 6d.; roan, 6s. and 5s.; calf or morocco, 10s. 6d.
—— *The Master's Home-Call; or, Brief Memorials of Alice Frances Bickersteth.* 20th Thousand. 32mo, cloth gilt, 1s.
—— *The Master's Will.* A Funeral Sermon preached on the Death of Mrs. S. Gurney Buxton. Sewn, 6d.; cloth gilt, 1s.
—— *The Shadow of the Rock.* A Selection of Religious Poetry. 18mo, cloth extra, 2s. 6d.
—— *The Shadowed Home and the Light Beyond.* New Edition, crown 8vo, cloth extra, 5s.
—— *The Reef, and other Parables.* Crown 8vo, 2s. 6d.
—— *Wreath.* New Edition, 18mo, 2s. 6d.
Bilbrough (E. J.) "Twixt France and Spain." Crown 8vo, 7s. 6d.
Biographies of the Great Artists (Illustrated). Crown 8vo, emblematical binding, 3s. 6d. per volume, except where the price is given.

Claude Lorrain.*
Correggio, by M. E. Heaton, 2s. 6d.
Della Robbia and Cellini, 2s. 6d.
Albrecht Dürer, by R. F. Heath.
Figure Painters of Holland.

Fra Angelico, Masaccio, and Botticelli.
Fra Bartolommeo, Albertinelli, and Andrea del Sarto.
Gainsborough and Constable.
Ghiberti and Donatello, 2s. 6d.

* *Not yet published.*

Biographies of the Great Artists (continued) :—

Giotto, by Harry Quilter.
Hans Holbein, by Joseph Cundall.
Hogarth, by Austin Dobson.
Landseer, by F. G. Stevens.
Lawrence and Romney, by Lord Ronald Gower, 2s. 6d.
Leonardo da Vinci.
Little Masters of Germany, by W. B. Scott.
Mantegna and Francia.
Meissonier, by J. W. Mollett, 2s. 6d.
Michelangelo Buonarotti, by Clément.
Murillo, by Ellen E. Minor, 2s. 6d.
Overbeck, by J. B. Atkinson.
Raphael, by N. D'Anvers.
Rembrandt, by J. W. Mollett.
Reynolds, by F. S. Pulling.
Rubens, by C. W. Kett.
Tintoretto, by W. R. Osler.
Titian, by R. F. Heath.
Turner, by Cosmo Monkhouse.
Vandyck and Hals, by P. R. Head.
Velasquez, by E. Stowe.
Vernet and Delaroche, by J. Rees.
Watteau, by J. W. Mollett, 2s. 6d.
Wilkie, by J. W. Mollett.

Bird (F. J.) American Practical Dyer's Companion. 8vo, 42s.

Bird (H. E.) Chess Practice. 8vo, 2s. 6d.

Black (Wm.) Novels. See "Low's Standard Library."

Blackburn (Charles F.) Hints on Catalogue Titles and Index Entries, with a Vocabulary of Terms and Abbreviations, chiefly from Foreign Catalogues. Royal 8vo, 14s.

Blackburn (Henry) Breton Folk. With 171 Illust. by RANDOLPH CALDECOTT. Imperial 8vo, gilt edges, 21s.; plainer binding, 10s. 6d.

—— *Pyrenees (The).* With 100 Illustrations by GUSTAVE DORÉ, corrected to 1881. Crown 8vo, 7s. 6d.

Blackmore (R. D.) Lorna Doone. Édition de luxe. Crown 4to, very numerous Illustrations, cloth, gilt edges, 31s. 6d.; parchment, uncut, top gilt, 35s. Cheap Edition, small post 8vo, 6s.

—— *Novels.* See "Low's Standard Library."

—— *Remarkable History of Sir T. Upmore.* New Edition, 2 vols., crown 8vo, 21s.

Blaikie (William) How to get Strong and how to Stay so. Rational, Physical, Gymnastic, &c., Exercises. Illust., sm. post 8vo, 5s.

—— *Sound Bodies for our Boys and Girls.* 16mo, 2s. 6d.

Boats of the World, Depicted and Described by one of the Craft. With Coloured Plates, showing every kind of rig, 4to, 3s. 6d.

Bock (Carl). The Head Hunters of Borneo: Up the Mahakkam, and Down the Barita; also Journeyings in Sumatra. 1 vol., super-royal 8vo, 32 Coloured Plates, cloth extra, 36s.

—— *Temples and Elephants.* A Narrative of a Journey through Upper Siam and Lao. Coloured, &c., Illustrations, 8vo, 21s.

Bonwick (J.) First Twenty Years of Australia. Crown 8vo, 5s.

—— *Lost Tasmanian Race.* Small 8vo, 4s.

Bonwick (J.) Port Philip Settlement. 8vo, numerous Illustrations, 21*s.*

Bosanquet (Rev. C.) Blossoms from the King's Garden : Sermons for Children. 2nd Edition, small post 8vo, cloth extra, 6*s.*

Bourke (J. G.) Snake Dance of the Moquis of Arizona. A Journey from Santa Fé. With Chromo and other Illustrations. 8vo, 21*s.*

Boussenard (L.) Crusoes of Guiana. Illustrated. 7*s.* 6*d.*

——— *Gold-seekers, a Sequel.* Illustrated. 16mo, 7*s.* 6*d.*

Boy's Froissart. King Arthur. Mabinogion. Percy. See LANIER.

Bracken (T.) Lays of the Land of the Maori and Moa. 16mo, 5*s.*

Bradshaw (J.) New Zealand as it is. 8vo, 12*s.* 6*d.*

Brassey (Lady) Tahiti. With 31 Autotype Illustrations after Photos. by Colonel STUART-WORTLEY. Fcap. 4to, 21*s.*

Braune (W.) Gothic Grammar. Translated by G. H. BULG. 3*s.* 6*d.*

Brisse (Baron) Ménus (366). In French and English, with recipes. Translated by Mrs. MATTHEW CLARKE. 2nd Edition. Crown 8vo, 5*s.*

British Fisheries Directory, 1883-84. Small 8vo, 2*s.* 6*d.*

Brittany. See BLACKBURN.

Broglie's Frederick II. and Maria Theresa. 2 vols., 8vo, 30*s.*

Browne (G. Lathom) Narratives of Nineteenth Century State Trials. Period I.: 1801—1830. 2nd Edition, 2 vols., cr. 8vo, cloth, 26*s.*

Browne (G. Lennox) Voice Use and Stimulants. Sm. 8vo, 3*s.* 6*d.*

Browne (Lennox) and Behnke (Emil) Voice, Song, and Speech. Illustrated, 3rd Edition, medium 8vo, 15*s.*

Bryant (W. C.) and Gay (S. H.) History of the United States. 4 vols., royal 8vo, profusely Illustrated, 60*s.*

Bryce (Rev. Professor) Manitoba. With Illustrations and Maps. Crown 8vo, 7*s.* 6*d.*

Bull (J. W.) Early Experiences of Life in Australia. Crown 8vo, 7*s.* 6*d.*

Bunyan's Pilgrim's Progress. With 138 original Woodcuts. Small post 8vo, cloth gilt, 3*s.* 6*d.*; gilt edges, 4*s.*

Burgoyne. Operations in Egypt, 1798—1802. Small 8vo, 5*s.*

Burnaby (Capt.) On Horseback through Asia Minor. 2 vols., 8vo, 38*s.* Cheaper Edition, 1 vol., crown 8vo, 10*s.* 6*d.*

Burnaby (Mrs. F.) High Alps in Winter; or, Mountaineering in Search of Health. By Mrs. FRED BURNABY. With Portrait of the Authoress, Map, and other Illustrations. Handsome cloth, 14*s.*

Butler (W. F.) The Great Lone Land; an Account of the Red River Expedition, 1869-70. New Edition, cr. 8vo, cloth extra, 7s. 6d.

—— *Invasion of England, told twenty years after, by an Old* Soldier. Crown 8vo, 2s. 6d.

—— *Red Cloud; or, the Solitary Sioux.* Imperial 16mo, numerous illustrations, gilt edges, 5s.

—— *The Wild North Land; the Story of a Winter Journey* with Dogs across Northern North America. 8vo, 18s. Cr. 8vo, 7s. 6d.

Buxton (H. J. W.) Painting, English and American. Crown 8vo, 5s.

CADOGAN (Lady A.) Illustrated Games of Patience. Twenty-four Diagrams in Colours, with Text. Fcap. 4to, 12s. 6d.

California. See "Nordhoff."

Cambridge Staircase (A). By the Author of "A Day of my Life at Eton." Small crown 8vo, cloth, 2s. 6d.

Cambridge Trifles; from an Undergraduate Pen. By the Author of "A Day of my Life at Eton," &c. 16mo, cloth extra, 2s. 6d.

Carleton (Will) Farm Ballads, Farm Festivals, and Farm Legends. 1 vol., small post 8vo, 3s. 6d.

—— See "Rose Library."

Carlyle (T.) Irish Journey in 1849. Crown 8vo, 7s. 6d.

Carnegie (A.) American Four-in-Hand in Britain. Small 4to, Illustrated, 10s. 6d. Popular Edition, 1s.

—— *Round the World.* 8vo, 10s. 6d.

Carr (Mrs. Comyns) La Fortunina. 3 vols., cr. 8vo, 31s. 6d.

Chairman's Handbook (The). By R. F. D. PALGRAVE, Clerk of the Table of the House of Commons. 5th Edition, 2s.

Challamel (M. A.) History of Fashion in France. With 21 Plates, coloured by hand, imperial 8vo, satin-wood binding, 28s.

Changed Cross (The), and other Religious Poems. 16mo, 2s. 6d.

Charities of London. See Low's.

Chattock (R. S.) Practical Notes on Etching. Sec. Ed., 8vo, 7s. 6d.

Chess. See BIRD (H. E.).

Children's Praises. Hymns for Sunday-Schools and Services. Compiled by LOUISA H. H. TRISTRAM. 6d.

China. See COLQUHOUN.

Choice Editions of Choice Books. 2s. 6d. each. Illustrated by
C. W. COPE, R.A., T. CRESWICK, R.A., E. DUNCAN, BIRKET
FOSTER, J. C. HORSLEY, A.R.A., G. HICKS, R. REDGRAVE, R.A.,
C. STONEHOUSE, F. TAYLER, G. THOMAS, H. J. TOWNSHEND,
E. H. WEHNERT, HARRISON WEIR, &c.

Bloomfield's Farmer's Boy. | Milton's L'Allegro.
Campbell's Pleasures of Hope. | Poetry of Nature. Harrison Weir.
Coleridge's Ancient Mariner. | Rogers' (Sam.) Pleasures of Memory.
Goldsmith's Deserted Village. | Shakespeare's Songs and Sonnets.
Goldsmith's Vicar of Wakefield. | Tennyson's May Queen.
Gray's Elegy in a Churchyard. | Elizabethan Poets.
Keat's Eve of St. Agnes. | Wordsworth's Pastoral Poems.

"Such works are a glorious beatification for a poet."—*Athenæum.*

Christ in Song. By PHILIP SCHAFF. New Ed., gilt edges, 6s.

Chromo-Lithography. See "Audsley."

Cid (Ballads of the). By the Rev. GERRARD LEWIS. Fcap. 8vo, parchment, 2s. 6d.

Clay (Charles M.) Modern Hagar. 2 vols., crown 8vo, 21s. See also "Rose Library."

Collingwood (Harry) Under the Meteor Flag. The Log of a Midshipman. Illustrated, small post 8vo, gilt, 6s.; plainer, 5s.

Colquhoun (A. R.) Across Chrysê; From Canton to Mandalay. With Maps and very numerous Illustrations, 2 vols., 8vo, 42s.

Colvile (H. E.) Accursed Land: Water Way of Edom. 10s. 6d.

Composers. See "Great Musicians."

Confessions of a Frivolous Girl. Cr. 8vo, 6s. Paper boards, 1s.

Cook (Dutton) Book of the Play. New Edition. 1 vol., 3s. 6d.

—— *On the Stage: Studies of Theatrical History and the Actor's Art.* 2 vols., 8vo, cloth, 24s.

Coote (W.) Wanderings South by East. Illustrated, 8vo, 21s. New and Cheaper Edition, 10s. 6d.

—— *Western Pacific.* Illustrated, crown 8vo, 2s. 6d.

Costume. See SMITH (J. MOYR).

Cruise of the Walnut Shell (The). In Rhyme for Children With 32 Coloured Plates. Square fancy boards, 5s.

Curtis (C. B.) Velazquez and Murillo. With Etchings, &c. Royal 8vo, 31s. 6d.; large paper, 63s.

Curzon (G.) Violinist of the Quartier Latin. 3 vols., 31s. 6d.

Custer (E. B.) Boots and Saddles. Life in Dakota with General Custer. Crown 8vo, 8s. 6d.

Cutcliffe (H. C.) Trout Fishing in Rapid Streams. Cr. 8vo, 3s. 6d.

D'ANVERS (N.) An Elementary History of Art. Crown 8vo, 10s. 6d.
—— *Elementary History of Music.* Crown 8vo, 2s. 6d.
—— *Handbooks of Elementary Art—Architecture; Sculpture; Old Masters; Modern Painting.* Crown 8vo, 3s. 6d. each.
Davis (C. T.) Manufacture of Bricks, Tiles, Terra-Cotta, &c. Illustrated. 8vo, 25s.
Dawidowsky (F.) Glue, Gelatine, Isinglass, Cements, &c. 8vo, 12s. 6d.
Day of My Life (A); or, Every-Day Experiences at Eton. By an ETON BOY. 16mo, cloth extra, 2s. 6d.
Day's Collacon: an Encyclopædia of Prose Quotations. Imperial 8vo, cloth, 31s. 6d.
Decoration. Vols. II. to VIII. New Series, folio, 7s. 6d. each.
—— See also BATLEY.
De Leon (E.) Egypt under its Khedives. Illust. Cr. 8vo, 4s.
Deverell (F. H.) All Round Spain, by Road or Rail. Visit to Andorra, &c. Crown 8vo, 10s. 6d.
Donnelly (Ignatius) Atlantis; or, the Antediluvian World. 7th Edition, crown 8vo, 12s. 6d.
—— *Ragnarok: The Age of Fire and Gravel.* Illustrated, Crown 8vo, 12s. 6d.
Dos Passos, Law of Stockbrokers and Stock Exchanges. 8vo, 35s.
Dougall (James Dalziel) Shooting: its Appliances, Practice, and Purpose. New Edition, revised with additions. Crown 8vo, 7s. 6d.
 "The book is admirable in every way. .... We wish it every success."—*Globe.*
 "A very complete treatise. .... Likely to take high rank as an authority on shooting."—*Daily News.*
Drama. See ARCHER, COOK (DUTTON), WILLIAMS (M.).
Durnford (Col. A. W.) A Soldier's Life and Work in South Africa, 1872-9. 8vo, 14s.
Dyeing. See BIRD (F. J.).

EDUCATIONAL Works published in Great Britain. A Classified Catalogue. Second Edition, 8vo, cloth extra, 5s.
Egypt. See "De Leon," "Foreign Countries," "Senior."
Eidlitz, Nature and Functions of Art and Architecture. 8vo, 21s.
Electricity. See GORDON.
Emerson Birthday Book. Extracts from the Writings of R. W. Emerson. Square 16mo, illust., very choice binding, 3s. 6d.
Emerson (R. W.) Life. By G. W COOKE. Crown 8vo, 8s. 6d.

English Catalogue of Books. Vol. III., 1872—1880. Royal 8vo, half-morocco, 42*s*. See also "Index."

English Philosophers. Edited by E. B. IVAN MÜLLER, M.A.
A series intended to give a concise view of the works and lives of English thinkers. Crown 8vo volumes of 180 or 200 pp., price 3*s*. 6*d*. each.

Francis Bacon, by Thomas Fowler.
Hamilton, by W. H. S. Monck.
Hartley and James Mill, by G. S. Bower.

*John Stuart Mill, by Miss Helen Taylor.
Shaftesbury and Hutcheson, by Professor Fowler.
Adam Smith, by J. A. Farrer.

* *Not yet published.*

Esmarch (*Dr. Friedrich*) *Treatment of the Wounded in War.*
Numerous Coloured Plates and Illust., 8vo, strongly bound, 1*l*. 8*s*.

Etcher. Examples of Original Work of Celebrated Artists— BIRKET FOSTER, J. E. HODGSON, R.A., COLIN HUNTER, J. P. HESELTINE, ROBERT W. MACBETH, R. S. CHATTOCK, &c. Vols. for 1881 and 1882, imperial 4to, gilt edges, 2*l*. 12*s*. 6*d*. each ; 1883, 36*s*.

Etching. See BATLEY, CHATTOCK.

Etchings (*Modern*) *of Celebrated Paintings.* 4to, 31*s*. 6*d*.

FARM Ballads, Festivals, and Legends. See "Rose Library."

Fashion (*History of*). See "Challamel."

Fawcett (*Edgar*) *A Gentleman of Leisure.* 1*s*.

Feilden (*H. St. C.*) *Some Public Schools, their Cost and* Scholarships. Crown 8vo, 2*s*. 6*d*.

Felkin (*R. W.*) *and Wilson* (*Rev. C. T.*) *Uganda and the* Egyptian Soudan. With Map, Illust., and Notes. 2 vols., cr. 8vo, 28*s*.

Fenn (*G. Manville*) *Off to the Wilds: A Story for Boys.* Profusely Illustrated. Crown 8vo, 7*s*. 6*d*.

—— *The Silver Cañon: a Tale of the Western Plains.* Illustrated, small post 8vo, gilt, 6*s*.; plainer, 5*s*.

Fennell (*Greville*) *Book of the Roach.* New Edition, 12mo, 2*s*.

Ferguson (*John*) *Ceylon in* 1883. With numerous Illustrations. Crown 8vo, 7*s*. 6*d*. "Ceylon in 1884," 7*s*. 6*d*.

Ferns. See HEATH.

Fields (*J. T.*) *Yesterdays with Authors.* New Ed., 8vo, 10*s*. 6*d*.

Fleming (*Sandford*) *England and Canada: a Summer Tour.* Crown 8vo, 6*s*.

Florence. See "Yriarte."

Flowers of Shakespeare. 32 beautifully Coloured Plates, with the passages which refer to the flowers. Small 4to, 5s.

Folkard (R., Jun.) Plant Lore, Legends, and Lyrics. Illustrated, 8vo, 16s.

Forbes (H. O.) Naturalist's Wanderings in the Eastern Archipelago. Illustrated, 8vo, 21s.

Foreign Countries and British Colonies. A series of Descriptive Handbooks. Crown 8vo, 3s. 6d. each.

Australia, by J. F. Vesey Fitzgerald.
Austria, by D. Kay, F.R.G.S.
*Canada, by W. Fraser Rae.
Denmark and Iceland, by E. C. Otté.
Egypt, by S. Lane Poole, B.A.
France, by Miss M. Roberts.
Germany, by S. Baring-Gould.
Greece, by L. Sergeant, B.A.
Holland, by R. L. Poole.
Japan, by S. Mossman.
*New Zealand.
*Persia, by Major-Gen. Sir F. Goldsmid.
Peru, by Clements R. Markham, C.B.
Russia, by W. R. Morfill, M.A.
Spain, by Rev. Wentworth Webster.
Sweden and Norway, by F. H. Woods.
*Switzerland, by W. A. P. Coolidge, M.A.
*Turkey-in-Asia, by J. C. McCoan, M.P.
West Indies, by C. H. Eden, F.R.G.S.

* *Not ready yet.*

Fortunes made in Business. 2 vols., demy 8vo, cloth, 32s.

Franc (Maud Jeanne). The following form one Series, small post 8vo, in uniform cloth bindings, with gilt edges :—

Emily's Choice. 5s.
Hall's Vineyard. 4s.
John's Wife : A Story of Life in South Australia. 4s.
Marian ; or, The Light of Some One's Home. 5s.
Silken Cords and Iron Fetters. 4s.
Vermont Vale. 5s.
Minnie's Mission. 4s.
Little Mercy. 4s.
Beatrice Melton's Discipline. 4s.
No Longer a Child. 4s.
Golden Gifts. 4s.
Two Sides to Every Question. 4s.

Francis (F.) War, Waves, and Wanderings, including a Cruise in the "Lancashire Witch." 2 vols., crown 8vo, cloth extra, 24s.

Frederick the Great. See "Broglie."

French. See "Julien."

Froissart. See "Lanier."

GENTLE Life (Queen Edition). 2 vols. in 1, small 4to, 6s.

THE GENTLE LIFE SERIES.

Price 6s. each ; or in calf extra, price 10s. 6d. ; Smaller Edition, cloth extra, 2s. 6d., except where price is named.

The Gentle Life. Essays in aid of the Formation of Character of Gentlemen and Gentlewomen.

About in the World. Essays by Author of "The Gentle Life."
Like unto Christ. A New Translation of Thomas à Kempis' "De Imitatione Christi."
Familiar Words. An Index Verborum, or Quotation Handbook. 6s.
Essays by Montaigne. Edited and Annotated by the Author of "The Gentle Life."
The Gentle Life. 2nd Series.
The Silent Hour: Essays, Original and Selected. By the Author of "The Gentle Life."
Half-Length Portraits. Short Studies of Notable Persons. By J. HAIN FRISWELL.
Essays on English Writers, for the Self-improvement of Students in English Literature.
Other People's Windows. By J. HAIN FRISWELL. 6s.
A Man's Thoughts. By J. HAIN FRISWELL.
The Countess of Pembroke's Arcadia. By Sir PHILIP SIDNEY. New Edition, 6s.

George Eliot: a Critical Study of her Life. By G. W. COOKE. Crown 8vo, 10s. 6d.
German. See BEUMER.
Germany. By S. BARING-GOULD. Crown 8vo, 3s. 6d.
Gibbs (J. R.) British Honduras. Crown 8vo, 7s. 6d.
Gilder (W. H.) Ice-Pack and Tundra. An Account of the Search for the "Jeannette." 8vo, 18s.
—— *Schwatka's Search.* Sledging in quest of the Franklin Records. Illustrated, 8vo, 12s. 6d.
Gilpin's Forest Scenery. Edited by F. G. HEATH. Post 8vo, 7s. 6d.
Glas (John) The Lord's Supper. Crown 8vo, 4s. 6d.
Gordon (J. E. H., B.A. Cantab.) Four Lectures on Electric Induction at the Royal Institution, 1878-9. Illust., square 16mo, 3s.
—— *Electric Lighting.* Illustrated, 8vo, 18s.
—— *Physical Treatise on Electricity and Magnetism.* 2nd Edition, enlarged, with coloured, full-page, &c., Illust. 2 vols., 8vo, 42s.
Gouffé (Jules) Royal Cookery Book. Translated and adapted for English use by ALPHONSE GOUFFÉ, Head Pastrycook to the Queen. New Edition, with plates in colours, Woodcuts, &c., 8vo, gilt edges, 42s.
—— Domestic Edition, half-bound, 10s. 6d.
Great Artists. See "Biographies."

Great Historic Galleries of England (The). Edited by LORD RONALD GOWER, Trustee of the National Portrait Gallery. *Permanent* Photographs of celebrated Pictures. Vol. I., imperial 4to, gilt edges, 36s. Vol. II., 2l. 12s. 6d.; III., 2l. 12s. 6d.; IV., 2l. 12s. 6d.

Great Musicians. Edited by F. HUEFFER. A Series of Biographies, crown 8vo, 3s. each:—

Bach.	Handel.	Purcell.
*Beethoven.	Haydn.	Rossini.
*Berlioz.	*Marcello.	Schubert.
English Church Composers. By BARETT.	Mendelssohn.	Schumann.
	Mozart.	Richard Wagner.
*Glück.	*Palestrina.	Weber.

* *In preparation.*

Grohmann (W. A. B.) Camps in the Rockies. 8vo, 12s. 6d.

Groves (J. Percy) Charmouth Grange: a Tale of the Seventeenth Century. Illustrated, small post 8vo, gilt, 6s.; plainer 5s.

Guizot's History of France. Translated by ROBERT BLACK. Super-royal 8vo, very numerous Full-page and other Illustrations. In 8 vols., cloth extra, gilt, each 24s. This work is re-issued in cheaper binding, 8 vols., at 10s. 6d. each.

"It supplies a want which has long been felt, and ought to be in the hands of all students of history.'—*Times.*

—————— *Masson's School Edition.* Abridged from the Translation by Robert Black, with Chronological Index, Historical and Genealogical Tables, &c. By Professor GUSTAVE MASSON, B.A. With 24 full-page Portraits, and other Illustrations. 1 vol., 8vo, 600 pp., 10s. 6d.

Guizot's History of England. In 3 vols. of about 500 pp. each, containing 60 to 70 full-page and other Illustrations, cloth extra, gilt, 24s. each; re-issue in cheaper binding, 10s. 6d. each.

"For luxury of typography, plainness of print, and beauty of illustration, these volumes, of which but one has as yet appeared in English, will hold their own against any production of an age so luxurious as our own in everything, typography not excepted."—*Times.*

Guyon (Mde.) Life. By UPHAM. 6th Edition, crown 8vo, 6s.

HALL (W. W.) How to Live Long; or, 1408 Health Maxims, Physical, Mental, and Moral. 2nd Edition, small post 8vo, 2s.

Hamilton (E.) Recollections of Fly-fishing for Salmon, Trout, and Grayling. With their Habits, Haunts, and History. Illustrated, small post 8vo, 6s.; large paper (100 numbered copies), 10s. 6d.

Hands (T.) Numerical Exercises in Chemistry. Cr. 8vo, 2s. 6d. and 2s.; Answers separately, 6d.

Hardy (Thomas). See LOW'S STANDARD NOVELS.

Hargreaves (Capt.) Voyage round Great Britain. Illustrated. Crown 8vo, 5s.

Harland (Marian) Home Kitchen: a Collection of Practical and Inexpensive Receipts. Crown 8vo, 5s.

Harper's Monthly Magazine. Published Monthly. 160 pages, fully Illustrated. 1s.
    Vol. I. December, 1880, to May, 1881.
    ,, II. June to November, 1881.
    ,, III. December, 1881, to May, 1882.
    ,, IV. June to November, 1882.
    ,, V. December, 1882, to May, 1883.
    ,, VI. June to November, 1883.
    ,, VII. December, 1883, to May, 1884.
    ,, VIII. June to November, 1884.
    ,, IX. December, 1884, to May, 1885.
Super-royal 8vo, 8s. 6d. each.

"'Harper's Magazine' is so thickly sown with excellent illustrations that to count them would be a work of time; not that it is a picture magazine, for the engravings illustrate the text after the manner seen in some of our choicest *éditions de luxe.*"—*St. James's Gazette.*

"It is so pretty, so big, and so cheap. . . . An extraordinary shillingsworth— 160 large octavo pages, with over a score of articles, and more than three times as many illustrations."—*Edinburgh Daily Review.*

"An amazing shillingsworth . . . combining choice literature of both nations."—*Nonconformist.*

Harrison (Mary) Skilful Cook: a Practical Manual of Modern Experience. Crown 8vo, 5s.

Harrison (Mrs. Burton) The Old-fashioned Fairy Book. Illustrated by ROSINA EMMETT. 16mo, 2s. 6d.

Hatton (Joseph) Journalistic London: with Engravings and Portraits of Distinguished Writers of the Day. Fcap. 4to, 12s. 6d.

—— *Three Recruits, and the Girls they left behind them.* Small post 8vo, 6s.

"It hurries us along in unflagging excitement."—*Times.*

—— See also "Low's Standard Novels."

Heath (Francis George) Autumnal Leaves. New Edition, with Coloured Plates in Facsimile from Nature. Crown 8vo, 14s.

—— *Fern Paradise.* New Edition, with Plates and Photos., crown 8vo, 12s. 6d.

—— *Fern Portfolio.* Section I. Coloured Plates. Folio, 5s.

—— *Fern World.* With Nature-printed Coloured Plates. New Edition, crown 8vo, 12s. 6d.

—— *Gilpin's Forest Scenery.* Illustrated, 8vo, 12s. 6d.; New Edition, 7s. 6d.

—— *Our Woodland Trees.* With Coloured Plates and Engravings. Small 8vo, 12s. 6d.

Heath (Francis George) Peasant Life in the West of England. New Edition, crown 8vo, 10s. 6d.
——— *Sylvan Spring.* With Coloured, &c., Illustrations. 12s. 6d.
——— *Trees and Ferns.* Illustrated, crown 8vo, 3s. 6d.
——— *Where to Find Ferns.* Crown 8vo, 2s.
Heber (Bishop) Hymns. Illustrated Edition. With upwards of 100 beautiful Engravings. Small 4to, handsomely bound, 7s. 6d. Morocco, 18s. 6d. and 21s. New and Cheaper Edition, cloth, 3s. 6d.
Heldmann (Bernard) Mutiny on Board the Ship "Leander." Small post 8vo, gilt edges, numerous Illustrations, 5s.
Henty (G. A.) Winning his Spurs. Illustrations. Cr. 8vo, 5s.
——— *Cornet of Horse: A Story for Boys.* Illust., cr. 8vo, 5s.
——— *Jack Archer: Tale of the Crimea.* Illust., crown 8vo, 6s.
Herrick (Robert) Poetry. Preface by AUSTIN DOBSON. With numerous Illustrations by E. A. ABBEY. 4to, gilt edges, 42s.
Hill (Staveley, Q.C., M.P.) From Home to Home: Two Long Vacations at the Foot of the Rocky Mountains. With Wood Engravings and Photogravures. 8vo, 21s.
Hitchman, Public Life of the Right Hon. Benjamin Disraeli, Earl of Beaconsfield. 3rd Edition, with Portrait. Crown 8vo, 3s. 6d.
Hodson (J. S.) Art Illustration for Books, Periodicals, &c. 8vo, 15s.
Hole (Rev. Canon) Nice and her Neighbours. Small 4to, with numerous choice Illustrations, 16s.
Holmes (O. Wendell) Poetical Works. 2 vols., 18mo, exquisitely printed, and chastely bound in limp cloth, gilt tops, 10s. 6d.
Hoppus (J. D.) Riverside Papers. 2 vols., 12s.
Hugo (Victor) "Ninety-Three." Illustrated. Crown 8vo, 6s.
——— *Toilers of the Sea.* Crown 8vo, fancy boards, 2s.
——— *History of a Crime. Story of the Coup d'État.* Cr. 8vo, 6s.
Hundred Greatest Men (The). 8 portfolios, 21s. each, or 4 vols., half-morocco, gilt edges, 10 guineas. New Ed., 1 vol., royal 8vo, 21s.
Hurrell (H.) and Hyde. Law of Directors and Officials of Joint Stock Companies. 8vo, 3s. 6d.
Hutchinson (Thos.) Diary and Letters. Demy 8vo, cloth, 16s.
Hutchisson (W. H.) Pen and Pencil Sketches: Eighteen Years in Bengal. 8vo, 18s.
Hygiene and Public Health. Edited by A. H. BUCK, M.D Illustrated. 2 vols., royal 8vo, 42s.
Hymnal Companion of Common Prayer. See BICKERSTETH.

ILLUSTRATED Text-Books of Art-Education. Edited by EDWARD J. POYNTER, R.A. Each Volume contains numerous Illustrations, and is strongly bound for Students, price 5s. Now ready :—

PAINTING.

Classic and Italian. By PERCY R. HEAD.
German, Flemish, and Dutch.
French and Spanish.
English and American.

ARCHITECTURE.

Classic and Early Christian.
Gothic and Renaissance. By T. ROGER SMITH.

SCULPTURE.

Antique : Egyptian and Greek.

Index to the English Catalogue, Jan., 1874, *to Dec.*, 1880. Royal 8vo, half-morocco, 18s.

Irish Birthday Book; from Speeches and Writings of Irish Men and Women, Catholic and Protestant. Selected by MELUSINE. Small 8vo, 5s.

Irving (Henry) Impressions of America. By J. HATTON. 2 vols., 21s.; New Edition, 1 vol., 6s.

Irving (Washington). Complete Library Edition of his Works in 27 Vols., Copyright, Unabridged, and with the Author's Latest Revisions, called the "Geoffrey Crayon" Edition, handsomely printed in large square 8vo, on superfine laid paper. Each volume, of about 500 pages, fully Illustrated. 12s. 6d. per vol. *See also* "Little Britain."

———————————— ("American Men of Letters.") 2s. 6d.

JAMES (C.) Curiosities of Law and Lawyers. 8vo, 7s. 6d.

Japan. See AUDSLEY.

Jarves (J. J.) Italian Rambles. Square 16mo, 5s.

Johnson, W. Lloyd Garrison and his Times. Cr. 8vo, 12s. 6d.

Johnston (H. H.) River Congo, from its Mouth to Bolobo. New Edition, 8vo, 21s.

Johnston (R. M.) Old Mark Langston: a Tale of Duke's Creek. Crown 8vo, 5s.

Jones (Major) The Emigrants' Friend. A Complete Guide to the United States. New Edition. 2s. 6d.

Jones (Mrs. Herbert) Sandringham: Past and Present. Illustrated, crown 8vo, 8s. 6d.

Joyful Lays. Sunday School Song Book. By LOWRY and DOANE. Boards, 2s.

Julien (F.) English Student's French Examiner. 16mo, 2s.
────── *First Lessons in Conversational French Grammar.* Crown 8vo, 1s.
────── *French at Home and at School.* Book I., Accidence, &c. Square crown 8vo, 2s.
────── *Conversational French Reader.* 16mo, cloth, 2s. 6d.
────── *Petites Leçons de Conversation et de Grammaire.* New Edition, 3s.
────── *Phrases of Daily Use.* Limp cloth, 6d.

KELSEY *(C. B.) Diseases of the Rectum and Anus.* Illustrated. 8vo, 18s.
Kempis *(Thomas à) Daily Text-Book.* Square 16mo, 2s. 6d.; interleaved as a Birthday Book, 3s. 6d.
Khedives and Pashas. Sketches of Contemporary Egyptian Rulers and Statesmen. Crown 8vo, 7s. 6d.
Kielland. Skipper Worsé. By the Earl of Ducie. Cr. 8vo, 10s. 6d.
Kingston *(W. H. G.) Dick Cheveley.* Illustrated, 16mo, gilt edges, 7s. 6d.; plainer binding, plain edges, 5s.
────── *Heir of Kilfinnan.* Uniform, 7s. 6d.; also 5s.
────── *Snow-Shoes and Canoes.* Uniform, 7s. 6d.; also 5s.
────── *Two Supercargoes.* Uniform, 7s. 6d.; also 5s.
────── *With Axe and Rifle.* Uniform, 7s. 6d.; also 5s.
Knight *(E. F.) Albania and Montenegro.* Illust. 8vo, 12s. 6d.
Knight *(E. J.) Cruise of the "Falcon."* A Voyage round the World in a 30-Ton Yacht. Illust. New Ed. 2 vols., crown 8vo, 24s.

LANGSTAFF-HAVILAND *(R. J.) Enslaved.* 3 vols., 31s. 6d.
Lanier *(Sidney) Boy's Froissart.* Illus., cr. 8vo, gilt edges, 7s. 6d.
────── *Boy's King Arthur.* Uniform, 7s. 6d.
────── *Boy's Mabinogion; Original Welsh Legends of King Arthur.* Uniform, 7s. 6d.
────── *Boy's Percy: Ballads of Love and Adventure, selected* from the "Reliques." Uniform, 7s. 6d.
Lansdell *(H.) Through Siberia.* 2 vols., 8vo, 30s.; 1 vol., 10s. 6d.
────── *Russia in Central Asia.* Illustrated. 2 vols, 42s.
Larden *(W.) School Course on Heat.* Second Edition, Illustrated, crown 8vo, 5s.
Lathrop *(G. P.) Newport.* Crown 8vo, 5s.
Legal Profession: Romantic Stories. 7s. 6d.

Lennard (T. B.) To Married Women and Women about to be Married, &c. 6*d.*

Lenormant (F.) Beginnings of History. Crown 8vo, 12*s.* 6*d.*

Leonardo da Vinci's Literary Works. Edited by Dr. JEAN PAUL RICHTER. Containing his Writings on Painting, Sculpture, and Architecture, his Philosophical Maxims, Humorous Writings, and Miscellaneous Notes on Personal Events, on his Contemporaries, on Literature, &c.; published from Manuscripts. 2 vols., imperial 8vo, containing about 200 Drawings in Autotype Reproductions, and numerous other Illustrations. Twelve Guineas.

Lewald (Fanny) Stella. Translated. 2 vols., 18mo, 4*s.*

Library of Religious Poetry. Best Poems of all Ages. Edited by SCHAFF and GILMAN. Royal 8vo, 21*s.*; re-issue in cheaper binding, 10*s.* 6*d.*

Lindsay (W. S.) History of Merchant Shipping. Over 150 Illustrations, Maps, and Charts. In 4 vols., demy 8vo, cloth extra. Vols. 1 and 2, 11*s.* each; vols. 3 and 4, 14*s.* each. 4 vols., 50*s.*

Lillie (Lucy E.) Prudence: a Story of Æsthetic London. 5*s.*

Little Britain, The Spectre Bridegroom, and *Legend of Sleeepy* Hollow. By WASHINGTON IRVING. An entirely New *Edition de luxe.* Illustrated by 120 very fine Engravings on Wood, by Mr. J. D. COOPER. Designed by Mr. CHARLES O. MURRAY. Re-issue, square crown 8vo, cloth, 6*s.*

Logan (Sir Wm. E.) Life. By B. J. HARRINGTON. 8vo, 12*s.* 6*d.*

Long (Mrs.) Peace and War in the Transvaal. 12mo, 3*s.* 6*d.*

Lorne (Marquis of) Memories of Canada and Scotland. Speeches and Verses. Crown 8vo, 7*s.* 6*d.*

Low's Standard Library of Travel and Adventure. Crown 8vo, uniform in cloth extra, 7*s.* 6*d.*, except where price is given.
1. **The Great Lone Land.** By Major W. F. BUTLER, C.B.
2. **The Wild North Land.** By Major W. F. BUTLER, C.B.
3. **How I found Livingstone.** By H. M. STANLEY.
4. **Through the Dark Continent.** By H. M. STANLEY. 12*s.* 6*d.*
5. **The Threshold of the Unknown Region.** By C. R. MARKHAM. (4th Edition, with Additional Chapters, 10*s.* 6*d.*)
6. **Cruise of the Challenger.** By W. J. J. SPRY, R.N.
7. **Burnaby's On Horseback through Asia Minor.** 10*s.* 6*d.*
8. **Schweinfurth's Heart of Africa.** 2 vols., 15*s.*
9. **Marshall's Through America.**
10. **Lansdell's Through Siberia.** Illustrated and unabridged, 10*s.* 6*d.*

Low's Standard Novels. Small post 8vo, cloth extra, 6s. each, unless otherwise stated.

A Daughter of Heth. By W. BLACK.
In Silk Attire. By W. BLACK.
Kilmeny. A Novel. By W. BLACK.
Lady Silverdale's Sweetheart. By W. BLACK.
Sunrise. By W. BLACK.
Three Feathers. By WILLIAM BLACK.
Alice Lorraine. By R. D. BLACKMORE.
Christowell, a Dartmoor Tale. By R. D. BLACKMORE.
Clara Vaughan. By R. D. BLACKMORE.
Cradock Nowell. By R. D. BLACKMORE.
Cripps the Carrier. By R. D. BLACKMORE.
Erema; or, My Father's Sin. By R. D. BLACKMORE.
Lorna Doone. By R. D. BLACKMORE.
Mary Anerley. By R. D. BLACKMORE.
Tommy Upmore. By R. D. BLACKMORE.
An English Squire. By Miss COLERIDGE.
A Story of the Dragonnades; or, Asylum Christi. By the Rev E. GILLIAT, M.A.
A Laodicean. By THOMAS HARDY.
Far from the Madding Crowd. By THOMAS HARDY.
Pair of Blue Eyes. By THOMAS HARDY.
Return of the Native. By THOMAS HARDY.
The Hand of Ethelberta. By THOMAS HARDY.
The Trumpet Major. By THOMAS HARDY.
Two on a Tower. By THOMAS HARDY.
Three Recruits. By JOSEPH HATTON.
A Golden Sorrow. By Mrs. CASHEL HOEY. New Edition.
Out of Court. By Mrs. CASHEL HOEY.
History of a Crime: Story of the Coup d'État. VICTOR HUGO.
Ninety-Three. By VICTOR HUGO. Illustrated.
Adela Cathcart. By GEORGE MAC DONALD.
Guild Court. By GEORGE MAC DONALD.
Mary Marston. By GEORGE MAC DONALD.
Stephen Archer. New Ed. of "Gifts." By GEORGE MAC DONALD.
The Vicar's Daughter. By GEORGE MAC DONALD.
Weighed and Wanting. By GEORGE MAC DONALD.
Diane. By Mrs. MACQUOID.
Elinor Dryden. By Mrs. MACQUOID.
My Lady Greensleeves. By HELEN MATHERS.
Alaric Spenceley. By Mrs. J. H. RIDDELL.
Daisies and Buttercups. By Mrs. J. H. RIDDELL.
The Senior Partner. By Mrs. J. H. RIDDELL.
A Struggle for Fame. By Mrs. J. H. RIDDELL.
Jack's Courtship. By W. CLARK RUSSELL.
John Holdsworth. By W. CLARK RUSSELL.
A Sailor's Sweetheart. By W. CLARK RUSSELL.
Sea Queen. By W. CLARK RUSSELL.

Low's Standard Novels—continued.
    Watch Below. By W. CLARK RUSSELL.
    Wreck of the Grosvenor. By W. CLARK RUSSELL.
    The Lady Maud. By W. CLARK RUSSELL.
    Little Loo. By W. CLARK RUSSELL.
    My Wife and I. By Mrs. BEECHER STOWE.
    Poganuc People, their Loves and Lives. By Mrs. B. STOWE.
    Ben Hur: a Tale of the Christ. By LEW. WALLACE.
    Anne. By CONSTANCE FENIMORE WOOLSON.
    For the Major. By CONSTANCE FENIMORE WOOLSON. 5s.
    French Heiress in her own Chateau.

Low's Handbook to the Charities of London. Edited and revised to date by C. MACKESON, F.S.S., Editor of "A Guide to the Churches of London and its Suburbs," &c. Yearly, 1s. 6d.; Paper, 1s.

*M*cCORMICK (R.). *Voyages of Discovery in the Arctic* and Antarctic Seas in the "Erebus" and "Terror," in Search of Sir John Franklin, &c., with Autobiographical Notice by the Author, who was Medical Officer to each Expedition. With Maps and Lithographic, &c., Illustrations. 2 vols., royal 8vo, 52s. 6d.

Macdonald (A.) "*Our Sceptred Isle*" *and its World-wide* Empire. Small post 8vo, cloth, 4s.

MacDonald (G.) Orts. Small post 8vo, 6s.

—— See also "Low's Standard Novels."

Macgregor (John) "*Rob Roy*" *on the Baltic.* 3rd Edition, small post 8vo, 2s. 6d.; cloth, gilt edges, 3s. 6d.

—— *A Thousand Miles in the "Rob Roy" Canoe.* 11th Edition, small post 8vo, 2s. 6d.; cloth, gilt edges, 3s. 6d.

—— *Voyage Alone in the Yawl "Rob Roy."* New Edition, with additions, small post 8vo, 5s.; 3s. 6d. and 2s. 6d.

Macquoid (Mrs.). See LOW'S STANDARD NOVELS.

Magazine. See DECORATION, ETCHER, HARPER.

Magyarland. Travels through the Snowy Carpathians. By a Fellow of the Carpathian Society, and Author of "The Indian Alps." With about 120 Woodcuts from the Author's drawings. 2 vols., 8vo, 38s.

Manitoba. See BRYCE and RAE.

Maria Theresa. See BROGLIE.

Marked "In Haste." A Story of To-day. Crown 8vo, 8s. 6d.

Markham (Adm.) Naval Career during the Old War. 8vo, 14s.

Markham (C. R.) The Threshold of the Unknown Region. Crown 8vo, with Four Maps, 4th Edition. Cloth extra, 10s. 6d.

—— *War between Peru and Chili,* 1879-1881. Third Ed. Crown 8vo, with Maps, 10s. 6d. See also "Foreign Countries."

Marshall (W. G.) Through America. New Ed., cr. 8vo, 7s. 6d.

Martin (J. W.) Float Fishing and Spinning in the Nottingham Style. Crown 8vo, 2s. 6d.

Marvin (Charles) Russian Advance towards India. 8vo, 16s.

Maury (Commander) Physical Geography of the Sea, and its Meteorology. New Edition, with Charts and Diagrams, cr. 8vo, 6s.

Men of Mark: a Gallery of Contemporary Portraits of the most Eminent Men of the Day, specially taken from Life. Complete in Seven Vols., 4to, handsomely bound, cloth, gilt edges, 25s. each.

Mendelssohn Family (The), 1729—1847. From Letters and Journals. Translated. New Edition, 2 vols., 8vo, 30s.

Mendelssohn. See also "Great Musicians."

Mesney (W.) Tungking. Crown 8vo, 3s. 6d.

Millard (H. B.) Bright's Disease of the Kidneys. Illustrated. 8vo, 12s. 6d.

Mitchell (D. G.; Ik. Marvel) Works. Uniform Edition, small 8vo, 5s. each.
Bound together.
Doctor Johns.
Dream Life.
Out-of-Town Places.

Reveries of a Bachelor.
Seven Stories, Basement and Attic.
Wet Days at Edgewood.

Mitford (Mary Russell) Our Village. With 12 full-page and 157 smaller Cuts. Cr. 4to, cloth, gilt edges, 21s.; cheaper binding, 10s. 6d.

Mollett (J. W.) Illustrated Dictionary of Words used in Art and Archæology. Terms in Architecture, Arms, Bronzes, Christian Art, Colour, Costume, Decoration, Devices, Emblems, Heraldry, Lace, Personal Ornaments, Pottery, Painting, Sculpture, &c. Small 4to, 15s.

Morley (H.) English Literature in the Reign of Victoria. 2000th volume of the Tauchnitz Collection of Authors. 18mo, 2s. 6d.

Muller (E.) Noble Words and Noble Deeds. By PHILIPPOTEAUX. Square imperial 16mo, cloth extra, 7s. 6d.; plainer binding, 5s.

Music. See "Great Musicians."

NEW Child's Play (A). Sixteen Drawings by E. V. B Beautifully printed in colours, 4to, cloth extra, 12s. 6d.

New Zealand. See BRADSHAW.

Newbiggin's Sketches and Tales. 18mo, 4s.

Newfoundland. See RAE.

Nicholls (J. H. Kerry) The King Country: Explorations in New Zealand. Many Illustrations and Map. New Edition, 8vo, 21s.

Nicholson (C.) Work and Workers of the British Association. 12mo, 1s.

Nixon (J.) Complete Story of the Transvaal. 8vo, 12s. 6d.

Nordhoff (C.) California, for Health, Pleasure, and Residence. New Edition, 8vo, with Maps and Illustrations, 12s. 6d.

Northbrook Gallery. Edited by Lord Ronald Gower. 36 Permanent Photographs. Imperial 4to, 63s.; large paper, 105s.

Nothing to Wear; and Two Millions. By W. A. BUTLER. New Edition. Small post 8vo, in stiff coloured wrapper, 1s.

Nursery Playmates (Prince of). 217 Coloured Pictures for Children by eminent Artists. Folio, in coloured boards, 6s.

O'BRIEN *(P. B.) Fifty Years of Concessions to Ireland.* Vol. I., 8vo, 16s.

—— *Irish Land Question, and English Question.* New Edition, fcap. 8vo, 2s.

Orvis (C. F.) Fishing with the Fly. Illustrated. 8vo, 12s. 6d.

Our Little Ones in Heaven. Edited by the Rev. H. ROBBINS. With Frontispiece after Sir JOSHUA REYNOLDS. New Edition, 5s.

Outlines of Ornament in all Styles. A Work of Reference for the Architect, Art Manufacturer, Decorative Artist, and Practical Painter. By W. and G. A. AUDSLEY. Small folio, 60 plates, with text, cloth gilt, 31s. 6d.

Owen (Douglas) Marine Insurance Notes and Clauses. New Edition, 14s.

PALLISER *(Mrs.) A History of Lace.* New Edition, with additional cuts and text. 8vo, 21s.

—— *The China Collector's Pocket Companion.* With upwards of 1000 Illustrations of Marks and Monograms. Small 8vo, 5s.

Pascoe (C. E.) London of To-Day. Illust., crown 8vo, 3s. 6d.

Perseus, the Gorgon Slayer. With Col. Plates, square 8vo, 5s.

Pharmacopœia of the United States of America. 8vo, 21s.

Philpot (H. J.) Diabetes Mellitus. Crown 8vo, 5s.

────── *Diet System.* Three Tables, in cases, 1s. each.

Photography. See TISSANDIER.

Pinto (Major Serpa) How I Crossed Africa. With 24 full-page and 118 half-page and smaller Illustrations, 13 small Maps, and 1 large one. 2 vols., 8vo, 42s.

Poe (E. A.) The Raven. Illustr. by DORÉ. Imperial folio, 63s.

Poems of the Inner Life. Chiefly from Modern Authors. Small 8vo, 5s.

Polar Expeditions. See GILDER, KOLDEWEY, MARKHAM, McCORMICK, MACGAHAN, NARES, NORDENSKIÖLD.

Politics and Life in Mars. 12mo, 2s. 6d.

Powell (W.) Wanderings in a Wild Country; or, Three Years among the Cannibals of New Britain. Illustr., 8vo, 18s.; cr. 8vo, 5s.

Power (Frank) Letters from Khartoum during the Siege. Fcap. 8vo, boards, 1s.

Prisons, Her Majesty's, their Effects and Defects. New Ed., 6s.

Poynter (Edward J., R.A.). See " Illustrated Text-books."

Publishers' Circular (The), and General Record of British and Foreign Literature. Published on the 1st and 15th of every Month, 3d.

RAE (W. Fraser) From Newfoundland to Manitoba; Canada's Maritime, Mining, and Prairie Provinces. Crown 8vo, 6s.

Rambaud (A.) History of Russia. 2 vols., 8vo, 36s.

Reade (A.) Tea and Tea-Drinking. Illustrated. Crown 8vo, 1s.

Reber (F.) History of Ancient Art. 8vo, 18s.

Redford (G.) Ancient Sculpture. Crown 8vo, 5s.

Richer than Wealth. 3 vols., crown 8vo, 31s. 6d.

Richter (Dr. Jean Paul) Italian Art in the National Gallery. 4to. Illustrated. Cloth gilt, 2l. 2s.; half-morocco, uncut, 2l. 12s. 6d.

────── See also LEONARDO DA VINCI.

Riddell (Mrs. J. H.) See Low's STANDARD NOVELS.

Robin Hood; Merry Adventures of. Written and illustrated by HOWARD PYLE. Imperial 8vo, 15s.

Robinson (Phil.) Chasing a Fortune, &c.: Stories. 1s. 6d. and 1s.

——— *In my Indian Garden.* Crown 8vo, limp cloth, 3s. 6d.

——— *Noah's Ark. A Contribution to the Study of Unnatural History.* Small post 8vo, 12s. 6d.

——— *Sinners and Saints: a Tour across the United States of America, and Round them.* Crown 8vo, 10s. 6d.

——— *Under the Punkah.* Crown 8vo, limp cloth, 5s.

Robinson (Serjeant) Wealth and its Sources. Stray Thoughts. 5s.

Rockstro (W. S.) History of Music. 8vo, 14s.

Roe (E. P.) Nature's Serial Story. Illustrated, 4to, 24s.

Roland; the Story of. Crown 8vo, illustrated, 6s.

Romantic Stories of the Legal Profession. Crown 8vo, 7s. 6d.

Roosevelt (Blanche) Stage-struck; or, She would be an Opera Singer. 2 vols., crown 8vo, 21s.

Rose (F.) Complete Practical Machinist. New Ed., 12mo, 12s. 6d.

——— *Mechanical Drawing.* Illustrated, small 4to, 16s.

Rose Library (The). Popular Literature of all Countries. Each volume, 1s.; cloth, 2s. 6d. Many of the Volumes are Illustrated—

Little Women. By LOUISA M. ALCOTT.
Little Women Wedded. Forming a Sequel to "Little Women."
Little Women and Little Women Wedded. 1 vol., cloth gilt, 3s. 6d.
Little Men. By L. M. ALCOTT. 2s.; cloth gilt, 3s. 6d.
An Old-Fashioned Girl. By LOUISA M. ALCOTT. 2s.; cloth, 3s. 6d.
Work. A Story of Experience. By L. M. ALCOTT. 3s. 6d.; 2 vols., 1s. each.
Stowe (Mrs. H. B.) The Pearl of Orr's Island.
——— The Minister's Wooing.
——— We and our Neighbours. 2s.; cloth gilt, 6s.
——— My Wife and I. 2s.; cloth gilt, 6s.
Hans Brinker; or, the Silver Skates. By Mrs. DODGE.
My Study Windows. By J. R. LOWELL.
The Guardian Angel. By OLIVER WENDELL HOLMES.
My Summer in a Garden. By C. D. WARNER.

Rose Library (The)—continued.

 Dred. By Mrs. BEECHER STOWE. 2*s.*; cloth gilt, 3*s.* 6*d.*
 Farm Ballads. By WILL CARLETON.
 Farm Festivals. By WILL CARLETON.
 Farm Legends. By WILL CARLETON.
 The Clients of Dr. Bernagius. 3*s.* 6*d.*; 2 parts, 1*s.* each.
 The Undiscovered Country. By W. D. HOWELLS. 3*s.* 6*d.* and 1*s.*
 Baby Rue. By C. M. CLAY. 3*s.* 6*d.* and 1*s.*
 The Rose in Bloom. By L. M. ALCOTT. 2*s.*; cloth gilt, 3*s.* 6*d.*
 Eight Cousins. By L. M. ALCOTT. 2*s.*; cloth gilt, 3*s.* 6*d.*
 Under the Lilacs. By L. M. ALCOTT. 2*s.*; also 3*s.* 6*d.*
 Silver Pitchers. By LOUISA M. ALCOTT. 3*s.* 6*d.* and 1*s.*
 Jimmy's Cruise in the "Pinafore," and other Tales. By LOUISA M. ALCOTT. 2*s.*; cloth gilt, 3*s.* 6*d.*
 Jack and Jill. By LOUISA M. ALCOTT. 5*s.*; 2*s.*
 Hitherto. By the Author of the "Gayworthys." 2 vols., 1*s.* each; 1 vol., cloth gilt, 3*s.* 6*d.*
 Friends: a Duet. By E. STUART PHELPS. 3*s.* 6*d.*
 A Gentleman of Leisure. A Novel. By EDGAR FAWCETT. 3*s.* 6*d.*; 1*s.*
 The Story of Helen Troy. 3*s.* 6*d.*; also 1*s.*

Round the Yule Log: Norwegian Folk and Fairy Tales. Translated from the Norwegian of P. CHR. ASBJÖRNSEN. With 100 Illustrations after drawings by Norwegian Artists, and an Introduction by E. W. Gosse. Imperial 16mo, cloth extra, gilt edges, 7*s.* 6*d.*

Rousselet (Louis) Son of the Constable of France. Small post 8vo, numerous Illustrations, 5*s.*

 ——— *King of the Tigers: a Story of Central India.* Illustrated. Small post 8vo, gilt, 6*s.*; plainer, 5*s.*

 ——— *Drummer Boy.* Illustrated. Small post 8vo, 5*s.*

Russell (W. Clark) English Channel Ports and the Estate of the East and West India Dock Company. Crown 8vo, 1*s.*

 ——— *Jack's Courtship.* 3 vols., 31*s.* 6*d.*; 1 vol., 6*s.*

 ——— *The Lady Maud.* 3 vols., 31*s.* 6*d.*; 1 vol., 6*s.*

 ——— *Little Loo.* New Edition, small post 8vo, 6*s.*

 ——— *My Watch Below; or, Yarns Spun when off Duty.* Small post 8vo, 6*s.*

 ——— *Sailor's Language.* Illustrated. Crown 8vo, 3*s.* 6*d.*

Russell (W. Clark) Sea Queen. 3 vols., 31s. 6d.; 1 vol., 6s.
——— *Wreck of the Grosvenor.* 4to, sewed, 6d.
——— See also Low's STANDARD NOVELS.
Russell (W. H., LL.D.) Hesperothen: Notes from the Western World. A Ramble through part of the United States, Canada, and the Far West, in 1881. By W. H. RUSSELL, LL.D. 2 vols., crown 8vo, 24s.
——— *The Tour of the Prince of Wales in India.* By W. H. RUSSELL, LL.D. Fully Illustrated by SYDNEY P. HALL, M.A. Super-royal 8vo, gilt edges, 52s. 6d.; large paper, 84s.

SAINTS and their Symbols: A Companion in the Churches and Picture Galleries of Europe. Illustrated. Royal 16mo, 3s. 6d.
Salisbury (Lord) Life and Speeches. By F. S. Palling, M.A. 2 vols., crown 8vo, 21s.
Saunders (A.) Our Domestic Birds: Poultry in England and New Zealand. Crown 8vo, 6s.
Scherr (Prof. J.) History of English Literature. Cr. 8vo, 8s. 6d.
Schuyler (Eugène). The Life of Peter the Great. By EUGÈNE SCHUYLER, Author of "Turkestan." 2 vols., 8vo, 32s.
Schweinfurth (Georg) Heart of Africa. Three Years' Travels and Adventures in the Unexplored Regions of Central Africa, from 1868 to 1871. Illustrations and large Map. 2 vols., crown 8vo, 15s.
Scott (Leader) Renaissance of Art in Italy. 4to, 31s. 6d.
Sea, River, and Creek. By GARBOARD STREYKE. *The Eastern Coast.* 12mo, 1s.
Sedgwick (Major W.) Light the Dominant Force of the Universe. 7s. 6d.
Senior (Nassau W.) Conversations and Journals in Egypt and Malta. 2 vols., 8vo, 24s.
Senior (W.) Waterside Sketches. Imp. 32mo, 1s.6d., boards, 1s.
Shadbolt and Mackinnon's South African Campaign, 1879. Containing a portrait and biography of every officer who lost his life. 4to, handsomely bound, 2l. 10s.
——— *The Afghan Campaigns of* 1878—1880. By SYDNEY SHADBOLT. 2 vols., royal quarto, cloth extra, 3l.
Shakespeare. Edited by R. GRANT WHITE. 3 vols., crown 8vo, gilt top, 36s.; *édition de luxe*, 6 vols., 8vo, cloth extra, 63s.

Shakespeare. See also " Flowers of Shakespeare."

Sidney (Sir Philip) Arcadia. New Edition, 6s.

Siegfried: The Story of. Illustrated, crown 8vo, cloth, 6s.

Sikes (Wirt). Rambles and Studies in Old South Wales. 8vo, 18s.

—— *British Goblins, Welsh Folk Lore.* New Ed., 8vo, 18s.

—— *Studies of Assassination.* 16mo, 3s. 6d.

Sir Roger de Coverley. Re-imprinted from the "Spectator." With 125 Woodcuts and special steel Frontispiece. Small fcap. 4to, 6s.

Smith (G.) Assyrian Explorations and Discoveries. Illustrated by Photographs and Woodcuts. New Edition, demy 8vo, 18s.

—— *The Chaldean Account of Genesis.* With many Illustrations. 16s. New Edition, revised and re-written by PROFESSOR SAYCE, Queen's College, Oxford. 8vo, 18s.

Smith (J. Moyr) Ancient Greek Female Costume. 112 full-page Plates and other Illustrations. Crown 8vo, 7s. 6d.

—— *Hades of Ardenne: a Visit to the Caves of Han.* Crown 8vo, Illustrated, 5s.

Smith (Sydney) Life and Times. By STUART J. REID. Illustrated. 8vo, 21s.

Smith (T. Roger) Architecture, Gothic and Renaissance. Illustrated, crown 8vo, 5s.

—————————— *Classic and Early Christian.* Illustrated. Crown 8vo, 5s.

Smith (W. R.) Laws concerning Public Health. 8vo, 31s. 6d.

Somerset (Lady H.) Our Village Life. Words and Illustrations. Thirty Coloured Plates, royal 4to, fancy covers, 5s.

Spanish and French Artists. By GERARD SMITH. (Poynter's Art Text-books.) 5s.

Spiers' French Dictionary. 29th Edition, remodelled. 2 vols., 8vo, 18s.; half bound, 21s.

Spry (W. J. J., R.N.) Cruise of H.M.S. "Challenger." With many Illustrations. 6th Edition, 8vo, cloth, 18s. Cheap Edition, crown 8vo, 7s. 6d.

Spyri (Joh.) Heidi's Early Experiences: a Story for Children and those who love Children. Illustrated, small post 8vo, 4s. 6d.

—— *Heidi's Further Experiences.* Illust., sm. post 8vo, 4s. 6d.

Stack (E.) Six Months in Persia. 2 vols., crown 8vo, 24s.

Stanley (H. M.) Congo, and Founding its Free State. Illustrated, 2 vols., 8vo, 42s.

—— *How I Found Livingstone.* 8vo, 10s. 6d.; cr. 8vo, 7s. 6d.

—— *"My Kalulu," Prince, King, and Slave.* With numerous graphic Illustrations after Original Designs by the Author. Crown 8vo, 7s. 6d.

—— *Coomassie and Magdala.* A Story of Two British Campaigns in Africa. Demy 8vo, with Maps and Illustrations, 16s.

—— *Through the Dark Continent.* Crown 8vo, 12s. 6d.

Stanton (T.) Woman Question in Europe. A Series of Original Essays. Introd. by FRANCES POWER COBBE. 8vo, 12s. 6d.

Stenhouse (Mrs.) An Englishwoman in Utah. Crown 8vo, 2s. 6d.

Stevens. Old Boston: a Romance of the War of Independence. 3 vols., crown 8vo, 31s. 6d.

Stirling (A. W.) Never Never Land: a Ride in North Queensland. Crown 8vo, 8s. 6d.

Stockton (Frank R.) The Story of Viteau. With 16 page Illustrations. Crown 8vo, 5s.

Stoker (Bram) Under the Sunset. Crown 8vo, 6s.

Story without an End. From the German of Carové, by the late Mrs. SARAH T. AUSTIN. Crown 4to, with 15 Exquisite Drawings by E. V. B., printed in Colours in Fac-simile of the original Water Colours; and numerous other Illustrations. New Edition, 7s. 6d.

—— with Illustrations by HARVEY. Square 4to, 2s. 6d.

Stowe (Mrs. Beecher) Dred. Cloth, gilt edges, 3s. 6d.; boards, 2s.

—— *Little Foxes.* Cheap Ed., 1s.; Library Edition, 4s. 6d.

Stowe (Mrs. Beecher) My Wife and I. Small post 8vo, 6s.

———— *Old Town Folk.* 6s.; Cheap Edition, 3s.

———— *Old Town Fireside Stories.* Cloth extra, 3s. 6d.

———— *Our Folks at Poganuc.* 6s.

———— *We and our Neighbours.* Small post 8vo, 6s.

———— *Poganuc People: their Loves and Lives.* Crown 8vo, 6s.

———— *Chimney Corner.* 1s.; cloth, 1s. 6d.

———— *The Pearl of Orr's Island.* Crown 8vo, 5s.

———— *Woman in Sacred History.* Illustrated. 4to, 25s.

———— See also ROSE LIBRARY.

Sullivan (A. M.) Nutshell History of Ireland. Paper boards, 6d.

Sutton (A. K.) A B C Digest of the Bankruptcy Law. 8vo, 3s. and 2s. 6d.

TAINE (H. A.) "Les Origines de la France Contemporaine." Translated by JOHN DURAND.

    Vol. 1. **The Ancient Regime.** Demy 8vo, cloth, 16s.
    Vol. 2. **The French Revolution.** Vol. 1. do.
    Vol. 3. Do. do. Vol. 2. do.

Talbot (Hon. E.) A Letter on Emigration. 1s.

Tangye (R.) Australia, America, and Egypt. New Edition, Crown 8vo, 2s. 6d.

Tauchnitz's English Editions of German Authors. Each volume, cloth flexible, 2s.; or sewed, 1s. 6d. (Catalogues post free.)

Tauchnitz (B.) German and English Dictionary. 2s.; paper, 1s. 6d.; roan, 2s. 6d.

———— *French and English Dictionary.* 2s.; paper, 1s. 6d.; roan, 2s. 6d.

———— *Italian and English Dictionary.* 2s.; paper, 1s. 6d.; roan, 2s. 6d.

———— *Spanish and English.* 2s.; paper, 1s. 6d.; roan, 2s. 6d.

———— *Spanish and French.* 2s.; paper, 1s. 6d.; roan, 2s. 6d.

Taylor (W. M.) Paul the Missionary. Crown 8vo, 7s. 6d.

——— *Moses the Lawgiver.* Crown 8vo, 7s. 6d.

Thausing (Prof.) Malt and the Fabrication of Beer. 8vo, 45s.

Theakston (M.) British Angling Flies. Illustrated. Cr. 8vo, 5s.

Thoreau. American Men of Letters. Crown 8vo, 2s. 6d.

Tolhausen (Alexandre) Grand Supplément du Dictionnaire Technologique. 3s. 6d.

Tolmer (A.) Adventurous and Chequered Career. 2 vols., 21s.

Tourist Idyll, and other Stories. 2 vols., crown 8vo, 21s.

Tracks in Norway of Four Pairs of Feet, delineated by Four Hands. Fcap. 8vo, 2s.

Treloar (W. P.) The Prince of Palms. With Coloured Frontispiece of the Cocoa-Nut Palm, also Engravings. Royal 8vo, 1s. 6d.

Trials. See BROWNE.

Tristram (Rev. Canon) Pathways of Palestine : A Descriptive Tour through the Holy Land. First Series. Illustrated by 44 Permanent Photographs. 2 vols., folio, cloth extra, gilt edges, 31s. 6d. each.

Tunis. See REID.

Turner (Edward) Studies in Russian Literature. Cr. 8vo, 8s. 6d.

UNION Jack (The). Every Boy's Paper. Edited by G. A. HENTY. Profusely Illustrated with Coloured and other Plates. Vol. I., 6s. Vols. II., III., IV., 7s. 6d. each.

Up Stream : A Journey from the Present to the Past. Pictures and Words by R. ANDRÉ. Coloured Plates, 4to, 5s.

VELAZQUEZ and Murillo. By C. B. CURTIS. With Original Etchings. Royal 8vo, 31s. 6d.; large paper, 63s.

Victoria (Queen) Life of. By GRACE GREENWOOD. With numerous Illustrations. Small post 8vo, 6s.

Vincent (F.) Norsk, Lapp, and Finn. By FRANK VINCENT, Jun., Author of "The Land of the White Elephant," "Through and Through the Tropics," &c. With Frontispiece and Map, 8vo, 12s.

BOOKS BY JULES VERNE.

WORKS. (LARGE CROWN 8vo.)	Containing 350 to 600 pp. and from 50 to 100 full-page illustrations.		Containing the whole of the text with some illustrations.	
	In very handsome cloth binding, gilt edges.	In plainer binding, plain edges.	In cloth binding, gilt edges, smaller type.	Coloured boards
	s. d.	s. d.	s. d.	
20,000 Leagues under the Sea. Parts I. and II.	10 6	5 0	3 6	2 vols., 1s. each
Hector Servadac	10 6	5 0	3 6	2 vols., 1s. each
The Fur Country	10 6	5 0	3 6	2 vols., 1s. each
The Earth to the Moon and a Trip round it	10 6	5 0	2 vols. 2s. ea.	2 vols., 1s. each
Michael Strogoff	10 6	5 0	3 6	2 vols., 1s. each
Dick Sands, the Boy Captain	10 6	5 0	3 6	2 vols., 1s. each
Five Weeks in a Balloon	7 6	3 6	2 0	1s. 0d.
Adventures of Three Englishmen and Three Russians	7 6	3 6	2 0	1 0
Round the World in Eighty Days	7 6	3 6	2 0	1 0
A Floating City	7 6	3 6	2 0	1 0
The Blockade Runners			2 0	1 0
Dr. Ox's Experiment	—	—	2 0	1 0
A Winter amid the Ice	—	—	2 0	1 0
Survivors of the "Chancellor"	7 6	3 6	2 0	2 vols., 1s. each
Martin Paz			2 0	1s. 0d.
The Mysterious Island, 3 vols:—	22 6	10 6	6 0	3 0
I. Dropped from the Clouds	7 6	3 6	2 0	1 0
II. Abandoned	7 6	3 6	2 0	1 0
III. Secret of the Island	7 6	3 6	2 0	1 0
The Child of the Cavern	7 6	3 6	2 0	1 0
The Begum's Fortune	7 6	3 6	2 0	1 0
The Tribulations of a Chinaman	7 6	3 6	2 0	1 0
The Steam House, 2 vols.:—				
I. Demon of Cawnpore	7 6	3 6	2 0	1 0
II. Tigers and Traitors	7 6	3 6	2 0	1 0
The Giant Raft, 2 vols.:—				
I. 800 Leagues on the Amazon	7 6	3 6		
II. The Cryptogram	7 6	3 6		
The Green Ray	6 0	5 0	—	1 0
Godfrey Morgan	7 6	3 6		
Kéraban the Inflexible:—				
I. Captain of the "Guidara"	7 6			
II. Scarpante the Spy	7 6			
The Archipelago on Fire (shortly)	7 6			

CELEBRATED TRAVELS AND TRAVELLERS. 3 vols. 8vo, 600 pp., 100 full-page illustrations, 12s. 6d. gilt edges, 14s. each:—(1) THE EXPLORATION OF THE WORLD. (2) THE GREAT NAVIGATORS OF THE EIGHTEENTH CENTURY. (3) THE GREAT EXPLORERS OF THE NINETEENTH CENTURY.

Viollet-le-Duc (E.) Lectures on Architecture. Translated by BENJAMIN BUCKNALL, Architect. With 33 Steel Plates and 200 Wood Engravings. Super-royal 8vo, leather back, gilt top, 2 vols., 3*l.* 3*s.*

Vivian (A. P.) Wanderings in the Western Land. 3rd Ed., 10*s.* 6*d.*

WAHL *(W. H.) Galvanoplastic Manipulation for the* Electro-Plater. 8vo, 35*s.*

Wallace (L.) Ben Hur: A Tale of the Christ. Crown 8vo, 6*s.*

Waller (Rev. C. H.) The Names on the Gates of Pearl, and other Studies. New Edition. Crown 8vo, cloth extra, 3*s.* 6*d.*

—— *A Grammar and Analytical Vocabulary of the Words in* the Greek Testament. Compiled from Brüder's Concordance. For the use of Divinity Students and Greek Testament Classes. Part I. Grammar. Small post 8vo, cloth, 2*s.* 6*d.* Part II. Vocabulary, 2*s.* 6*d.*

—— *Adoption and the Covenant.* Some Thoughts on Confirmation. Super-royal 16mo, cloth limp, 2*s.* 6*d.*

—— *Silver Sockets; and other Shadows of Redemption.* Sermons at Christ Church, Hampstead. Small post 8vo, 6*s.*

Walton (Iz.) Wallet Book, CIƆIƆLXXXV. 42*s.*; 21*s.*

Warner (C. D.) Back-log Studies. Boards, 1*s.* 6*d.*; cloth, 2*s.*

Warren (W. F.) Paradise Found; the North Pole the Cradle of the Human Race. Illustrated. Crown 8vo, 12*s.* 6*d.*

Washington Irving's Little Britain. Square crown 8vo, 6*s.*

Watson (P. B.) Marcus Aurelius Antoninus. Portr. 8vo, 15*s.*

Webster. (American Men of Letters.) 18mo, 2*s.* 6*d.*

Wells (H. P.) Fly Rods and Fly Tackle. Illustrated. 10*s.* 6*d.*

Weismann (A.) Studies in the Theory of Descent. With a Preface by CHARLES DARWIN, and Coloured Plates. 2 vols., 8vo, 40*s.*

Wheatley (H. B.) and Delamotte (P. H.) Art Work in Porce- lain. Large 8vo, 2*s.* 6*d.*

—— *Art Work in Gold and Silver. Modern.* Large 8vo, 2*s.* 6*d.*

—— *Handbook of Decorative Art.* 10*s.* 6*d.*

White (R. G.) England Without and Within. Crown 8vo, 10*s.* 6*d.*

—— *Every-day English,* crown 8vo, 10*s.* 6*d.*

White (R. G.) Fate of Mansfield Humphreys, the Episode of Mr Washington Adams in England, an Apology, &c. Crown 8vo, 6s.

―――― *Words and their uses.* New Edit., crown 8vo, 10s. 6d.

Whittier (J. G.) The King's Missive, and later Poems. 18mo, choice parchment cover, 3s. 6d.

―――― *The Whittier Birthday Book.* Extracts from the Author's writings, with Portrait and Illustrations. Uniform with the "Emerson Birthday Book." Square 16mo, very choice binding, 3s. 6d.

―――― *Life of.* By R. A. UNDERWOOD. Cr. 8vo, cloth, 10s. 6d.

Wild Flowers of Switzerland. Coloured Plates, life-size, and Botanical Descriptions of each Example. Imperial 4to, 63s. nett.

Williams (C. F.) Tariff Laws of the United States. 8vo, 10s. 6d.

Williams (H. W.) Diseases of the Eye. 8vo, 21s.

Williams (M.) Some London Theatres. Crown 8vo, 7s. 6d.

Wills, A Few Hints on Proving, without Professional Assistance. By a PROBATE COURT OFFICIAL. 7th Edition, revised, with Forms of Wills, Residuary Accounts, &c. Fcap. 8vo, cloth limp, 1s.

Winckelmann (John) History of Ancient Art. Translated by JOHN LODGE, M.D. Many Plates and Illustrations. 2 vols., 8vo, 36s.

Winks (W. E.) Illustrious Shoemakers. Crown 8vo, 7s. 6d.

Witcomb (C.) Structure of English Verse. Crown 8vo, 3s.

Witthaus (R. A.) Medical Student's Chemistry. 8vo, 16s.

Woodbury, History of Wood Engraving. Illustrated. 8vo, 18s.

Woolsey (C. D., LL.D.) Introduction to the Study of International Law. 5th Edition, demy 8vo, 18s.

Woolson (Constance F.) See "Low's Standard Novels."

Wright (H.) Friendship of God. Portrait, &c. Crown 8vo, 6s.

Written to Order; the Journeyings of an Irresponsible Egotist. Crown 8vo, 6s.

*Y*RIARTE *(Charles) Florence: its History.* Translated by C. B. PITMAN. Illustrated with 500 Engravings. Large imperial 4to, extra binding, gilt edges, 63s.; or 12 Parts, 5s. each.

History; the Medici; the Humanists; letters; arts; the Renaissance; illustrious Florentines; Etruscan art; monuments; sculpture; painting.

London:
SAMPSON LOW, MARSTON, SEARLE, & RIVINGTON,
CROWN BUILDINGS, 188, FLEET STREET, E.C.

www.ingramcontent.com/pod-product-compliance
Lightning Source LLC
Chambersburg PA
CBHW030425300426
44112CB00009B/859